Expert Praise for
The New Media Driver's License®

You wouldn't get in a car in a foreign county without a map or GPS. For the same reason it makes sense to have a comprehensive roadmap when it comes to navigating the ever changing landscape of the new media world. The New Media Drivers License Resource Guide is your starting point. Happy trails!

JOSEPH JAFFE
Author of "Flip the Funnel" @jaffejuice

Richard Cole expertly organizes and aggregates the a vast array of social media thinking into a single primer, offering tips to leverage and pitfalls to avoid, reminding us all along the way how important it is to monitor and measure the value of any marketing program, including those delivered via social media.

LAURA PATTERSON
President, VisionEdge Marketing
Author, Marketing Metrics in Action

This book is a treasure trove of up-to-date information on the fast-moving social media marketing landscape. Cleverly connecting the print edition with a robust list of linked online resources, it lets readers dip into hundreds of useful articles and how-to guides on the latest techniques and strategies. My beat being B-to-B, I delved into Chapter 4, on LinkedIn, and picked up plenty of new ideas. Social media is here to stay, and this book provides you a handy road map.

RUTH P. STEVENS
Author of *Maximizing Lead Generation* and
Trade Show and Event Marketing
Customer Acquisition and Retention Consultant
Adjunct at business schools in the US and around the world.

The New Media Driver's License® Resource Guide

Using Social Media and Digital Marketing for Business

Blogging, Social Networking, Google Tools, Facebook, LinkedIn, Search Engine Marketing, Search Engine Optimization, Online Public Relations, Foursquare, Twitter and more . . .

Richard T. Cole
Michigan State University

Derek Mehraban
Ingenex Digital

Foreword by Michal Lorenc
Head, Dedicated Client Services, Google Canada, Inc.

Companion Link Listings to More than 500 Articles and Posts see
www.NewMediaDriversLicenseResources.com

RĀCOM
COMMUNICATIONS

Editor: Richard Hagle
Cover and interior design by Sans Serif, Inc., Saline, MI

Published by:
Racom Books/Racom Communications
150 N. Michigan Ave. Suite 2800
Chicago, IL 60601
312-494-0100/800-247-6553
www.racombooks.com

ISBN: 978-1-933199-35-1

Featuring Favorite Resource Lists from...

Ross Johnson
CEO, 3.7 Designs

Nick Lucido
Digital Strategy Team Member, Edelman PR

Andrew Miller
CEO, *Your Search Advisor*

Katie Delahaye Paine
CEO, KD Paine & Partners

Steve Rubel
SVP and Director of Insights, Edelman Digital

David Meerman Scott
Author, *Real Time Marketing and PR*

Greg Verdino
Author, *microMARKETING: Get Big Results by Thinking and Acting Small*

Dedication

This book is dedicated to the more than 700 individuals who, since 2009, have received "New Media Driver's Licenses" through our classes at Michigan State University in East Lansing. This selection of resources is significantly influenced by a great many of these "licensed drivers" who, during the course of their training, were charged with identifying and sharing publicly-accessible resources in the wide variety of subject areas that constitute New Media Driver's License® training. These students are listed on the back pages of this book.

Acknowledgments

The authors wish to acknowledge our publisher, editor, and "inspirer," Rich Hagle. We also want to thank Alan Stokes, a new media driver's license® holder and social media leader at the Children's Trust Fund of Michigan, for his editorial assistance. Lauren Marie Schneider, an Ingenex Digital intern, did significant research and was instrumental in the selection of many of the resources in this book. Ingenex Digital intern David Weight constructed our "link history." Dean emeritus of Michigan State University's College of Communication Arts and Sciences, Dr. Charles Salmon, deserves a great deal of credit for allowing us to create and operate the New Media Driver's License® classes, as does current Dean Pamela Whitten for supporting our departmental social media initiatives. Dr. Jef Richards, chairperson of the Department of Advertising, Public Relations, and Retailing at MSU, has supported our efforts since his arrival on campus in early 2011, and we owe him, also, a debt of gratitude.

We want to provide special acknowledgment to the authors of various postings that we reference in this resource guide.

CONTENTS

Foreword

Would TV's ultimate mad man, Don Draper, survive in the age of the Social Media?

Social Media—

- Where a mere "text link" can be more powerful than the 30 second TV Spot;
- Where a 140-character "tweet" can have higher reach and impact than a full-page ad in nation's largest daily paper;
- Where potential consumers are connected, always; and,
- Where consumers are more than willing to chime in and express their opinions on any brand, product, or service they chose.

The pace of this technological innovation is breathtaking, and the seismic change in the marketing and PR landscape it is creating is…well…it's unprecedented.

New media has changed nearly everything. It has changed the way individuals and businesses communicate. It has changed the way we conduct transactions, interact with one another, learn (continuously), and are entertained.

And most importantly, and pertaining especially to this important book, social media has changed the way we market with, and to, one-another.

So, who is leading this change? Is it the academic community or the innovators at Google? Well, as much as the academics or practitioners would like to think they are in charge, the real change in social media is driven by and, to a large extent, designed by the consumer.

And in no greater way is this consumer-driven change obvious than in the fact that the consumer is writing the new rules for when, how, and for what purpose companies are allowed to advertise to her or him. The consumer is in charge.

Just think about this simple question. Where does a marketer go to find the consumer today?

There she is on AOL, GeoCities or TheGlobe. No wait. He's over there. He's on Friendster or MySpace or, more likely, Facebook. Now there she goes over to Google+, something that didn't even exist a few months ago.

Does the consumer still IM and email, or have text messaging and online sharing and posting taken over?

Does he or she still tune in every Thursday night for "Must See TV," or has online access to video content changed the way all of us watch TV, and altered what advertising we see or don't see?

Is the consumer still online only while sitting at the desk using the 28.8 modem plugged into Gateway desktop computer, or is the consumer on a tablet, or a phone, everywhere he or she goes, 24x7?

With nearly two billion online consumers around the globe, and more than three billion smart phones, when we talk about social media we are no longer talking about a niche discipline for geeks.

Google alone has one billion consumers. Facebook boasts three-quarters of a billion. Every minute there are more than two days worth of new video content uploaded to YouTube. Online consumption continues to grow, and it is central to our lives. Some people even believe that online access is a human right.

Simply put social media and online marketing and public relations needs to be more than an add-on. It needs to be the cornerstone of any company's overall business strategy.

With such a head-spinning pace of innovation, coupled with unprecedented access to data and ability to "measure" nearly everything, it's no wonder advertising and PR are still struggling. There is a seismic shift underfoot to overcome the imbalance between all disciplines using social media. The best evidence of this imbalance may be the fact that companies are changing their ad and PR agencies more frequently than ever, and that the average tenure of a Fortune 1000 chief marketing officer (CMO) is measured in fish fly years—the shortest of any of the "C-level executives."

Companies large and small not only want to learn, better understand and leverage the new media, but increasingly they recognize they need to change. Yet so many are struggling to find the right resources and the right talent to help them do so.

I've heard that story time and again, all over the world, while meeting with companies and speaking at various events during my many years at AOL and now Google. I've heard that story from students and scores of executives as they struggle to figure out the world of advertising industry. They notice that change is all round them, and they even recognize they are part of that change, but they want to understand it. And most of all, they want to take advantage of it.

Yet, despite the change going on all around us, the traditional way that advertising, marketing and PR have been taught at US universities hasn't seemed to change that much over the years.

Professor Richard Cole and my marketing colleague Derek Mehraban share my passion for new technology, especially in the way it empowers consumers, and in how it opens up great new opportunities for conversation-based promoting, selling and relationship building. After all, imagine knowing not only your potential consumers' demographic characteristics (how boring) but also his or her likes and dislikes, moods, location and, perhaps, intent.

Almost " all-of-a-sudden" we are able to connect with our consumer at the "Moment of Relevance" — What can I wear? Where can we eat? What should we drive? This almost entirely new concept is made possible by new media.

So, here's the key question. Would Don Draper embrace new media?

I think he would. He'd take a drag on a Marlboro and embrace technology and social media for what it is. It's a tool (an extremely powerful one) to connect. Draper would throw back his head, drawing down a shot of Scotch whisky, and opine that "you need to get connected and stay connected."

I think Don Draper would use this wonderful resource sampler as the authors suggest it be used—to jumpstart his journey into the exciting world of new and social media.

I think you should too.

Sincerely
Michal Lorenc
Google Canada, Inc.

Introduction

If you are looking to understand social media marketing, search engine optimization, blogging, digital public relations, Google, and more, then this book is for you.

Whatever your job title, these skills will help you go far in this new world of digital media. After following this resource sampler, you will be better equipped to:

- Build your personal brand through new media and position yourself for success.
- Use digital marketing to help sell products or find new volunteers.
- Start a new blog or develop content for blogs that already exist but are dead in the water.
- Write digital public relations (PR) news releases.
- Be a master of social media sites like Facebook, LinkedIn, Twitter and YouTube.
- Build communities of interest with customers or other audiences.
- Practice search engine optimization and search engine marketing.
- Understand how Google and Yahoo search rankings have an impact on your business bottom line, and prove it with Google Analytics.

This book won't make you an expert in social media just by reading it. You need to practice social media day-in and day-out.

Our goal in writing this new media driver's book is to get you ready to go out into the world of social media on your own. The resources and commentary in this book will encourage you to visit some new territory and explore the best of the thousands of resources we examined for this first edition.

With the *New Media Driver's License Resource Guide* by your side, you will begin your journey into social media and new media marketing, and you will not be alone. You will have the advice and commentary of great bloggers, professors, journalists, social media professionals, and Michigan State University students who have all shared their experience in this book, and on our resource guide website.

Speaking of MSU students, the New Media Driver's License® Seminar was just one ripple in a huge new wave in education that began for us in 2008 at Michigan State University when we decided to get fully engaged in learning how social media can be used to advance companies, causes, and careers. We use a process we call "guided experience" in our classes. And we used much the same approach in creating this book.

For the past three years we have guided hundreds of students to get their New Media Driver's License® certificate, certifying them as a successful driver in social media and new media marketing. All our students do the work online, start their own blogs, practice SEO for real, and participate in online marketing and public relations.

This isn't a book for the unmotivated, and it's not a "book for dummies" either. This book is an outline for self-instruction. And it requires your active participation.

Think of this book as you would think of a handy travel guide, and you'll make tremendous progress in starting a lifetime "continuing education process." Use this book as recommended and you will find a vast array of valuable, publicly available tools. This guide will also help you find new tools as they surface on the Internet every day. Take this approach and you'll be better equipped to:

- Become an effective and safe driver in a wide variety of social networks, media tools and online technology.
- Get to know the ins and outs of blogging and become a regular blogger.
- Engage with others through social media, including LinkedIn, Twitter and Facebook.
- Understand what social media marketing is and how it can work for you.
- Understand how to listen to and participate in and start online conversations.
- Learn the rules of online public relations, and how PR is quite different than marketing.
- Become part of the online community.
- Understand Google and how search engine optimization (SEO) works.
- Learn to develop a digital marketing strategy.
- Understand and use Google AdWords, and Google Analytics and more than 50 other Google applications.
- Learn about location-based services.

We said this before, and it bears repeating: If you take this challenge seriously, you'll begin a lifetime process of learning and teaching and using and developing new uses for social media as a business tool that so many of us already take for granted as part of our *social life*.

How to Use This Book

The book is laid out in a simple format that allows you to take maximum advantage of the most basic tools and applications we already know so much about.

To get started, it helps if you are connected. It is possible to read this book on an airplane or in a car (preferably while you are a passenger), but generally, we designed this book to be read in such a manner that you can get easy access to resources that may be of special interest to you through links provided on our website in the order that they appear in the book.

Turn your computer on and connect to our website (www.NewMedia DriversLicenseResources.Com) or download the "link listing" so that you can click through to any resource that interests you. The links appear in the order they appear in the book. This listing will be a very useful tool to you over the years as you want to make sure you're doing everything you can to exploit the wonderful world of social media. We'll do our best to add new links as "new and improved" resources become available.

Part 1
SOCIAL MEDIA

CHAPTER 1

What Makes Social Media Social?

There are about as many definitions for social media as there are for public relations, and that's a lot. About.com says the best way to define social media is (or "are" if you're using social media in the plural sense) to break it down. Media is something that is used for communication. Newspaper, radio and television fall into that category. So social media, says About.com, "would be a social instrument of communication." Okay, in order to understand this point of differentiation, one would have to have a pretty clear description of "social."

"Think of regular media as a one-way street where you can read a newspaper or listen to a report on television, but you have very limited ability to give your thoughts on the matter. Social media, on the other hand, is a two-way street that gives you the ability to communicate too." http://webtrends. about.com/od/web20/a/social-media.htm

We're willing to accept this definition so long as the reader is willing to accept the possibility that, over time, virtually every media has been engaged in a struggle to be increasingly social. That's why, for example, newspapers created pages to print "Letters to the Editor." Newspapers understood for a long time that, in order for true communication to occur, they needed to introduce some component of listening and responding to their audience, as well as just reporting on news and offering their editorial opinion.

Radio stations understood the importance of giving voice to one's audience by incorporating another separate media into their programming—the telephone. The call-in talk show, in fact the all-talk radio station, is a concession to the importance of give and take for true communication to occur, and it wasn't until radio stations started taking on-air audience calls that the power of this "social" media began to emerge.

But it wasn't until the development and emergence of the Internet, in which media could become truly "social," that our world really changed, and the socializing of these media is expanding daily as dramatically as are the new uses for these media.

Consider what we learn from the latest edition of "The Social Habit

To ease your exploration of the resources identified in this book, please go to the Link Listing—www.NewMediaDriversLicenseResources.com

3

2011," the study conducted by Edison Research and Arbitron, and reported by Edison VP Tom Webster. http://webtrends.about.com/od/web20/a/social-media.htm:

> Social Media now reaches the majority of Americans 12 (years or older), with 52% having a profile on one or more social networks. This figure is driven largely by Facebook, which is now used by more than half (51%) of Americans 12 and older.
>
> Further, Twitter is as familiar to Americans as Facebook (with 92% and 93% familiarity, respectively). However, Twitter usage stands at 8% of Americans 12 and older. Approximately 46 million Americans 12 and older now check their social media sites and services several times every day.

In what is described as the most-viewed Social Media video series, "Social Media Revolution," author Erik Qualman provides clear evidence of the significance and size of the social media revolution. If you haven't viewed the most recent version, search it on YouTube or go to this link. http://www.socialnomics.net/2011/06/08/social-media-revolution-video-2011/

To find out what's driving this unprecedented adoption of social media, we turn to social media maven Brian Solis who says we need to understand what he calls "behavior-graphics" in order to understand that the many reasons we "share and interact online, and the motivation for doing so, changes with circumstances, intentions, and experiences." http://www.briansolis.com/2010/11/the-three-cs-of-social-networking-consumption-curation-creation/

"The social landscape is populated by individual presences," Solis says, "but charted by its connections and how in turn they move information between them. These conduits represent the opportunities for brands and media to participate in and steer the sharing of usefully and mutually beneficial content."

Solis credits Forrester Research's introduction of Social Technographics http://forrester.typepad.com/groundswell/2007/04/forresters_new_.html with giving us a template for better understanding different use patterns among social media consumers. Reminiscent of Everett Rogers's "Diffusion of Innovations" scale, Forrester characterizes social media consumers as moving up a "Social Technographics® Ladder from Inactives through Spectators, Joiners, Collectors, Critics, Conversationalists, and, ultimately, to Creators."

Solis believes that good content creation is an essential component of a brand or individual's likeability in social media and, acting on that hunch, worked with Vocus http://www.vocus.com/content/index.asp (another significant force in American research) to test his theory.

Solis believes that it is the discovery and consumption of compelling content that helps a consumer move to the "contributor role of curator. . . . Curation drives a significant volume of Tweets, and it is also curation that balances the art and science of engagement between creation and conversation."

http://www.briansolis.com/2010/11/the-three-cs-of-social-networking-con-sumption-curation-creation/

"There's a reason why people 'like' you. The networks realize that as our networks both grow and contextualize, your presence increases exponentially in value and they can sell against it."

Stephanie Schwab, posting in socialmediaexplorer.com, says the first question any brand manager should be asking is: "Are we in the stream?"

"In the coming year people are going to be much more diligent about curating their own content into a more manageable form. Consumers are realizing that following 'eleventy-hundred' brands on Twitter and Facebook is getting them some good coupons and deals, but it's also turning their walls into malls, which is getting overwhelming."

The solution to being overwhelmed by content is one of the new trends in social media, Schwab says. http://www.socialmediaexplorer.com/social-media-marketing/five-social-media-trends-for-2011/

"In Twitter, a company called Cadmus (http://thecadmus.com/) aims to change the way we view our streams by determining what content is most relevant to you based on your Twitter usage patterns. Other tools, such as Paper.li and Flipboard (for iPad), also curate Twitter, primarily based on content popularity, and make that content much more reader-friendly."

"For brands," Schwab says, "this means it's not going to be enough to create content. You have to create content that gets curated into people's streams. If your content is truly compelling and share-worthy, it'll get noticed and 'liked,' it will generate 'comments' and 're-tweets,' and you'll be okay. . . ."

Social Media: The Phenomena

Social Media Resource 1-1: Did You Know 4.0

http://www.youtube.com/watch?v=6ILQrUrEWe8

This video is one of many available in cyberspace that attempts to put numbers on the immensity of the impact of new media. By the time you see this there will be a 5.0 or 6.0 out there, but this resource remains a reminder as to how fast everything is changing.

Social Media Resource 1-2: The Top Three Ways Social Media Has Changed Our Lives

http://www.socialmediatoday.com/brettgreene/200560/top-3-ways-social-media-has-changed-our-lives

There doesn't seem to be a lot of reflection about the impact of social media on the overall quality of our lives. But Brett Greene's SocialMediaToday.com post confirms that there is at least some deep thinking going on. He's been thinking deeply about some of the prophecies that were made with the emergence of Facebook as a force majeure—great force with world-changing implications.

Has Facebook and other social media truly summoned the grim reaper to the villages of traditional media—newspapers, radio, and TV? Are we working at such a rapid pace that we are killing off the kind of thinking that yields great innovation and creativity? Is privacy a thing of the past and what are the implications.

Like us, Greene puts a lot of stake in the wisdom of Brian Solis, and he leans upon this social media maven to remind us that as it relates to privacy, the question may not be so much as to whether or not it is dead, as to whether social media has created conditions in which privacy, and many other things with which we are comfortable, will never quite be the same.

Social Media Resource 1-3: 50 Definitions of Social Media

http://thesocialmediaguide.com/social_media/50-definitions-of-social-media/

If you are still unclear about what social media is TheSocialMediaGuide.com can help.

"If you ask a heap of different people, What is Social Media? they will all give you a different answer," says post writer Matthew Tommasi.

He compiled a list of 50 social media definitions from different industry websites to help.

This list will give you that ability to frame your own definition of social media. And it might also cause you to consider purchasing a copy of Tomassi's *Social Media Guide* within which you will find his definition: "Social media is user generated content that is shared over the internet via technologies that promote engagement, sharing and collaboration." http://thesocialmediaguide.com/

Social Media Resource 1-4: Don't Confuse Social Networking With Social Media

http://adage.com/digitalnext/article?article_id=143232

As the web becomes more social, the meaning of different social terms increasingly is becoming blurred.

"Today, there is a lot of confusion about . . . terms such as *social media* and *social networking* buzzing through the Twitterverse," says Patrick Keane.

Keane, CEO of Associated Content, uses an Adage.com post to explain the differences between the two phrases. And he stresses that these are not distinctions without differences. In fact, Keane says, how you understand the terms will, to a large degree, govern your behavior. How you behave in the commercial Internet will govern your success.

"Until brands understand how to authentically join, rather than crash, the conversation, they will continue to throw their money away," says Keane.

Social Media Resource 1-5: 90+ Essential Social Media Resources

http://mashable.com/2010/05/31/92-essential-social-media-resources/

This is among the most complete list of social media resources we found on the web. The social media gurus at Mashable.com compiled this list of resources on topics ranging from mobile to business. Mashable.com is a resource we trust. Mashable calls this resource a holy grail of social media information.

Find links to funny YouTube videos and other more traditional educational resources and adopt this resource to help you get the most out of social media.

Social Media Resource 1-6: Viralblog Provides Updates with Social Media Trends and News

http://www.viralblog.com/

Be inspired on everything social and viral on Viralblog.com. The blog is ranked #56 on Ad Age's Power 150 as a top media and marketing blog and is a very interesting and credible spot to check out fresh, hot, and up-and-coming social media topics.

The goal of Viral Blog is to bring interested businessmen and women the newest and best social media marketing ideas and strategies and to examine viral campaigns. It's a great resource for social media entrepreneurs and experts to share their wisdom, predictions and suggestions.

Social Media Resource 1-7: What Old McDonald Can Teach You about Social Media

http://www.socialmediaexaminer.com/what-old-mcdonald-can-teach-you-about-social-media/

Old McDonald Had a Farm, E-I-E-I-0.

Social media is the tune marketers are singing today according to Bill Seaver who wrote this clever post for SocialMediaExaminer.com.

Evolution, some say revolution, has taken a toll on advertising as consumers are developing the ability to block and ignore promotions they are confronted with every day. They are shunning persuasion in favor of conversation and fluff in favor of facts.

"Consumers have developed extremely sophisticated filters. As a marketer, you're fighting that filter every day," says Seaver.

Founder of Micro Explosion Media, a social media marketing consulting firm, Seaver obviously wants you to have the benefit of experience in order to know how to get the attention of an increasingly reluctant and discerning audience.

To break this barrier, he uses the pre-school jingle *Old McDonald Had a Farm* to help gain consumer attention by providing valuable content. He uses this pneumonic device "E-I-E-I-O" to remind us that we must *Entertain, Inspire, Educate, Inform and* (even occasionally) *Outrage* if we want to create valuable and memorable content.

Social Media Resource 1-8: Justin Bieber: A Social Media Case Study

http://socialmediatoday.com/eric-goldstein/305692/justin-bieber-social-media-case-study

Love him or hate him, Justin Bieber is a famous entertainer who skyrocketed to fame in what seemed like a matter of seconds. What's the key to his fame? Social media.

Business Development Manager for One To One, Eric Goldstein wrote an article on SocialMediaToday.com examining the undeniable influence social media has had Bieber's career:

> Justin was just starting out—singing on the street with a guitar case in front of him and entering small talent competitions—when he decided to start uploading some of his videos into YouTube.

Bieber's YouTube videos eventually caught the attention of big name music producers and of course the famous Usher (Raymond IV). Once he was found, Bieber and team used Twitter and other social media tools to connect with fans and leverage the star's success. The rest, some may say, is history. His success just proves why you should *never say never* regarding the potential of social media.

Bieber's story is inspirational and a great learning tool for aspiring entertainers and individuals who want to leverage their social media platforms to stardom or success.

Social Media Resource 1-9: Which Boomers Are Using Social Media the Most?

http://adage.com/adagestat/post?article_id=147013

This is a great resource from Ad Age. Post author Matt Carmichael reports on a study social media consultant Laurel Kennedy conducted for her book "*The Daughter Trap.*"

The book discusses the plight of the Baby-Boomer, generally people aged 50 to 65, often referred to as the Sandwich Generation. They are like the meat in the sandwich being squeezed between their children, in one way or the other, while also looking after aged and ill parents.

Kennedy worked with market research firm comScore www.comScore.com

to study a group of "Boomer" caregivers. She found "a great niche for marketers," according to Carmichael.

Roughly 20% of the country's boomers fall into the category of caregivers, and they are increasingly turning to social media, viewing 70% more pages per month than the average Internet user. Why would this be?

The answer might not be what you would expect. It turns out that the number one reason caregivers are turning to social media is, well, the social aspect of it. Says Carmichael:

> Being a caregiver, especially for the parents that always cared for you, causes all kinds of relationship stresses.

Finding *people communities* in similar situations is key for this group.

Strategies and Campaigns in Social Media

Social Media Resource 1-10: How To Start a Social Media Campaign

http://samhowat.com/small-business-social-media-marketing/

A lot of people are weary of social media usefulness for business and marketing. Developing a campaign will alleviate some of this fear and start a social media campaign in the right direction.

SamHowat.com will show you how to start your social media campaign:

> Though establishing a social media presence for your business can be a daunting task, there are several proven strategies for both establishing your campaign and tracking it's results that you can use to get started on the right path.

Helping you to set up an effective social media campaign, Howat demonstrates several goal-setting techniques and ideas for creating a strategic plan. The article discusses different media options to incorporate into a social media campaign like local search, contests, and giveaways.

Social Media Resource 1-11: Social Media— Four Steps to an Effective Marketing Strategy

http://www.practicalecommerce.com/articles/2244-Social-Media-4-Steps-to-an-Effective-Marketing-Strategy

Forget about the four or five Ps of marketing. Paul Chaney, writing in PracticalECommerce.com, says as far as social media is concerned the four Ps don't count, but the four Cs do: *content, communication, conversation,* and *conversion.*

A lot of this and related professional advice gets down to understanding the shift that is occurring in buyer-seller relationships from a persuasion-based model to one in which information and conversation is infinitely more interesting, and profitable.

This is a strong resource in that provides the reader with a usable mental model to help shape their Internet marketing strategy. Chaney also, generously, lists five other great PracticalECommerce.com posts that will be helpful to the start-up or the veteran retailer or other socially inclined marketers.

Social Media Resource 1-12: How to Integrate Social Media with Traditional Media

http://www.socialmediaexaminer.com/how-to-integrate-social-media-with-traditional-media/

Founder of Converse Digital, Tom Martin works with companies and ad agencies, helping them monitor, create, and engage in digital conversations to grow market share or increase customer loyalty. Martin believes that "knowing how to use social media isn't enough."

"So instead of asking how to integrate all of it, maybe a better question would be to ask 'how to think' about integrating social media, digital media, old media and the blending of all of it," says Martin. "We need to be asking for a framework, not a solution."

The post on SocialMediaExaminer.com provides tips to integrate social media marketing with traditional marketing in the right way.

Learning a strategic planning approach and identifying the goals of a social media marketing campaign is something marketers and advertisers should think about when meshing together social media and traditional media.

Social Media Resource 1-13: Social Media Budgeting

http://www.newmediasocial.com/profiles/blogs/social-media-budgeting

Money matters. Creating a budget for a social media campaign is often difficult because it is hard to determine how much money actually is required to do the job. Only spending half enough is like only taking half the pill the physician prescribes to cure your illness. Half a pill probably won't be enough, and shorting the dose in this way might lead you to believe that the medicine was useless. You'd be wrong.

Ray Spellerberg describes how important effective social media budgeting has become in providing the resources necessary to reach your goal.

In his NewMediaSocial.com article Spellerberg says that, "up to 79% of retail/ecommerce companies will increase their social media budgets, as the retail/ecommerce category is known to be leading indicators of marketing and advertising trends, and the rest of the business categories will surely follow."

There is a real shift in marketing with new media.

"The good news is that when budgeting for social media (marketing), businesses do not need to add new dollars to the mix but rather reallocate existing dollars," says Spellerberg.

Check out the comments under the post. We think Robin really has a handle on how more and more of us ought to be thinking about return on social media investment, and to do that, you have to know how much it costs going in.

Social Media Resource 1-14: Social Media Marketing Strategy Study: Twitter vs. Facebook Business Application

http://www.onlineprnews.com/news/30315-1271088215-social-media-marketing-strategy-study-twitter-vs-facebook-business-applications.html

We're not entirely certain why a businessperson would feel a need to choose between a Twitter and a Facebook social media marketing strategy, although one certainly could argue that you ought to pick one of the two to start with. This report of such a comparison in "Online PR Media" (formerly onlineprnews.com) deals with both business-to-business (B2B) and business-to-consumer (B2C) strategies.

As you travel through the links of this release, you can get deeper and deeper into Irbtrax SEO studies that take you through a variety of different aspects of the comparison, beginning with "Traffic and User Metrics."

Their initial release on the study says:

> Facebook was declared to have the advantage (in this category) because its format allows for the inclusion of photos, detailed information, multiple outbound links, videos and other business to consumer applications.

But don't stop here. In the seven-category comparison, the fight ends in a split decision.

Perhaps the most important category is not included, probably for common-sense reasons. One way to settle the dispute as to where to start might involve answering the question: "Which platform is our current customer base and prospect list using today?"

Social Media Resource 1-15: Social Media Marketing Campaign No-Nos

http://business.ezinemark.com/7-social-media-marketing-campaign-no-nos-16de57ad1d7.html

Talk about resources! This link has some great insights about social media.

This EzineMark.com site (the Free Content and Article Directory) is actually the vestibule in their large library of hundreds of bright and brief videos, and many more interesting articles, on virtually every aspect of social marketing.

Just on the landing page, for example, you'll find everything from a brief presentation on "social media mantras" by Patrick Schwerdtfeger to articles on the "Primary Components of a Social Media Marketing Campaign" by Saki S.

Social Media Resource 1-16: President Obama's New Campaign Begins With Social Media Strategy
http://www.siliconrepublic.com/new-media/item/21224-obama-launches-2012/

With more than a year to go before the 2012 US presidential elections, the reelection campaign of sitting President Barack Obama emphasized one dramatic way in which social media has changed our world. You might think it would be enough just to use social media as a central force in a campaign to select the leader of the free world. But there's more.

As Laura O'Brien points out in her article in SiliconRepublic.com, the unprecedented campaign that made Mr. Obama the US's first African-American president "was praised for how it used the web and social media to gain support." Example: As we write, President Obama's Facebook following is approaching 20 million people.

But the 2012 initiative is not only promising to be better and bigger, but it also will boast numerous innovations. For example, the President's homepage has a YouTube video, lists of online groups to join, lists of upcoming events and links to donate or volunteer for the campaign http://www.barack obama.com/im-in-splash-2

Social Media Resource 1-17: A Variety of Hot Social Media Tips from CommProBiz
http://blog.commpro.biz/socialmediazone/category/social-media-how-to/

Library of Congress look out. The world is changing so rapidly that it doesn't seem possible that even our greatest institutions could possibly keep up with the information freely available online. Come to think of it, many of these great institutions (read: dead newspapers) haven't. You already know that one of our favorite resources is CommPro.Biz. In fact, not a day goes by that we don't get a number of great articles delivered via good old-fashioned email from CommProBiz.Biz.

Before you get started in this "library," click to the *about page* of Social Media Zone. Vicki Flaughter, CEO of B2B SocialMediaTraining.com facilitates the site. We guess that means she is the editor and manager. We know she's a wonderful observer of the social media scene.

According to CommPro.Biz: "The mission we gave her was to create a space where the professionals that visit CommPro.Biz can find relevant and helpful information about social media—how to do it, what's working and what's not, how the field is evolving, and let you meet the people beyond the gurus who are living it every day in their businesses."

So, use this exercise as an excuse to drill into the Social Media Zone, and while you are at it, you might just decide to subscribe to this wonderfully enriching new media library.

Social Media Resource 1-18: Top Ten Social Media Tips for Big Ten Plus News Directors

Here's co-author Derek Mehraban's social media advice for the news directors attending the Big Ten Plus News Directors Conference 2011, which was held in June 2011 in East Lansing.

Rick thought the advice was right on the money, and rather than send you to Derek's blog http://www.thedigialbus.com to get the full story, we thought we'd reprint the post in its entirety right here, right now:

Top Ten Social Media (Marketing) Tips for Big Ten News

1. **Optimize yourself first and foremost.** And that includes your team. As a Big Ten news director it's important to be able to find you with ease—and I mean by Googling you. So be sure you have a strong profile. Be sure you have links from your university. Take a screen shot of your search results and build from there. What happens when I search for Derek Mehraban on Google?

2. **Create great content.** First and foremost you need to create great content for your organizations. Interesting. Fun. Funny. Relevant. News content. Blur the lines of news and entertainment. The more interesting the information is the better. What is the most interesting and entertaining thing you have covered? And then think where do you post that? Facebook? Twitter? Blogs? How do you disseminate your news?

3. **Lead with your best SEO terms.** Figure out what people are searching for and lead with that. Put your keywords at the front of your titles on pages, and through out your copy. Use one phrase or 3-5 keywords per post or news release. Use the keywords at the beginning, middle, and end. Next, link to that article from other places using those keywords. This means—don't waste your prime real estate w/ words that won't help you. Search the phrase "Digital Marketing Firm" on Google and see what happens.

4. **Tweet. Follow. And ReTweet.** Using Twitter to build community is a lot like being at a tailgate—everyone has fun. So put out your content. But share and promote others content too. Use your University Twitter accounts for the greater good. And then use your personal accounts to further promote and build relationships. Be real.

5. **Know your audience.** Figure out with whom you want to communicate. Where do they spend time? What interests them? You can use analytics to help you with this. Also, you can ask them with surveys. Once you find out the "who, what, when, where, and why", you can communicate much more effectively and get more traction from your news. Can you track your audiences? Think about remote check-in services like Foursquare, Gowalla, or Facebook check in. What can you do to capitalize on this trend?

6. **Be known for the smallest things.** And track it. The beauty of SEO and the Internet is that you can create micro-content that relates to your university. You can show up in the search results for the smallest and most obscure search phrases. Whether it's a certain type of rare spider, or a micro-fusion technique that is being pioneered by your university. Why not pick three interesting keyword phrases per university department that you want to be known for and develop a content strategy to get page one Google ranking for them?

7. **Video, Photos, and Text Oh My!** These days you need all three to be relevant. Think about events. What can you document? What is the social play? When you publish video, photos and text—you have a much better chance of showing up on people's radar.

8. **"Coopetition" as my friends Terry Bean and Charlie Wollborg like to say, is imperative.** Work together to build the reputation of the best conference in the United States—the Big Ten. Why not have cooperative competition between the Big Ten Universities. In fact you have a great opportunity to help one another. Why not create a #hashtag or use #BigTen and then you can promote and Tweet or share other information from your Big Ten counterparts. This type of arrangement could be really beneficial. Linking to one another's articles could really boost SEO. Ask for people to RT, Share on Facebook, or +1 your content on Google.

9. **Monitor and track your success.** Metrics like time on site, time watching videos, views of pages or releases are all very important—track them. I encourage you to share your best practices for how you do it—by commenting on this blog post so others can see it. We use Trackur or Radian6 for tracking trends and keywords. You can too. Also simple things like Google Alerts can really help you track. In addition to using HootSuite or some sort of social content producing site that allows you to track users and #hashtags.

10. **Mobile browsing and interaction is KING.** How does your university look in the mobile environment? Mobile browsing, especially for students, is going to surpass traditional Internet browsing. Be very aware of how you show up on mobile devices. Think Apps. iPhone, Android, Windows Mobile, Blackberry. Test, and refine and promote to mobile audiences. Who is doing the best job at Mobile in the Big Ten?

Social Media Resource 1-19: Twitter Talk Draws Dantonio's Ire
http://www.lansingstatejournal.com/apps/pbcs.dll/article?AID=2011107310486

Related to the role of social media and athletics, comes this article in the *Lansing State Journal*, the hometown paper of Michigan State University:

> You are always representing Michigan State. On the field, in class, on the streets of East Lansing—and yes, even when you are sitting at home using social media on your handheld device.

These are the sentiments Coach Mark Dantonio expressed to his Big Ten champ football players, according to LSJ sportswriter Joe Rexrode. It was a tough message designed for one purpose and one purpose alone. There is way too much information being tweeted by the players, and it's starting to get the coach riled up.

"I don't want to stop them from doing something, but I want them to understand that they represent all of us," Dantonio said Friday when asked by sportswriters if he has considered banning his players from Twitter. "If somebody makes (a comment)—which you read, you guys read them—and they think they're talking to their buddies and they're talking to all you guys, it's ridiculous. It's a reflection on all of us."

Social Media Resource 1-20: Ten Blended Social Media Marketing Strategies a Company Might Want to Consider
http://directmarketingobservations.com/2009/07/29/10-blended-social-media-marketing-strategies-a-company-might-want-to-consider/

You've made a Twitter account, Facebook, LinkedIn and created some Search Engine optimized content. Now what?

Using these platforms is only a small piece of the social media marketing pie. An even larger piece involves understanding how these tools are incorporated into marketing strategies.

Clients were requesting "that I should supply a document that mapped out the ways that you can blend social media into your marketing mix," said Marc Meyer, a Digital and Social Media Strategist at Ernst and Young.

To help, Meyer posted an article on DirectMarketingObservations.com that "supplied the tool or the platform, how I used it, what was the time suck and what were the results."

This post is an awesome resource and gave us a new way of looking at the process for integrating the right social media into our overall campaigns.

"This is what has worked and works for me when working with clients." Hopefully this resource will be as helpful to you as it apparently has been for Meyer's clients.

Social Media Resource 1-21: The Ten Stages of Social Media Business Integration

http://mashable.com/2010/01/11/social-media-integration/

We know it's starting to sound repetitive, but we simply have to push you to another Brian Solis piece. His Mashable.com posts are the cream of the crop, and he did it again with this "Kubler-Ross" stages of grief-like sequencing of what a business should go through to fully integrate its social strategy.

Solis never really explains what he means by integration, but he obviously knows it when he sees it: It becomes clear as you walk through the steps he feels are necessary for a business to be on the leading new media edge of its business segment.

One thing is clear. Solis believes, as do KD Paine (who you will read about later) and others, that true business integration of social media cannot occur until you have a full understanding of the "volume, locations, and nature of online interaction, the true impact of our digital footprint, and its relationship to the bottom line. . . ."

"Business Performance Metrics" is the tenth stage in the Solis/Kubler-Ross model. Getting from steps one to nine may cause lots of grieving. It is never, ever, as easy to do this stuff as it seems on paper, but Solis makes a very credible case that there's something very important to experiencing all the stages along the way to full acceptance.

Social Media Resource 1-22: How to Plan and Promote Events with Social Media

http://mashable.com/2009/04/29/events-social-media/

Event planners spend countless hours organizing and planning events, picking the invitations, catering, picking a venue, budget issues, and picking the décor.

You'll see that we have selected Mashable.com editor Ben Parr's writings as among many of the best resources for social media and marketing we've found.

This post provides a step-by-step guide teaching you everything from choosing the right social media tools for an event to tips for e-invitations: "Whether you need to work with organizers, generate buzz, or share post-party photos, social media should be a primary weapon in your arsenal."

He describes how using social media for an event is a great way to create conversation and keep people updated before, during and even after the event is over. The Children's Trust Fund of Michigan has used some of these techniques in generating buzz for its annual Pam Posthumus Signature Auction Event, a "must attend" event in the State of Michigan capital city.

Social Media Resource 1-23: Seven Traits of
Successful Social Media Campaigns

http://www.adrants.com/2010/10/seven-traits-of-successful-social-
media.php?utm_source=feedburner&utm_medium=feed&utm_
campaign=Feed%3A+adrants+%28Adrants%29

Adrants.com "provides marketing and advertising news . . . with insightful, informed, experiential, no-holds-barred commentary on the state of advertising. . . ." Its publisher, Steve Hall, has "done time," (in his words) in a variety of advertising agency-related jobs.

We thought his list of traits of a successful "social" campaign is a great "common sense" way to start this discussion because it's almost entirely about the concept of authenticity. From "platitudes don't work" to the importance of avoiding "blatant self promotion," Hall's no-B.S. approach to campaigns should be required reading.

Social Media Resource 1-24: Why Social Media Is Perfect for
Brand Ambassador Campaigns

http://mashable.com/2010/10/25/bran3d-ambassador-campaigns/

Jared from Subway, the Snapple lady, and the mothers of Walmart are benefitting from social media.

Stephanie Marcus, posting in yet another Mashable.com site, describes how social media can amplify "real people" advertising campaigns:

> The public, having grown wary of traditional advertising, has become more difficult to convince. That's where the brand ambassador—the person who creates a sense of credibility, likability, or interest—comes in.
>
> Brands have realized that *people like real people* and social media has the ability to take that one step further.

We suspect that the "dialogic ability" of social media—when I get a tweet from a celebrity it feels like it's from her to me—is the driving force behind this phenomenon.

Marcus praises successful ad campaigns that mix social and traditional media. Her Mashable.com post describes how you can create a lasting image, generate positive feedback and share content with others to promote your brand using ordinary people as the face of a social media campaign.

Social Media Resource 1-25: Warning Signs of a Weak Social Media
Strategy

http://www.socialmediatoday.com/SMC/195884

"Instead of watching a train wreck hurt your brand, here are warning signs of a weak social media strategy that you need to be aware of before things really get bad," says social media and marketing enthusiast Nehal Kazim.

You may be able to fix a failing social media campaign if you know the warning signs.

Ryerson University (Toronto) student Kazim's list of warning signs of a weak social media strategy contains a bit of a tautology, but we can handle that. His warning sign number five of a weak social media strategy is "There is No Social Media Strategy in the First Place!!" And that's a point worth emphasizing.

"Ask yourself or your team, 'do we really have a social media strategy?' If you're not honest about this, all of your hard work will mean nothing. If you don't have a social media strategy, stop putting it off and get started," Kazim says.

What are the key components to consider?

- "Why are you participating in social media? Exposure? Sales? Creating bonds with your clients?

- "What's the expected ROI (Return on Investment)? Are you expecting too much too soon?

- "What's the content strategy? What will you post? Why are you posting that content? How is the content aligned with the reason why you're on social media?"

Social Media: The Emerging Tool for Business

Social Media Resource 1-26: Social Media Profiles Increase Trust in e-Commerce Sites

http://www.businesswire.com/news/hoime/20110411006240/en/Social-Media-Profiles-Increase-Consumer-Trust-e-Commerce

One of our favorite resources is Business Wire, a Berkshire Hathaway Company. http://www.businesswire.com/portal/site/home/ We don't see everything that they put out—they are a news release distribution enterprise, of course. But what we do see from BW is normally in plain English, capable of being understood by a man who would say, as would Berkshire's Warren Buffet, "never invest in something you don' understand."

"With three million fraudulent or fake websites entering the World Wide Web every year, consumers are understandably wary about buying from sites that are away from the mainstream," PR social and search agency Punch Communications said in a presser released through Business Wire.

So what's the answer for companies in a category that may be a bit suspect, if you will, or at least seen as being too large to fail, like Buffet's GEICO, for example? Social media, that's what. And, now that you know this little

GEICO gecko has a Facebook page, doesn't that make you trust the company just a bit more?

Turns out it might.

Social Media Resource 1-27: Eight Ways Businesses Should Use Social Media

http://kikolani.com/8-ways-businesses-social-media.html

This great resource is guaranteed to help you become a better business-savvy social media marketer.

Social networking blogger and creator of Kikolani.com Kristi Hines's post can help you identify different ways your business should be using social media. But you have to put her ideas into practice. Hoping won't help.

Hines offers "eight ways that businesses can use social media to learn more about themselves and their industry as well as get more involved with their clients and communities interested in what they have to offer."

Start out, Hines implores, by monitoring conversations about your business through Google Alerts http://www.google.com/alerts and Social Mention. http://www.socialmention.com/

"Many businesses hear about the advantages of social media in terms of marketing their products or services, but some forget to look at other major benefits of social media beyond finding leads or making a sale," says Hines.

Her Kikolani.com post gives you customer service tips and ideas for monitoring industry trends through social media to help your business thrive.

Sometimes the only thing keeping you from controlling content and driving traffic to your website is just doing it. You might say: "Well, there's not much new here." We think that's right because this article applies traditional business principles with traditional social media models to help you create a marketing plan that will work for your business.

And just like any business strategy, hoping won't make it happen.

Social Media Resource 1-28: Five Stages of Social Media Maturity

http://socialmediatoday.com/billives/305522/five-stages-social-media-maturity?ref=popular_posts–

Every organism has a life cycle and matures through different stages. Social media isn't any different.

Bill Ives, consultant and writer in on SocialMediaToday.com and elsewhere, examined the natural cycle social media goes through as they adopt new social media technologies.

His article is based on the Forrester research that was the basis for the strong-selling book, *Groundswell*. It would be very easy to misinterpret both the Forrester research and Ives article to suggest that there is a logical sequence of development that companies go through in adopting social media, but we don't think this is the point.

Ives (and presumably, though we haven't read the Forrester report, or even *Groundswell*, for that matter) has companies moving from the Laggard stage, through testing to coordinating "where management recognizes the risks and rewards of social media."

From there, Ives says companies move to "scaling and optimizing . . . when firms 'have already coordinated their social organization and are now focusing on optimizing their social media activities.'"

"Finally," Ives says, "the Innovators are truly empowering their employees. This final stage is where an easy to use social media awareness tool . . . can have a real impact."

Communications scholar Everett Rogers spent three or four decades of his academic career expounding upon and elaborating the Diffusion of Innovations theory (Google: Diffusion of Innovations), for which he became internationally known. A very similar concept to the one described above by Ives, Rogers looked at approach to the adoption of processes, consumer products, ideas—even the Internet of which he wrote in 2003—as moving through stages, for sure, with increasing percentages of a population acquiescing.

Innovators, those who are inclined to embrace change, may constitute as low a percentage as 2.5% of a normal population while Rogers's laggards—the last to move—maybe be more than 6 times that percentage (16%). In between are early adopters, early majority and late adopters.

As you are examining the resources presented and, to a limited extent, discussed in this book, it might be wise for you to ask yourself where you fit on Ives's adaptation of Rogers's scale. Are you willing to make the changes necessary to get on the cutting edge of the curve? As you might also, correctly, observe the cutting edge is not always the best place to be. Just ask Julius Caesar.

Social Media Resource 1-29: Answered: 10 Common Social Media Marketing Questions

http://blog.hubspot.com/blog/tabid/6307/bid/7093/Answered-10-Common-Social-Media-Marketing-Questions.aspx

Social media marketing and its role in the business mix are often misunderstood. In fact, that's a bit of an understatement. Given the embryonic stage of social media compared to other forms of media, for example, most effective social media applications for business have not yet been discovered.

Magdalena Georgieva posted on Hubspot.com to help us clear up some of the obvious misconceptions about social media and business.

In her post, she gives some strong hints as to how she goes about judging the effectiveness of a social media campaign; how to create and maintain a blog; and even details like how to incorporate social media buttons into web content.

Georgieva's blog post also discusses how to evaluate the best channels to use for reaching your target audience.

Social Media Resource 1-30: Top Five Enterprises Using Social Media

http://mashable.com/2010/10/05/top-enterprises-social-media/

That people are using social media for business is old news. Exactly how businesses are *going social* is a different story.

"There are countless enterprises—from mega brands promoting campaigns, to small business owners growing their presences—maximizing social media in their day-to-day," says Zachary Sniderman, Assistant Features Editor at Mashable.com

Sniderman provides examples from The National Wildlife Federation to Ann Taylor and Whole Foods to show how these for-profit and not-for-profit organizations create a sense of community using individualized forms of social media.

Sniderman's insightful post will help you generate your own ideas to take control of your brand's online image through social media marketing.

Social Media Resource 1-31: Three Steps to Improving Client Retention With Social Media 101

http://www.accountingsoftware411.com/Press/Insider/InsiderArticleView.aspx?iid=10
49&docid=12153

Rick's always thought that *elegance is best defined by its simplicity*. Here's what he says is an elegant post on ways to keep clients interested in you and to form the kinds of relationships that will power your company over the years.

Author Brett Owens is CEO and co-founder of Chrometa, a provider of time-tracking software that records and categorizes activity in real time. Probably nothing will create a stronger bond with a client than accurate and timely activity reports—or that will lose a client's trust faster than late or insufficient ones. We got that, but we're partial to Owens's second point in this post: "Set up a Blog and Write Informative Articles on a Weekly Basis":

> You have a lot of expertise floating around in your head, so much that you might not realize it. Your clients tap this vast pool of knowledge when they meet with you and engage your services—it's the value they receive from doing business with you.

Social Media Resource 1-32: Five Ways Companies are Using Social Media to Lower Costs

http://mackcollier.com/5-ways-companies-are-using-social-media-to-lower-costs/

Before you dig into this resource, remember that the one thing the author may be missing is that *it takes several more dollars, generally, to get a new customer than it does to keep an existing one.* So, on our list of ways that companies can use social media, retaining existing relationships scores number one.

Almost everyone loves to make money and no one loves to spend money, especially businesses. (The fact that this is Derek's statement is attributable, in part, to the fact that he is a small businessman, and Rick is a professor. Also, the fact that he would say "no one loves to spend money" is irrefutable evidence that he doesn't have teenagers yet. Rick remembers when his then-teenaged daughter acted surprised to learn he had a Ph.D. after his name. "I always thought it was ATM," the daughter said.)

"There are two ways that social media can benefit your business: By generating sales, or by lowering costs," says social media marketing blogger Mack Collier.

In the MackCollier.com post Collier says businesses often overlook the potential of social media to lower their business costs. His aim, however, is to "highlight some ways that companies can lower costs via social media, with some examples of companies that are doing just that."

This is a great resource because provides real examples—tips from Fortune 500 companies, like Cisco, that use social media in their own business dealings, and are developing new client programs to cut costs and increase customer satisfaction.

Social Media Resource 1-33: 30 Tips for Using Social Media in Your Business

http://www.inc.com/articles/2010/01/30-tips-for-using-social-media.html

The author of this resource describes it as "a social media cheat sheet for the time-strapped entrepreneur."

Here's Joyner's tip #8.

> Don't try to create a stand-in for yourself.
>   With all the other tasks required within your company, it's tempting to outsource managing your social media or even to try automating the process. That can easily backfire, as Joe Pulizzi, founder of Cleveland marketing firm Junta42, learned when he tried sending automated welcome messages to new followers on Twitter. His online contacts quickly called him out for sending out what they perceived to be spam.

Here's another tip that will help resolve a growing dispute. Some social media-oriented marketing consultants believe it is "dangerous" to allow people to post comments that have not been pre-screened. Others, on the other hand, won't participate in a blog if they feel that someone is "approving." "Why," they say, "should I expect others to go along with censorship?"

Joyner puts it this way:

> Interact with visitors—really.
>
> Just putting up a blog or a Facebook fan page won't do much good if visitors sense the flow of conversation only goes one way.
>
> In fact, Matt Mullenweg, founder of blogging platform Wordpress, lists not participating in comments as a surefire way to kill a community. Mullenweg and his team field the many suggestions users have for Wordpress through his blog.

Social Media Resource 1-34: 90% of College Faculty Use Social Media in the Workplace

http://www.prnewswire.com/news-releases/new-survey-finds-more-than-ninety-per-cent-of-college-faculty-use-social-media-in-the-workplace-119626249.html

We still run into a few Luddites on college campuses. Nonetheless, we're not exactly surprised that college faculty are nearly "twice as likely as other workers to be using social media as part of their job," according to a recent survey conducted by Babson Survey Research Group.

"Faculty are big users of and believers in social media—nearly 80 % use at least one online social media site to support their professional career activities. More than three-quarters have visited a social media site within the past month for personal use, with half of them posting content," said Jeff Seaman, Ph.D., Co-director of the Babson Survey Research Group.

More than 40% of faculty members say they require students to read or view social media as part of a course assignment, and 20% assign students to comment or post to social media sites. Almost half of faculty use video and other sites in their teaching, with another one-third using video only.

Social Media Resource 1-35: Study—72% of Marketers Don't Outsource Social Media

http://www.prdaily.com/marketing/Articles/7875.aspx

Companies are outsourcing their call centers to India. They are outsourcing their janitorial services, their cafeterias, even their payroll management system. So why aren't most companies outsourcing their social media? Ragan's PRDaily.com raised this question in the post we cite above.

The post links to SocialMediaExaminer.com 2011 *Social Media Marketing Industry Report* (http://www.socialmediaexaminer.com/social-media-marketing-industry-report-2011/). This resource goes into a great many issues beyond outsourcing social media. "Where are my peers targeting their social media efforts? What benefits are they achieving? Where will they focus their future activities?"

Before you jump to a conclusion on this, check out the first comment on the article. Mayra Ruiz say: "If social media-anything was commonly NOT outsourced, man, my agency would be SOL and out of work. I've actually seen all kinds of combinations and approaches towards outsourcing and not outsourcing social."

We think that what the *SocialMediaExaminer* may be picking up is the tendency, like Ruiz says deeper in her comment, for organizations not to think of it as outsourcing when an outside firm is engaged to help set up and operate a social program. After all, admitting that you have your social media done outside your organization might sound a bit anti-social.

Social Media Resource 1-36: How to Develop a Social Media Policy

http://humanresources.about.com/od/socialmediaandwork/a/social_media.htm

As Susan M. Heathfield in this About.com post says: "Your employees are participating in social media." So, what are you going to do about it?

"Use social media to your company's advantage." Shama (Hyder) Kabani, author of *Zen of Social Media Marketing* asks a company's customers, clients, employees and other key constituencies:

> What are they saying about you, your company, and your practices? Better yet—how are you responding? Having a social media policy in place does not mean that you get to dictate your image. But, you do get to interact responsibly in the conversation that forms your image. And, you get to help your employees do the same.

Beyond this, Kabani says there are benefits to blogs and Twitter and other social media, but there are risks. Without a clear policy, you and your company can get into trouble with other government agencies, customers or the general public. In other words, without a policy, you can allow your company's brand name to be diminished, or worse.

Heathfield, again drawing heavily on the work of Kabani, lays out a step-by-step process for analyzing what your policy should be and how you should convey it. But don't expect the post to ruminate on whether or not such a policy should be put in place. It's how to—not *let's think about it.*

Social Media Resource 1-37: How Social Media Actually Improves Your Productivity at Work

http://www.socialmediatoday.com/suzannevara/237190/how-social-media-actually-improves-your-productivity-work

"With employees surrounded by thousands of ways to keep in touch with the outside world while working, are productivity levels doomed to slide into

Twitter oblivion?" Suzanne Vara examines this issue in a recent post in Social-MediaToday.com

This is a great resource if you want to tell your boss to get his facts straight when he tells you to get off Facebook at work. You might want to be somewhat diplomatic, but Vara argues that you should say that social media is helping you be more productive, not less, on the job.

"Social media is having a surprisingly opposite effect on work productivity. Social media is improving work productivity," says Vara.

Vara theorizes that productivity may increase through the use of social media because people who use social media while doing other work are able to multitask. She also suggests that scientific evidence supports the notion that says a "mental break" is good for productivity. Social media can provide that escape.

Social Media Resource 1-38: Going Global with Your Social Media Strategy

http://chiefmarketer.com/disciplines/international/1006-global-social/

Global social media is the new frontier for many international businesses.

"The reality for global marketers is that the rest of the world is just as engaged—if not more so—in the social media channels that Americans pioneer," says Rebecca Bernard Aguiar.

Social media's popularity transcends boundaries, but the way it is used differs greatly. Businesses hoping to go global with their social media marketing campaigns need to be cautious.

In her post in Chief Marketer.com, Aguiar cautions marketers hoping to capitalize on international social markets:

> Successful marketers know that the success of their brand messages hinge on speaking to their buyers directly, and regional language and cultural preferences can greatly impact this success.

Aguiar describes different global strategies—tackling the language barrier and tailoring cultural preferences to help your brand go global.

New Tactics, Tools and Tricks of the Trade

Social Media Resource 1-39: New Mobile App Aims to Make Social Media Your Friend

http://www.sciencedaily.com/releases/2011/04/110411121752.htm

People learn things in all kinds of ways. And there is a wealth of free information available on the Internet for folks who want to polish their new media skills, as this book is trying to emphasize.

Here's a new application that comes from a faculty member at England's Bournemouth University, Andy Pulman. It's designed to teach social media to those new to the idea.

A book author in his own right (*Blogs, Wikis, Podcasts and More*) ScienceDaily.com describes the new application as designed to "give brief and informative tips on a range of social media, and how you can get the best out of using it."

Social Media Resource 1-40: 90+ Essential Social Media Resources
http://mashable.com/2010/05/31/92-essential-social-media-resources/

This is a must-save Mashable site. You simply have to love Matt Silverman for putting together a list that links you to nearly 100 fabulous (most), fascinating (somewhat less), frivolous (a good many) resources that you can use:

- To turn a profit. The design community is always hungry for content, inspiration, and tutorials. These nine networks are a great place to discover and share creative resources.

- Boost non-profit. The National Wildlife Federation has been getting creative with their social media awareness campaigns, particularly when it comes to location-based technologies. This post discusses some of their innovations.

- Curate content. At times, content creators and content curators have been at odds, but the sheer volume of "stuff" and noise on the web has made curation essential. This post discusses the status of the curator on today's social web.

There are 87 more, at least.

Social Media Resource 1-41: Tools to Help Companies Manage Their Social Media
http://www.nytimes.com/2010/11/15/business/media/15social.html

The reason some accidental status updates, tweets, and photo uploads on a social network can be deadly is because *they are permanent*.

Twitter saves every tweet even after it's deleted, and, anyhow, instant dissemination to followers and friends means your message, with special emphasis on the 'mess' part, has already been broadcast. Corporations using social media need to be aware of what messages are posted and who is posting them.

Tanzina Vega, media reporter and multimedia journalist for *The New York Times*, describes how important social media management is.

In the rush for businesses "to leverage the keyboard," many companies are finding an unwanted side-effect—an inability to keep track of all the ephemeral thoughts and ideas they are sending into cyberspace.

"But," says Vega, "a small suite of emerging technologies offering solutions to help companies manage their social media presence, by archiving business communications or managing individual employees' posts on sites like Twitter and Facebook."

Besides every other reason for keeping track of every social media message released from a corporate account, one major argument is that it provides a way to avoid legal issues.

Here's the basic message. *Archive, archive, archive!* Understand how to keep track of everything on social networks and safeguard yourself from harming the company brand, and your own job security.

Social Media Resource 1-42: Nine Must-Have Gadgets for Social Media Nuts

http://thenextweb.com/gadgets/2010/11/13/9-must-have-gadgets-for-social-media-nuts/

Adam Mills of TheNextWeb.com is a gadget nut. That's all there is to it. Well, that's not all there is to it. He must also be a David Letterman fan because when he puts out a Top Nine list, he also starts from the bottom of the list and works up to number one.

We almost couldn't stand the suspense as he worked up from Gadget #9—a *Livescribe Echo SmartPen*. This is the pen that allows you to jot notes on special paper that picks up the writing with a camera in the pen's tip. The pen also records what's being said. (It's also smart legal strategy to disclose that you are recording a conversation at the beginning, not the end, of a meeting.)

Other more familiar items on the list include the *Samsung Galaxy* (tablet device), the *Apple iPad*, the *Microsoft Xbox 360*, the *Eye-Fi*, the *Flip Slide HD camcorder*, *Google TV, HTC EVO 4G* (Sprint), and revealing that this column is now about one year old (the puppy is now seven in human years) Gadget #1 . . . Well, you'll have to check out Mills's post to find out just what he picked.

But we will say this. We can't wait to see Mills 2011 update.

Social Media Resource 1-43: 11 Twitter and Social Media Tools to Try in 2011

http://www.commscorner.com/2010/11/11-twitter-social-media-tools-to-try-in.html

New tools are coming to social media much, much faster than we are able to keep track of them. That's why we put together this book. We, and our students, have found most of these resources, and we are reporting on them, among the many possibilities, to help you get started. This Commscorner.com (we assume its Comms Corner and not Comm Scorner) post showed us a couple of tools of which we'd never heard, and the writing is clean and to-the-point.

Here's an example about MentionMap, a "conversation-visualization tool."

Post author Adam Vincenzini puts it this way: "I think PR people will really like this one."

"MentionMap provides a 'live' analysis of what a particular person is talking about on Twitter and who they are talking to."

"When you take a look at a blogger or journalist's MentionMap, you can get a really clear idea of what they have been Tweeting about lately."

Social Media Resource 1-44: 5 Incredibly Useful Social Media Tools Making a Splash (This Week)

http://www.prdaily.com/Main/Articles/8920.aspx

This same Adam Vincenzini, PR Daily Europe contributing editor, shows you how a clever new tool, Twylah.com, can "turn your tweets into a fan page" and how Likester.com can help you "see what the world 'likes.'"

Beyond that, this social media maven leads you to three other very useful tools (and, in some cases, you might say tool boxes) that you may want to test drive.

Social Media Resource 1-45: The Number One Thing to Do to Go Viral on Social Media

http://blog.commpro.biz/socialmediazone/?p=1455

Here's another CommPro.Biz blog post that we found incredibly valuable. It's kind of a trick headline—there really is no one thing to do except "be sharable." So, the real question then is, "How do I make my posts or videos (or whatever) more shareable?"

The post gives eight ideas ranging from "lighten up" to "ask me to share." Sounds obvious? Well, we want to assure you that as elementary as many of the CommPro pointers are, this is a great checklist to go through so you're not wasting your time posting "dogs that won't hunt."

Social Media Resource 1-46: The 7 Secrets of Social Media Conversion

http://unbounce.com/social-media/the-7-secrets-of-social-media-conversion-info-graphic/

The secret's out! But Oli Gardner wants you to promise not to spread it around, at least until you talk to someone.

Improving your conversion rate is easier then you think. The website UnBounce.com and the people at Flowtown have compiled their secret sauce in a colorful infographic to push your next social media campaign to greater success.

Gardner believes "these seven secrets (shhh) will help you leverage social media in smarter ways to improve your conversions."

Infographic/narrative combination on UnBounce.com should help you create an ever-more engaging social media page that will produce even more positive results.

Gardner puts a great deal of emphasis on the importance of a landing page and how to use social media widgets to prove your validity and show the organization's popularity.

Social Media Resource 1-47: 10 Beautiful Social Media Infographics
http://mashable.com/2010/07/01/social-media-infographics/

Looking at a pretty picture is actually a great way to learn. You might even say it's worth a thousand words, we suppose.

"Infographics help communicate information in a digestible manner as they creatively present data in an understandable and engaging format," says experienced web designer Grace Smith. You might ask: "What do you expect a graphics designer to say? *Did you ever ask a barber if you need a haircut?*"

But, seriously folks, Smith's article on Mashable.com is much deeper than you might expect. She compiles a list of 10 infographics that are actually designed and, she says, tested, to help you learn and make sense of social media.

"With social media growing at an ever-increasing pace, there is now a wealth of data about how people are interacting with one another on the web," said Smith.

The list of infographics engages your inner creativity by organizing data into a colorful and playful format. Social media are represented on infographics like the Conversation Prism, which categorizes and organizes how people use social media according to how they are used for finance and human resources. This list can make social media even more fun and interesting then you already think it is.

Social Media Resource 1-48: 5 Social Media Marketing Tips That Will Get You Instant Results
http://www.businessinsider.com/5-social-media-marketing-tips-that-will-get-you-instant-results-2010-4

Creating a blog, Twitter and Facebook account is hardly the start of a social media marketing campaign.

"Sure, you can start publishing updates and sending friend requests, but

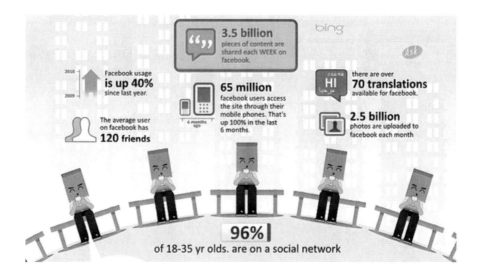

those communications are just the preliminary steps to social media marketing success," says Susan Gunelius.

As President and CEO of KeySplash Creative Inc., a marketing communications provider and branding consultancy with nearly 20 years of marketing, branding, and copywriting experience, Gunelius's BusinessInsider.com article is a great resource to learn how to improve your social media marketing results— fast.

Her article provides five simple tips that will help you achieve your goals with social media. Learn how to be more accessible to audience members to create an interactive and open environment. Create the right content for your social media platforms that can be shared and incorporated with other marketing efforts.

This is a great resource for learning how to mold information of your brand to the customer and keep them wanting more.

Social Media Resource 1-49: 16 Tactics for Building an Audience via Social Media

http://www.socialmediatoday.com/mikebrown-brainzooming/240629/16-tactics-building-audience-social-media

Mike Brown posted this great resource in socialmediatoday.com. Direct and to the point, Brown, the founder of Brainzooming Group, is described as a strategic brand builder, and we can see why after reading this piece. Here are just three of his key points:

1. **Regularly share strong, intriguing content, especially news & interesting links**—It's easy to say, "Don't be boring." Work hard

to make sure it's also easy for your audience to see you really follow the advice. And don't think you can share content once and then stop! Be consistent in your presence and sharing.

2. **Share content from intriguing people**—If you struggle generating enough rich content on your own, at least share and link to rich content others are creating.

3. **Don't overpromote yourself**—Nobody likes an aggressive salesperson in real life or online. Cool the sales pitch and attract followers at their pace.

It's worth reading, so go read it, and let Brown know how you found him while you are at it.

Social Media Resource 1-50: The New and Improved 2010 Social-Media and Mobile Glossary

http://adage.com/article/cmo-strategy/improved-2010-social-media-mobile-glossary/146161/

By the time you read this, no doubt Pete Blackshaw will have his 2011 jargon refresher out and published on Ad Age's CMO Strategy e-newsletter. Go ahead and Google him to find an update. But here are a few buzzwords and phrases he accumulated in 2010.

A *hash bragger*, for example, is "a person who consistently (and annoyingly) uses hash tags to brag about exploits, exclusive conferences, or envious travel—often uses multiple hash tags."

Then there's the *App rat*: "A relentless app collector who is known to download apps and then leave them to gather cobwebs. Related to *Appotato*, a compulsive app addict.

Then there is the *trail marker*. Picture the central character in Disney's version of the great Farley Mowat book *Never Cry Wolf*. You know, it features the guy who drank excessive amounts of tea so he'd have enough ammunition to mark off his territory from the wolf pack. (Well, maybe you had to be there.)

Social Media Resource 1-51: Top 10 Ways to Promote Your Social Media Presence Offline

http://www.toptenz.net/top-10-ways-to-promote-your-social-media-presence-offline.php

Here's *guerilla marketing* brought to cyberspace. We are not sure each and every idea in this TopTenz.net list is a great one. Like Thomas Edison said, every wrong idea is a step forward because it proves what won't work.

Ok. Here's one of the ideas, and you'll have to judge how good it is:

You know you are a social media enthusiast when you choose to steer away from the average Halloween costume shop and go (to the party after) dressing up as your Facebook profile instead.

Check this post out.

Social Media for Personal Brand Building

You know the expression that *the cobbler's kid goes without shoes?* Well, you do now, and you really ought to think about this within the context of social media. Here's a thought: "If you can't find yourself on Google, maybe you don't exist."

That may be a bit of an overstatement, but think about it in this way: You have to understand the *positive power* social media has for building your personal brand, and your personal brand is undeniably connected to your professional success. And parents and grandparents shouldn't forget what this BizReport points out—that children have an online presence even before they are born. http://www.bizreport.com/2010/10/avg-children-have-online-presence-before-birth.html

So, we've included just a couple of good resources to keep your family from going shoeless.

Social Media Resource 1-52: 101 Social Media Sites to Help Market Your Business or Yourself Online
http://www.seomoz.org/article/social-media-marketing-tactics

New social media websites seem to be popping up everywhere. And there is a social media site for just about everything. This is a great resource to guide your marketing efforts for a brand in the right direction utilizing the 101 websites outlined by SEOMoz.org.

With data provided from the EMarketer.com article, "Focusing on Social

Networks," the list ranks the popularity of various social networking, social bookmarking, social news, social directory, and education websites.

"Using this list, you can determine which sites to target and how to engage with them to earn mindshare, branding, customers, and links," SEOmoz tells us, encouraging readers to copy and paste the snippet (above) and others to your website or blog.

Each social site in the SEOmoz ranking is categorized by website primary value and size, and a link to more information about the website is provided. The top 25 social media sites are accompanied with marketing tips to help you create a social media marketing campaign.

Social Media Resource 1-53: How to Use Social Media to Improve Your Career

http://money.usnews.com/money/blogs/alpha-consumer/2010/11/03/how-to-use-social-media-to-improve-your-career.html

What could be more important, after all, than properly managing your career? Well, there probably a couple of crystal balls, as our friend former GM executive Roy Roberts used to say, that you have to be careful juggling. "All the other balls you juggle," Roy would say, "are probably rubber and will bounce if they hit the floor."

This post is written as a guest post in Money.USNews.com by the author of *All Moms Work: Short-Term Career Strategies for Long Term Success*, Sharon Reed Abboud.

She tells a variety of real-world stories about how people all over the country have landed jobs using social media. By the way, we have several similar stories from young people, and not so young people, who have taken our New Media Driver's License® course at Michigan State University, so nothing in this article surprised us.

We'll let you read the article—that is, read it if you are interested in making sure that career crystal ball you're juggling doesn't hit the floor, or if it already did, how you might get a second chance to juggle it again, this time more successfully.

Social Media Resource 1-54: How to Use Social Media for Personal Branding

http://www.techipedia.com/2010/social-media-personal-branding

Denying that your actions online build your personal brand won't make it not so. "Most people online are building 'a brand,'" says Dan Schwabel in this techniqedia.com post, "but sometimes people forget whose brand they are building. . . ."

"For instance," Schwabel says, "if your Twitter handle reads '@fastcar,'" then you aren't building your own personal brand. When people retweet you, they are viewing @fastcar, and not your full name." And please don't think the Twitter handle @needajob will land you your dream career.

Social Media Resource 1-55:
7 Tips to Give Your Social Media Career a Facelift
http://www.b2cmarketinginsider.com/social-media/7-tips-to-give-your-career-a-social-media-facelift-03996

Heidi Cohen, self-described "actionable marketing expert," provides seven steps to help build your social media presence.

"To develop an effective social media marketing presence requires accepting that social media has become an integral part of how we communicate and share information. Not participating means that you're missing a large part of the conversation."

So, you have to begin by giving your own perspective a facelift: "You must take control of own social media footprint."

Cohen's second point includes a link to an inventory of her favorite available social media marketing resources (newsletters, books, handbooks and posts, and special sections on Facebook, Twitter, LinkedIn, Blogging sources, and more).

Her list of newsletters begins with Mashable.com and moves to a great daily newsletter round up of the top social media stories of the day: "Smart Brief on Social Media." Just going through Heidi's resource list is a great education and is bound to make you a better social mediator.

Social Media Resource 1-56: What Your Social Network
Says about You
http://www.geeksugar.com/What-Your-Social-Network-Says-About-You-11184562

Here's a Geeksugar.com compilation of the findings, as they interpret them, of 10 things a person's social networking site and social media behavior may reveal about him or her. One of the things we like most about this column is that it is one of the rare posts that even references academic research.

Another interpretation might be that it is about the *only example of academic research* we found in looking at what others have told us are the best resources on the web.

A group of researchers from Germany (and one from Harvard) found that Facebook status messages "make us feel more connected with each other."

Another study, this one from Hewlett-Packard Laboratories demonstrates that most of us are relatively passive consumers of information on the Web, and it discusses the marketing implications of this information.

A Malaysian business school study demonstrated that peer or 'friend' movie recommendations seem to matter more than critic's reviews.

We found the study from the Psychology Department of Tufts University to be both encouraging and, also, somewhat common sense: "We like people more if they are expressive" in both real-life situations as well as online.

Social Media Resource 1-57:
What Companies Want in a Social Media Intern
http://mashable.com/2010/10/09/social-media-interns/

You know right now if you don't need to read this article. But, if you are a student or a young worker in an unsatisfying job who thinks that you may want to consider a job in the rapidly expanding world of social media, this Mashable.com post (and the comments that follow it) is for you. Or if you are in a business or a nonprofit organization and feel that sometime you may want to bring in an intern or a young employee or a consultant, to help you get up to the warp speed of social media, this post might be for you.

Ok. So our next question is why in the world would anyone be in possession of this book if you don't fall into one of these two categories?

Thank you, Amy-Mae Elliott, for what is bound to be a career-expanding piece of work (Would the phrase *life-saving* be hyperbole?) for a large number of our readers.

First, we love how you have organized this piece. Your first graphic—the one with the young lady holding up a cardboard handwritten sign that says "heart to work!" is precious, and it also emphasizes the first thing we tell our students. *You simply have to show that you love to work*, you love social media, and you are enthusiastic. Enthusiasm is actually one of the things you stress later in your post. But the picture is worth one thousand words.

And then there are the words. Your first point about good communication skills, followed by the admonition that you better make yourself a good writer if you're not one already, is supported by lots of experience and even some research Rick did involving a survey of PRSA practitioners a couple of years ago.

PR supervisors are often shocked and largely put off by the poor quality of writing they are seeing among entry-level practitioners.

You simply have to make yourself a better writer than you are today. And as Billy Crystal's character told Danny DeVito's character in "Throw Mama from the Train" when DeVito asked him words to the effect of "What's it take to be a good writer?"

Billy Crystal replied: "Writers write."

Writers write. That's it. That's all. And there has never been a greater time, or an easier way, to practice your writing skills than in this day and age of social media. So write away, and while you do, learn to be accurate, grammatically correct and, unlike perhaps these authors, brief and to the point.

Social Media Resource 1-58: 11 Essential Apps for Managing Your Real Life Social Network

http://mashable.com/2010/11/19/apps-real-life-social/

And after all is said and done, and you get supercharged on the idea of exploiting every possible social media tool that is at your disposal, you come to a point where you ask yourself the question: "How can I possibly manage all of my real-life networks?"

Well, again we turn to Mashable. This time it's Rich Aberman making the contribution and what a contribution it is.

His "essential apps" include the likes of *TeamSnap* for iPhone, and Facebook Groups, and for formal groups, *GroupSpaces*. There is *GroupMe*, Facebook Events (which, according to Aberman is not the greatest RSVP-management tool, but like many things in life, is defined by its "redeeming qualities.")

Link to this Mashable site, and while you're at it you might consider signing up with Mashable.

And then there is this . . .

Social Media Resource 1-59: Facebook is Fun for Recruiters Also

http://online.wsj.com/article_email/SB100014240531119034611045764648237627271 88-lMyQjAxMTAxMDIwNDEyNDQyWj.html

Could you pass a Facebook test with a perspective new employer? It's often been said that but for some questions of legality, one test every employer should give a perspective new hire is to stop by her or his apartment and pay a surprise visit. Would you see anything that might cause you to not want to go through with the hiring? A surprise visit might be a great idea, but it might also open up some legal challenges. Apartments are private, after all. But Facebook isn't.

Jennifer Waters, writing in the *Wall Street Journal*'s online publication, opens with this question: "Could you pass a Facebook background search?

"The next time you apply for a job, don't be surprised if you have to agree to a social-media background check. Many U.S. companies and recruiters are now looking at your Facebook, Twitter, Flickr, and other accounts and blogs—even YouTube—to paint a clearer picture of who you are," said Waters.

One employer told Waters he's not terribly concerned about party shots—as long as they are not outrageous. "I look at their Facebook and see how they approach what they put on it. Is it immature? Is it appropriate or inappropriate? I'm not judging their activity but looking at how they communicate what they do and their thoughts and their judgments to the public as a reflection of what they will do with their clients and team members."

Monitoring, Evaluation, and Security in Social Media

If you really want to become an expert in social media (and/or public relations) modern measurement techniques and applications, you simply have to meet K.D. Paine.

She's a firebrand on the subject of measurement, and you should consider her to be your first and, maybe, your last source; but certainly you should consider her one of your best sources.

Katie Delahaye Paine is CEO of KD Paine & Partners. She's a speaker (worldwide) and has a tremendous blog that covers the waterfront of measurement http://kdpaine.blogs.com/

K.D. Paine
5 measurement books you could sure take to the beach.

1. A great place to start your social media strategy is Stephen D. Rappaport's, *Listen First!*: Turning Social Media Conversations into Business Advantage. It's a detailed workbook of how to begin listening to your customers, how to manage a social media listening program, and how to use the research correctly.
2. Your next step up the measurement ladder is Katie Delahaye Paine's *Measure What Matters: Online Tools For Understanding Customers, Social Media, Engagement, and Key Relationships*. It takes you from first steps all the way through how-to-measure procedures for each of your audiences and projects. If you're a seasoned pro, it's your all-purpose reference: As Lee Odden says, "This is a measurement bible for the social media and public relations savvy professionals of the world."
3. Philip Sheldrake's *The Business of Influence*: Reframing Marketing and PR for the Digital Age is definitely not for the newcomer to social media. It does start with a great overview of where we are, but then quickly gets into the nitty-gritty of defining and mapping the influencers that are important to your strategy. Says Katie Delahaye Paine: "The Business of Influence should be found, dog-eared and jam-packed with marks in the margins, on every successful CMO's desk."
4. If you're in the b2b space, *Social Marketing to the Business Customer*: Listen to Your B2B Market, Generate Major Account Leads, and Build Client Relationships by Paul Gillin and Eric Schwartzman is an great read. It removes the "This doesn't apply to me excuse" beautifully. Chris Brogan says, "Finally, the book I was too lazy to write. Gillin and Schwartzman have broken open the code to how to approach B2B marketing with social media."
5. Finally, for anyone in marketing or media—practitioner or teacher—- you must read Timothy Wu's *The Master Switch*: The Rise and Fall of Information Empires. Every new communications medium or technology begins with an idea, an entrepreneur, and an explosion of free exchange of this technology. But, sooner or later, it is taken over and monopolized by a single person or company—too frequently with the collusion of the US government.

(Reprinted with permission: KD Paine & Partners)

"If you've ever wondered how to measure social media, public relations, public affairs, media relations, internal communications, or blogs," her KD Paine's Measurement Blog announces, "you are in the right spot."

As we write this, Paine's blog is reporting from the *Lisbon Amec European Summit on Measurement* (July 2011) in which she gives a complete run-down on the conference, discusses ways in which the Lisbon conference can "improve the life of the typical PR pro" and something she calls "The Tyra Banks Approach to Writing."

Paine's blog has a great list of the "Five Measurement Books You Could, Sure, Take to the Beach." As you might expect from Paine (she's a shameless promoter of her discipline—measurement—without shamelessly promoting herself), Paine did not put her book first on the list. Maybe that's a sign of her modesty. But actually as you review the list, you are going to get a pretty good idea that she had a reading sequence in mind as she put this list together.

By the way, Katie says: "O.K., we don't really expect you to take these measurement books along the next time you go to the beach." But any serious student of measurement should consider this a *must do* reading list.

Social Media Resource 1-60: Why You Need to Monitor and Measure Your Brand on Social Media

http://mashable.com/2010/07/29/monitor-measure-brand-social-media/

Maria Ogneva, Director of Social Media at Attensity, stresses the importance of social media brand monitoring, and how she does it in this Mashable.com post.

> Although there is no shortage of social media monitoring tools, each one is a bit different in its approach, methodology, metrics, depth of analysis, channels measured, reports and UI. The existence of this many tools and the fragmentation of the tools market is evidence of the fact that the space is not quite mature, and doesn't yet have a set of agreed-upon metrics and best practices.

To prove her point on the wonderful world of social media monitoring, Ogneva links to Ken Burbary's "Wiki of Social Media Monitoring Solutions" http://wiki.kenburbary.com/.

The current, but building, count of resources on this list alone is 201.

Social Media Resource 1-61:
3 New Ways to Measure the Social Web

http://mashable.com/2010/02/02/social-analytics/

Unfortunately traditional web analytics don't reveal anything about user social media habits. Tracking the page views and bounce are not particularly valuable.

Founder of real-time analytics service Mixpanel, Tim Trefren helps companies understand how users behave with web applications. He posted an article to help you understand how and why social web companies are developing their own data collecting systems:

> There's a reason for this: Social media is highly competitive, and the biggest advantage you can have is data. To improve and grow, these companies need to gather as much information as they can, and they need more than simple page view tracking.

If you're interested in learning about new social web measurements, this resource will help you understand what these new systems are, why they are useful, and how you can use this for your social media marketing campaign.

Trefren says, "There's a lot to learn about analytics from the frontrunners in social media. The intense competition has resulted in many new and innovative ways to track and analyze visitor data."

Social Media Resource 1-62: How to Catch the Social Media Buzz by Monitoring Your Brand Online

http://blog.opsecsecurity.com/commentary-how-to-catch-the-social-media-buzz-monitor-your-brand-online/

Nick Lucido, one of our stellar graduates, who became President of the national Public Relations Student Society of America (PRSSA) while he was at MSU, is now at Edelman PR in Chicago. One of his specialties, when he was still at MSU working in cyberspace for Edelman, was setting up what he told his classmates were social media *listening posts* for Edelman clients.

Alina Halloran, writing in the OpSecSecurity.com blog, opens her commentary post with these questions: "What are you doing? What's the latest trend? And what are you buying? (These are) just some of the questions being asked and answered through online platforms."

"As brand owners monitor their online presence, it is an opportune time to mine intelligence . . . weeding through vast amounts of information on social networking platforms can be cumbersome, but there are guidelines to help make your search a bit more manageable."

Alina shows us what we should be monitoring for and renders her expert opinion on what we can learn from the conversations that are occurring about our brand online. That's exactly what Nick does.

Social Media: Some of Edelman PR's Nick Lucido's Favorite Social Media Resources

Nick Lucido joined Edelman Digital in May 2009 after receiving the Daniel J. Edelman/PRSSA Outstanding PR Student Award. He is a member of the firm's digital strategy team, providing strategic counsel for clients in the technology, pharmaceutical, consumer packaged goods and restaurant industries. Prior to working for Edelman, he also completed internships in mid-sized and boutique agencies.

We love to point out that Nick was in the first class of New Media Driver's License® graduates at Michigan State University.

Lucido completed his undergraduate degree from MSU in December 2010. At MSU, he assisted co-author Professor Richard Cole in redesigning a graduate course in media relations to include a new media component, which he then co-instructed. He is active in the Public Relations Student Society of America (PRSSA) and currently serves as 2011-2012 Immediate Past President of this national organization.

ComScore—Social SEO

http://blog.comscore.com/2011/07/social_seo_facebook_twitter_be.html?utm_sourc
e=feedburner&utm_medium=feed&utm_campaign=Feed%3A+comscore-
blog+%28comScore+Voices%29

Nick says: "One emerging trend has been how an organization can leverage social media to improve SEO—or search engine optimization—rankings. This post lays the foundation on how an organization can use Facebook and Twitter to not only improve its social page ranking, but also to help your main website rank higher."

Logic + Influence—The Six Pillars of Influence

http://darmano.typepad.com/logic_emotion/2011/01/the-six-pillars-of-
influence.html?utm_source=feedburner&utm_medium=feed&utm_campaign=Feed
%3A+Logicemotion+%28Logic%2BEmotion%29

Nick likes this resource because his colleague, David Armano, points out the six key sources of influence. "This is particularly important to remember in order to iden-tify influencers in within your community, as one pillar has no more weight than others," Nick says.

The Digital Influence Mapping Project—Evaluating Markets for
Social Media Readiness

http://johnbell.typepad.com/weblog/2011/03/evaluating-markets-for-social-media-
readiness-.html

"One of the most daunting aspects of social media is how people use different online networks in different countries," Nick says. "It makes executing a global social media strategy seem very challenging, so I often reference this post from John Bell that encourages you evaluate your program through a critical eye."

Techipedia—17 Digital Marketing Experts Share Their Top Tips, Tricks, and Tools

http://www.techipedia.com/2011/digital-marketing-tips-tools/?utm_source=
feedburner&utm_medium=feed&utm_campaign=Feed%3A+techipedia+%28Techip
edia%3A+Tamar+Weinberg+on+Social+Media+Marketing+Strategy%29

"While it's important for companies and brands to find their own way in social media, looking up to see what the experts are doing and using in digital marketing is helpful," Nick says. This post, written by Blue Cross Blue Shield of Michigan social media manager, Shannon Paul, lists what Nick believes to be some relevant tools and tricks to help any new PR or digital professional navigate the space a little easier.

Jeff Esposito—23 Social Media Facts to Share with Executives

http://www.jeffesposito.com/2011/02/14/social-media-facts-share-executives/

Although stats are constantly changing, Nick feels it's important to know what kind of stats to share with someone you're trying to sell social media to. This is a solid guide on what stats executives care about and can guide you in the right direction if you're trying to sell in an online program.

Social Media Resource 1-63: 6 Social Media Mistakes to Avoid and How to Correct Miscalculation

http://www.ieplexus.com/company-news/5171-six-social-media-mistakes-to-avoid-and-how-to-correct-miscalculation/

Jamie Galvin writing in iePlexis.com says this about the future of social media: "What most people don't realize is that their lack of success with social media might be attributed to their own actions."

The article draws heavily from a SocialMediaExaminer.com post http://www.socialmediaexaminer.com/top-6-social-media-mistakes-and-how-to-fix-them/ with Galvin plugging in an interpretation of common errors and suggestions for avoiding them.

Social Media Resource 1-64: 5 Great Tips for Dealing with Complaints on Social Media

http://www.blinemarketing.com/social-media-complaints/

Controlling the conversation between consumers on social media websites is nearly impossible. It is important to monitor it and address any issues that may come up, especially complaints.

A BlineMarketing.com post says, "Social media can be a tricky endeavor and maintaining your accounts is the most important aspect."

The article asks, "What do you do when someone leaves a negative comment?"

The manner in which you deal with these complaints if done correctly can be beneficial to your brand. If complaints are handled incorrectly or not taken seriously they can really hurt your image.

It's been more than a dozen years since Karl Albrecht, in his classic book *Moment of Truth*, observed that it's not when things are going well that relationships with clients are strengthened; it's when something goes wrong. At that moment the customer is conscious of the fact that the problem is providing the retailer or service provider with the opportunity to demonstrate the depths of his or her commitment to customer service. "Just how important is my business?" That's what the customer is thinking, and that's the time the supplier can show him—or not.

Negative comments online are naturally harsher than face-to-face, mainly because of the lack of personal interaction and because the anonymity provides a safe way to emote. So the first thing any business needs to remember is that *it isn't personal.* And it's equally important to not be impersonal when responding to customer complaints.

Donald M.D. Thurber, a former board chair at Blue Cross and Blue Shield of Michigan, used to tell executives that *every knock is a boost.* It's when the customer doesn't feel like it's worth his or her time to complain that the business is in deep trouble.

Social Media Resource 1-65:
7 Reasons Why Your Social Media Campaign Is Failing

http://www.bitrebels.com/geek/7-reasons-why-your-social-media-campaign-is-failing/

There is this crazy idea that social media is easy and that it will work just because everyone is doing it. Wrong!

Listen to Misty Belardo and clear up these kinds of misconceptions. Her advice might prevent you from wasting a good deal of time and money in a half-hearted pursuit of new business in social media.

Belardo's post on BitRebels.com may just help your online social media efforts succeed. For example, she identifies reasons for social media failure as basic as having a sheer lack of knowledge about social media, which sounds like an endorsement for this book, doesn't it?

Belardo says: "not everyone is successful [in social media], and maybe that is because there are some things that they have overlooked." She goes on to offer several—more than seven actually—"practical tips and reasons why some social media strategies fail." The problem might also be that the business problem you are trying to solve isn't a problem that can be answered by a Facebook page or Twitter account.

In any event, once you choose to go into social media, you have to recognize this. Operating successfully in social media isn't as simple and clear cut as many try to make it out to be. After all: *If it was all fun, they wouldn't call it work.*

Social Media Resource 1-66:
8 Social Media Metrics You Should Be Measuring

http://www.socialmediaexaminer.com/8-social-media-metrics-you-should-be-measuring

Metrics can provide valuable information. Metrics can tell you what's working, what isn't and what needs to change. There are many different kinds of metrics besides return of investment that are important for any social media marketer.

Nichole Kelly is a social media measurement speaker, consultant, and coach.

Her SocialMediaExaminer.com post asks this. "Are you struggling to find measurements that are meaningful to your organization? Do you feel like you're searching for a needle in a haystack of metrics?"

If you've answered yes, then Kelly's post can help. There are many tools used for measuring data and the article describes what resources are used for different measurements.

Learn the importance of conversion rates and how these calculations are made, the importance of a control group, and how to measure social media growth against what's happening in the control group.

You can use your conversion rate to measure customer acquisition costs and retention rates once you understand how to calculate it. And this information may help boost the rate the success of your marketing campaign.

Social Media Resource 1-67: 11 Social Media Mistakes Your Company Must Avoid

http://www.businessinsider.com/social-media-mistakes-2010-2

Bianca Male wrote this post for BusinessInsider.com (War Room).

> In reality, there are common mistakes that business leaders unfamiliar with social media marketing seem to stumble into. These errors reveal a lack of social media savvy and often negate the effectiveness of those marketing efforts.

You might think the examples she cites are pretty much common sense, and then they are. But then, how often have you felt that common sense really isn't always all that common, like when you bump into sites that don't have "enough fresh content"? Do you return to those sites? We don't.

Or what about spamming? To some degree spam is in the eye of the beholder. But you shouldn't take chances.

Male advises:

> Tools like *Twitterfeed* allow you to automatically send certain updates to your account. Convenient, yes, but beware: If those are the only posts you have, your account is going to feel impersonal, and it will completely negate the interactive element of social media marketing. Think "Rescue Marketing." http://www.rescuemarketing.com/blog/2009/05/08/social-media-mistakes-small-business-owners-should-avoid/

Social Media Resource 1-68: 9 Social Media Marketing Sins
http://atomic5.com/9-social-media-marketing-sins

We suppose that to some people social media has become such a religion that screwing up can be seen as sinful behavior. Unfortunately, it's not as simple as showing up once a month for confession to get fresh start.

Atomic5.com, an Australia-based social marketing consultancy, summarizes *Art of Online Marketing* (AOOM—http://www.aoom.com.au/). Again, much of this advice is common sense, and some of it is absolutely no different than that which you would give a mentee who was looking to stay out of trouble in the workplace.

For example, AOOM Social Media Marketing Sin #1—*Not thinking before speaking.*

> In the online social media world, almost every conversation is transparent— that's one of the beauties of social media marketing as a marketing and communications tool. However, the flip side is—whatever you publish will be remembered, publicized and possibly held against you for a long, long time.
>
> Add to that the real time nature of social media—there's a real danger of speaking before thinking. For companies, this can lead to damaging consequences—you may unwittingly anger your audience, publish inaccurate information or state opinions that undermine the company's values and brands.

We could take you right down the list. The advice is solid: "Social Media Marketing Sin #2—*Lacking a plan and focus.*" Again, this advice may not be much different from any business or communication strategy, but it's worth putting into an online context as this resource does very well.

Social Media Resource 1-69: Social Media Screw-ups— A Brief History
http://adage.com/digitalnext/article?article_id=146314

Why is it that tragedy is often the underlying basis of stuff we think is funny? We don't know the answer to that and Matthew Yeomans didn't address it directly in this AdAgeDigital posting. But that doesn't make the article less funny, or the screw-ups less humorous.

In September, 2010, Burger King was forced to change the source of the palm oil it used in food preparation as a result of "fierce Greenpeace social-media protest pressure."

"Back in 2003," Yeomans says, "no one had heard of 'social-media swarm,' and the exploding business of social-media monitoring and measurement didn't exist. Of course neither did YouTube, Facebook, or Twitter and it is these three social-publishing platforms, with the personal publishing power of blogs, that have brought about a sea-change in the way companies have been forced (yes, forced) to communicate with their customers."

One of the reasons this is such a great resource is that within his very insightful commentary like that above, Yeomans has embedded a 43-slide presentation (which includes some great video) that you just have to look at.

Social Media Resource 1-70: 4 Must-Have Social Media Dashboards for Your Business

http://venturebeat.com/2010/10/04/social-media-dashboards

This VentureBeat.com "Entrepreneur Corner" post by Cody Barbierri highlights a list of dashboards that companies can use to track their social media sites including HootSuite, Netvibes, Jungle Torch, and Trackur:

> While big brands and agencies have the luxury of resources and money, local businesses don't. What they need is a social-media dashboard—an all-in-one, Web-based monitoring tool for Facebook, Twitter, and other social sites where customers hang out. . . .

Barbierri identifies three dashboard criteria: *cheap, easy to use,* and *automated.*

HootSuite is one of the original players in the dashboard market—allowing users to monitor all of their social profiles like Facebook, Twitter, and Linked In.

Social Media Resource 1-71: How to Stay Safe in a Social Media World

http://www.socialmediatoday.com/steve-olenski/205671/how-stay-safe-social-media-world

Use protection and be safe.

No, this isn't advice from Planned Parenthood or the National Rifle Association. It's social media advice from someone with experience.

Learn how to protect yourself against the dangers of social media. Child predators and identity thieves thrive on social media websites, where the age of users gets younger and younger, and the amount of personal information posted online gets larger and larger.

Steve Olenski, Creative Director of Digital Services for The Star Group, a marketing communications agency, says: "In today's social media gone amok world, everyone thinks they need to be and should be social and sociable with EVERYONE.

"For some reason many of us think of the Internet as somehow being different than the *real world.*"

This Olenski post will explain some of the dangers of social networking and when and where we need safeguards to protect our families, our children, and ourselves.

The post describes how to make a strong password, status updates you should never post, and how to use privacy controls.

Extra Point—Tracking the Trends

Social Media Resource 1-72: Burson-Marsteller PR Reports Social Media Trends at Fortune 500 Companies

http://www.burson-marsteller.com/Innovation_and_insights/blogs_and_podcasts/BM_Blog/Lists/Posts/Post.aspx?ID=160

This study is about a year old, but if it's pointing out a trend—and we think it is—a year shouldn't matter much. The international PR firm Burson-Marsteller studied the 100 largest companies in the Fortune 500 list.

Nearly 80% of the Fortune 500 firms were using Twitter, Facebook, YouTube, or corporate blogs to communicate with customers and other stake-holders.

That's just one finding, but the finding is not as important as is the fact that, as Marshall McLuhan might say, *it's the medium that's the massage.*

What we really like about this Burson-Marsteller release is its links to a detailed PDF of the study, and even more, to their "Evidence-Based Tool called the 'Social Media Check-up . . . which analyzes and measures . . . how a company's social media presence is impacting their overall online health and reputation."

Social Media Resource 1-73: The 10 Next Social Media Trends

http://www.smartcompany.com.au/internet/the-10-next-social-media-trends-2.html

Brad Howarth can't possibly really know everything there is to know about social media. No one can. But if you want to go to someone who, as far as social media is concerned, certainly *knows stuff*, even if he isn't a for-tuneteller, this might be your guy.

"Social media still dominates headlines as the new direction for business marketing, but it seems many businesses are resisting the call. A recent survey by Optus found that only 28% of small businesses (in contrast to the earlier reported study regarding Fortune 500 companies) used social media to pro-mote their business, while 56% had no near-term plans to start," Howarth says.

So, unless you just rode into town on a load of pumpkins, you can see this potential market for new users. And as grand as it will be, you almost have to imagine exponential growth to accurately characterize what is going to happen in the next few years in relation to new uses, new applications and new social media tools for small business.

We're not even going to attempt to summarize Howarth's ideas for *the 10 trends*. This is a book designed to lead you to important resources, not to regurgitate them. But if you're not motivated to go to this post and get a glimpse into what the future might look like, maybe you ought to consider getting on the next empty pumpkin truck and riding back out of town.

By the way, as a caveat, you need to understand that Howarth's predictions were written about a year before Google's recent "*Google+*" announcement.

We'll have more on *Google+–* and its potential impact—later.

Social Media Resource 1-74: 10 Creative Contests Powered by Social Media

http://mashable.com/2009/08/11/social-media-contests/

Contests are cool. Who doesn't like winning something for free or recognition on a national scale? Naturally, social media and content are an undeniable match. Social media contests, after all, allow people to show their creativity and loyalty to a brand, and do it in a fully engaged way.

Founder of Spark Media Solutions, David Spark, has produced a terrific Mashable.com post on creative and successful contests executed through social media:

> Now that social media is in vogue, there's no reason to limit a content sub-mission to just a one-way promotional mailing list. Social media contests are multi-directional—they allow for increased customer engagement and content generation.

This is a great resource to help you generate ideas to create your own contest through social media.

Don't forget, in this social media world, contests include trivial pursuits that can help raise the awareness of your brand and products, old and new. Video testimonial contests can help give your brand authority and recognition while promoting the contestants—a prize for everyone.

Social Media Resource 1-75: What Social Media Will Look Like in 2012

http://adage.com/digitalnext/post?article_id=143145

Freddie Laker's prediction in this AdAge.com post shares his insights into how social media will change, stay the same, and grow over the next few years. This is last year's list of predictions for next year's conditions, and there are always dangers in these kinds of lists.

We're not even sure Larry Page and Sergey Brin could have predicted *Google+* a year ago, and we were equally unsure that they know exactly what it's going to be next year. That's the nature of the fast-paced world in which we live.

But Laker's list is worth reading, as the 30 or 40 commenters on this post will largely attest.

Laker's boldest prediction, perhaps, is that privacy expectations will begin to shift significantly. "There will be a cultural shift, whereby people will begin to find it increasingly acceptable to expose more and more of their personal details on different forms of social media."

One has to wonder the degree to which otherwise unrelated and unpredictable events like the recent exposure of the allegedly illegal wire-tapping practices of the Murdoch family's News International organization, and subsequent revelations, might change our view of privacy, however unrelated the Murdoch organization's old media alleged snooping practices are to the world of new media.

Social Media Resource 1-76:
40 Most Popular Social Networking Sites of the World

http://www.socialmediatoday.com/soravjain/195917/40-most-popular-social-networking-sites-world

Here's a list you have to read. Thanks to Sorav Jain, posting in SocialMedia-Today.com, this link reminds us that Facebook, Twitter, and Google+ (which had not been announced as of this posting) are not the only games in town.

If a picture is, in fact, worth a thousand words as we said earlier, check

40 Most Popular Social Networking Sites of the World
www.soravjain.com

out Jain's graphic, and go immediately to his post to see the most popular social media sites in the world, as of late 2010, with a description of each site.

Here's an example of the kind of detail Jain provides:

31. Renren: (http://www.renren.com/)Renren (formerly called Xiaonei Network) is one of the largest social networking sites in China, and caters to people of Chinese origin. It is very popular amongst college students. Renren also has a WAP version, which users can access through mobile phones. It features an instant messaging service for its users. Users can use the same username to log in both Renren and Kaixin. Renren appeals more to Chinese college students who use Internet cafes, while Kaixin001 targets Chinese white-collar workers who have Internet access at work.

Social Media Resource 1-77:
10 Signs You Have Social Media Sickness
http://thestir.cafemom.com/entertainment/111020/10_signs_you_have_social

Do you need an intervention? You might "if your babies have Twitter and Facebook accounts that you post to regularly."

I'd say so. And so would Jill Smokler. She did, in fact, in a wonderful post in CafeMom.com.

This post is linked, as you can see, to CafeMom's entertainment section, but don't be put off by that. This isn't entertainment. This is therapy. Or at least, it's a self-evaluation you can use to see if you need therapy:

- "Are you more involved with your classmates than you were in high schools? Do you really care that they are not aware of your relationship?"

- Do you "snuggle your iPhone more closely than your husband, wife or significant other?"

- Don't tell us that you "can't remember the last time you read a book?"

There's more to this test, but we can't go on now without getting depressed.

But, I guess we shouldn't be depressed. One step in the long road to recovery is acceptance. *Do you have a problem?*

Remember, DENIAL is not a river in Egypt.

Social Media Resource:
Top Five "Picks" of Social Media Expert
and Author Greg Verdino

Greg Verdino is the author of *microMARKETING: Get Big Results by Thinking and Acting Small* (McGraw-Hill, 2010), a recognized marketing thought leader, and a popular conference speaker. His company, Verdino LLC, provides clients with strategic consulting and business innovation advisory services. Over the course of his twenty-plus year career he has held leadership and individual contributor roles at top advertising, direct marketing, digital, and social media marketing agencies; and has played key roles at a variety of technology and online media startups. Greg lives in New York, blogs at www.gregverdino, and tweets as @gregverdino.

Six Pixels of Separation
http://www.twistimage.com/blog/

Written (and recorded—Six Pixels is a blog *and* a long-running podcast) by Twist Image president Mitch Joel, Six Pixels casts a realist's eye on the latest in social media, mobile and more, all from the perspective of a seasoned digital marketer and recognized marketing thought leader. Mitch's book—also called *Six Pixels of Separation*—is a smart, easy-to-digest introduction to social media marketing, and he can always be counted on to look at new technologies and approaches within the context of digital marketing strategies that stand the test of time.

PR-Squared
http://www.pr-squared.com/

Todd Defren is a principal at SHIFT Communications and the man who conceived the original social media press release. After more than seven years blogging about social media from the PR practitioner's perspective, Todd still consistently delivers smart, no-nonsense thinking on the current and future state of public relations.

PSFK
http://www.psfk.com

PSFK isn't a marketing or PR blog per se, but it is my go-to source for a wide-ranging look at trends, ideas, and cool new stuff in general. Piers Fawkes and his team assembled dozens of short, inspiring posts each day—covering everything from branding and business to culture and design. If you're looking for a spark for your next innovative idea or simply want to keep your finger on the pulse of what's new and what's next, PSFK is a fertile field to sow.

Darren Herman
http://www.darrenherman.com

I first met Darren when he was running his in-game advertising startup, IGA Worldwide, and I was running the emerging channels group at Digitas. He has since gone on to become Chief Digital Media Officer at New York ad agency kirschenbaum bond senecal + partners, and looks at the media, marketing, and advertising scene with a compelling blend of big budget ad guy plus entrepreneurial spirit. His blog is a great source for marketers looking to understand the tools and technologies shaping the future of the ad business, and for sell-side startups interested in getting inside the heads of one of the most innovative digital media buyers in the industry.

We Are Social
http://www.wearesocial.net

This one is worth reading for two main reasons. First, We Are Social is among the top social agencies in Europe and Australia, so their team (led by managing director Robin Grant) brings a uniquely international perspective to their posts about the latest social media marketing campaigns, news and trends. Second, their Monday Mashup posts provide fantastic one-stop-shop reviews of each week's interesting global stories, technology developments, platform plays, marketer moves, and new social initiatives. While there's plenty of U.S.-oriented content, this blog provides American Marketers with a nice little reminder that there is plenty of interesting, innovative (and sometimes surprising) activity happening beyond the states.

Perfect Practice Makes Perfect:
Some tasks that will help you understand the concepts in Part I.

Exercise 1: Join LinkedIn and build your profile to 100% (or close to it). Every step of the way, LinkedIn tells you how to do it. Building a credible profile, loaded with keywords, may help propel your business career. Invite your friends. Request recommendations. Upload a photo. Your LinkedIn profile is your connection to the business social media world—and you need to be there. We'll show you more about LinkedIn in that section of the book, later.

Exercise 2: Start a Twitter page. Choose your handle (username) and launch your Twitter presence. (see: www.Twitter.com/username) Then you can tell your friends about your Twitter. Login to your Yahoo or Google mail and see how many of your friends are on Twitter. Make your first tweet. Follow some people. Join in the Conversation as Joseph Jaffe of www.jaffejuice.com likes to say. More is coming on Twitter later too.

Exercise 3: Create your Facebook profile. You need to have a presence there to understand this social media giant. Your Facebook profile can lead to hours of entertainment as you surf and connect with past people you thought you would never see again. You can also create a Business Page if you own a business, or a Professional Page instead of a profile if you wish to use Facebook strictly for business. Read more in our upcoming Facebook section.

Exercise 4: Join Google+ and see what it's all about. This new entry into the social media space gives you a nice alternative to Facebook. Invite your friends. See who is already on there. Group your friends into Circles and play along. You may just like it.

Exercise 5: Now that you have built all these profiles, commit to using them once a day for the next 90 days. If you really want to immerse yourself in social media, you need to do it. And a 90-day regimen will be a good start in joining the conversation, and building your social media brand.

Part II

BLOGGING

CHAPTER 2

The Ins and Outs of Blogging

As you must know by now, blogs were described as web logs when they first hit the Internet scene a decade or so ago.

Some people think about blogs as websites—simple websites perhaps, but websites nonetheless. But for those of you too young to remember, trust us when we tell you that much of what can be done on a free blog service today would have required hundreds, perhaps thousands, of programming hours to have been able to do on a website only a few years ago. In fact, a good deal of what goes on blogs—even the free services—simply could not have been done at all.

Why would someone want to set up a blog?

The basic motivation for setting up a blog is because the blogger wants to conduct a public conversation on a subject that is important to her or him and she wants to do it now.

Some people will point out that other bloggers may have different motivations. They want to be recognized by their peers as experts, or they want to collect information that will be useful to them as they pursue their hobby, their job, or their interest groups, or sell books they have written. Maybe some bloggers have a long-term goal of generating enough traffic so that they can eventually sell advertising or make a living in some other way from their blog. That's perfectly OK as far as we are concerned.

Normally, entries in blogs go in what is called reverse chronological order. In other words the most recent comment is at the top of a string of comments related to the particular subject of interest. There is much more about blogs available to you through a variety of online sources. Here's a useful Wikipedia entry on blogs:

> Most blogs are interactive, allowing visitors to leave comments and even message each other via widgets on the blogs and it is this interactivity that distinguishes them from other static websites.
>
> Many blogs provide commentary or news on a particular subject; others function as more personal online diaries. A typical blog combines text, images, and links to other blogs, web pages, and other media related to its

To ease your exploration of the resources identified in this book, please go to the Link Listing—www.NewMediaDriversLicenseResources.com

topic. The ability of readers to leave comments in an interactive format is an important part of many blogs. Most blogs are primarily textual, although some focus on visual or commercial art, photographs, videos, music, and audio. Micro-blogging is another type of blogging, featuring very short posts.

As of 16 February 2011, there were over 156 million public blogs in existence. http://en.wikipedia.org/wiki/Blog

You'll read a lot about Technorati in this chapter. One thing we recommend without hesitation is that you can dramatically broaden your perspective on blogging by going to the Technorati home page and click on the "blogging" button. Here http://technorati.com/blogging/ you'll find a steady stream of conversation and posts on a wide variety of issues you might want to consider, from why people are blogging to the benefits of a company blog and well beyond.

For example, here's Technorati's "Comments Policy," which seems very clear that while all comments will be allowed to post, Technorati reserves the right to remove any posts it deems inappropriate.

Technorati Comments Policy

Please think of the comments as a conversation between individuals and interact with civility.

We will edit/delete spam comments, duplicate comments, unsupported accusations, personal attacks of any kind, and terms offensive to groups when used in a pejorative manner.

In addition, we reserve the right to edit/delete comments that are some combination of pointlessly vulgar, vile, cruel, without redeeming qualities, and an embarrassment to the site.

We also ask that you not post comments under multiple names, and it is grounds for immediate banning to comment under someone else's name.

We will also ban repeat or particularly egregious offenders.

Please do not post phone numbers or email addresses in the body of your comment—you cannot assume the good intentions of everyone who reads them.

And please do not post URLs—which may be long and skew the page or the comment sidebar—but make the URL an actual HTML link.

Read on.

Blogging Resource 2-1: Technorati

http://technorati.com/technorati-comments-policy/#ixzz1RoEY2Rfw

Blogging Resource 2-2: Setting up a WordPress Blog

www.youtube.com/watch?v=MWYi4_COZMU

Especially if you are "visual learner," here's a great way to get an overall feel for just how easy it is to set up a blog using WordPress.com. This tutorial by Chris Abraham, of AbrahamPR is very much biased toward WordPress, but so are we, and this is a wonderful self-help resource.

The tutorial will take you about an hour to get Abraham's basic overview, and if you're not ready to commit to your own blog yet, just come back to this when you are.

Abraham makes a great case for selecting WordPress as your basic blogging tool. We recommend that you set up a word document so that you can take the basic notes you'll need to guide you through the actual process, once you are ready that is.

You may want to check this WordPress post out in order to understand the difference between Wordpress.com and WordPress.org—an important distinction in setting up your blog. http://en.support.wordpress.com/com-vs-org/

Blogging Resource 2-3: Blogging is Dead Just Like the Web is Dead

http://gigaom.com/2011/02/22/blogging-is-dead-just-like-the-web-is-dead/

Before you go any further, you really need to focus on just how likely it will be that you'll be blogging in the future. Mathew Ingram, writing in Gigaom.com (Feb. 22, 2011, *The New York Times*), citing research from the Pew Center's Internet and American Life Project, implied that blogging is on the decline.

"Except," says Mathew, "that the actual story said something quite different: even according to the figures used by the *New York Times* itself, blogging activity is actually increasing, not decreasing."

"What blogging is really doing is evolving," and if you want to get the full scoop on how the evolution is occurring and in which demographic blogging is showing the greatest increases (or decreases), check this next resource out.

Blogging Resource 2-4: The Future of Blogging

http://www.twistimage.com/blog/archives/the-future-of-blogging-might-surprise-you/

One of the reasons that it's a bit complicated to predict exactly what the future of blogging is relates to the fact that it's not all that easy to say what is, and what is not exactly, a blog.

Twist Image President Mitch Joel put it this way in his Six Pixels of Separation blog:

It's interesting to note that the true growth of blogging is not coming from individuals using this empowered publishing platform to share their insights with the world. The credibility and growth from blogs moving forward seems to be coming from the mainstream media's desire to have a cheaper, faster, and near-real-time platform to distribute their content.

Mitch quotes extensively from a 2010 study report titled, The Blogosphere—Colliding With Social And Mainstream Media, written by Paul Verna for eMarketer.com. http://www.emarketer.com/Report.aspx?code= emarketer_2000708

"Despite the success of other social media venues such as Facebook, Twitter and Flickr, blog readership has increased steadily and is expected to continue on an upward path," the Blogosphere report says. ''Just over half of U.S. Internet users are now reading blogs at least once a month, and this percentage will climb to 60 % in the next four years.''

We also like Technorati.com's annual "State of the Blogosphere Report," which in its most recent iteration http://technorati.com/blogging/article/ state-of-the-blogosphere-2010-introduction/ also provides an optimistic glimpse into the future of blogs.

The only thing we know for sure about this, or virtually any other subject relating to the Internet or anything else, is that no one really knows much of anything for sure. Well, there is one more thing we know for sure. If blogs are the be-all and end-all, which they are most certainly not, then being able to take maximum advantage of whatever the next thing is requires knowing as much as possible about this thing. Forearmed is forewarned.

Blogging Resource 2-5: Introduction to Blogging

http://codex.wordpress.org/Introduction_to_Blogging

Even for those who feel they are well versed in blogs and looking for more in-depth information and sources of inspiration, this is a great article. It is, after all, written by one of the leaders in free blog hosting, Wordpress.

Just look at the contents outline on the opening page if you need convincing that even the most experienced blogger could benefit from this review.

Becoming a Better Blog Writer

Blogging Resource 2-6: Creating Valuable Content

http://publicrelationsblogger.com/2009/11/blogging-tips-creating-valuable-content.html

Anyone can be a blogger, but not everyone can blog well. Bloggers must learn to both write well and to provide valuable content to get their blog noticed.

This resource lays out a series of seven helpful tips for being a good blogger. One tip suggests that good bloggers should offer some free content on their site.

True to their word, "blog-masters" Coleen Moffitt and Jennifer Gehrt, encourage readers to download a pretty smart mini-book on strategic blogging in public relations.

Blogging Resource 2-7:
Ways to Create Engaging Blog Content—Fast

http://www.ragan.com/Main/Articles/42830.aspx-

This is our kind of idea. Everyone, especially us it seems, is short on time. In this article, Heidi Cohen, provides five tips on how to keep up a blog if you are short on time or ideas.

Tips include using online video or expert interviews. They may take some time to produce, but don't get carried away.

Here's the benefit, according to Heidi: "Videos tend to be short, so they are less time consuming to produce. Further, videos are useful for search optimization. Just don't forget to add text for the search engines."

Shorter than what, we ask?

Blogging Resource 2-8:
7 Ways to Improve Your Writing . . . Right Now

http://www.copyblogger.com/fast-writing-improvement/

Let's be clear and concise, which is Copyblogger's tip number one.

Copyblogger is a very cool service you should check out for a lot of reasons. But the link that we are sending you to will give you seven quick and easy tips for becoming a better blog writer.

We hope that when James Chartrand, who wrote the post, reads our book he will say: "Gee, these guys did a pretty good job of following our advice."

Check this post out for yourself and let us know what you think, and then take a look at what Chris Lake has to say—a bit more detail.

Blogging Resource 2-9: How to Write for the Web: 23 Useful Tools

http://econsultancy.com/us/blog/6771-how-to-write-for-the-web-23-useful-rules

Chris Lake's very interesting post begins by suggesting that he lucked into a job as a technology journalist. Reading his 23 rules for writing on the web, it occurs to us that rather than dumb luck, Chris is a pretty good example of what happens when preparation and opportunity collide.

The advice he offers is spot on. We don't want to give too much away because we want you to go to his post, but we will share Chris's first rule. It should give you a little insight as to why we think this Ecoconsultancy.com post is valuable enough for you to drop everything and check out.

Chris says that one of the "best ways of writing an article is to quickly pour out your thoughts, and then to finesse the finer points once you have a structure for your post. That's how I'm writing this one: I've written out the rules and am now filling in the detail."

Well, Chris, that's exactly the strategy we are using to write this book, and we thank you for the advice.

By the way, we feel pretty lucky too, and what we've found out is how true the statement is that *the harder we work, the luckier we get.*

Blogging Resource 2-10: 10 Key Points to Remember in an Effective Blog Writing Checklist

http://socialmediatoday.com/georgepasswater/204248/10-key-points-remember-effective-blog-writing-checklist

Not to be outdone, copywriter and technologist George Passwater says: "Well, if you are like me, then you probably don't remember everything, all the time. This is why I have a checklist I use when I write my blog posts. It's just a simple reminder of the points I need to check off before I hit that publish button."

SocialMediaToday.com is another one of those cool companies that provide a wealth of free information to anyone trying to get better at what he does. It even offers a free newsletter to keep you up to speed on the latest and greatest in social media.

So, you may want to start with the Passwater checklist and move from there to becoming a SocialMediaToday.com regular.

Blogging Resource 2-11: Writing SEO-Friendly Blog Posts

http://www.practicalecommerce.com/articles/2679-Writing-SEO-Friendly-Blog-Posts-8-Suggestions

In this post, written by Paul Chaney for PracticalCommerce.com, you'll get eight clear and precise suggestions about writing blog posts that meet Google's "Farmer" algorithm thereby resulting in more favorable search results.

Rule number one is to frequently update your content.

Here's what Paul says about this: "A question I am routinely asked about blogging is, 'How often should I post?' The answer is, 'As often as you can.' If you are planning to use a blog for marketing and search engine optimization purposes, the more frequently you can update content, the better. Google thrives on fresh content. I recommend a minimum of three to five times per week. And blog posts don't have to be long—350 words is a good average length."

Other recommendations include how to "Think Keywords" including eight very specific recommendations for how to select and use keywords for maximum impact. But if being good is not enough, and you want to be great, check out Tracy Gold's post (below).

Blogging Resource 2-12: Tips on Being a Great Blogger

http://www.marketingtrenches.com/copywriting/how-to-be-a-great-blogger-even-if-you're-not-a-great-writer/

If you don't have any idea what to be blogging about, consider the possibility that you should not be blogging at all. And, as Tracy Gold's post in market-ingtrenches.com stresses, if you are a "horrible writer, or even worse, you hate writing, you probably shouldn't blog either."

But if you are simply struggling with keeping a consistent blog on a great topic going, and being good is not good enough, Tracy offers six helpful tips to steer you back in the right direction, and possibly even make you great.

Blogging Resource 2-13: What To Blog About?

http://www.businessinsider.com/what-to-blog-about-2011-4

OK. So you simply cannot be deterred. You are going to become a blogger come hell or high water. But you need to get started, and you are looking for a little help.

Beth Monaghan of InkHouse.com posted a very important set of ideas at BusinessInsider.com on April 1, 2011, and I don't think she was fooling around. She starts out where we should start most projects—setting clear goals. And she ends up by providing links to several of her favorite advice posts on blogging.

Blogging Resource 2-14: Fifty Can't-Fail Techniques for Finding Great Blog Topics

http://www.copyblogger.com/brainstorm-blog-topics

Every once in a while, and it seems very often, we come across resources that have a value that exceeds even their promise.

Here's an article by Carol Tice writing for CopyBlogger.com that would be just as valuable for Stephen King or Randy Newman as it for people who are trying to become successful bloggers.

That's right. Whether you are a great novelist, songwriter or blogger, you need ideas that capture the attention and the imagination of your audience. You need ideas that resonate with your fan base, ideas that have the ability to attract new readers or listeners.

Copyblogger.com is a service that is all about getting traffic and gaining readers and, as they say, helping their clients "sell stuff."

People want valuable online content, so compelling content becomes your advertising. And using the right words in an engaging, persuasive way (that's copywriting) determines not only how well your site converts visitors into sales, but also how much traffic you get and how well you rank in search engines.

Delivering quality online content is the smartest strategy for growing an authoritative website and your business, so it's your copywriting and content marketing skills that will set you apart for success.

Making Your Blog

Blogging Resource 2-15: If You Were Starting out in Blogging from Scratch—How Would You Promote Your Blog?

http://www.problogger.net/archives/2008/03/18/if-you-were-starting-out-in-blogging-from-scratch-how-would-you-promote-your-blog/

Here's another one from a familiar name, one of our favorites, Darren Rowse, founder and editor of ProBlogger.net. He identifies five strategies that he says if pursued together would give you a long leg up in becoming a viable blogger.

Again, this book is more of an hors d'oeuvres sampler platter than a main course, so we don't want to do anything that might distract you from going to Darren's site and getting the full scoop, but here's what Darren chose to make first on his list.

> Perhaps one of the most powerful ways of exposing your writing to a new group of people is to put some of your best content on other peoples' blogs—and not your own.
>
> Guest Posts have long been a feature of blogging, but it has been in the last year or two that I've really seen some wonderful examples of bloggers launching their own blogs and raising their own profiles through focusing their attention on writing guest posts on other blogs.

Good point, Darren. And this might imply that if you don't have anything valuable enough to put on other blogs, why would you even consider starting your own?

Blogging Resource 2-16: Growing a Blog Community

http://www.socialmediaexaminer.com/how-to-grow-a-blog-community-with-social-media/

Once you start your own blog, how do you grow it? Again, we turn to Darren Rowse, one of the world's blogging experts. His best-selling book, *ProBlogger*, is a must read for anyone who wants to be a competitive blogger. And after all, we're all competing for the attention of limited audiences. This video is a great way to get started moving to the next level.

You'll get some great tips from Darren on the video for sure, and you might even decide to enroll in Darren's latest project, the ProBlogger Academy, a platform that takes bloggers through the various aspects of blogging.

Blogging Resource 2-17: How to Attract More Traffic to Your Blog
http://www.flyte.biz/resources/newsletters/10/05-blog-traffic.php

It's an old saying in business (especially heard in sales departments): *Nothing happens until somebody sells something.* That's what generating visits to most websites is all about. At some level it's about selling something to somebody.

In this neat list of eight tips for generating more visits to your blog, Rich Brooks, President of Flyte.biz, a new media company, gives a world of useful information in just a few hundred words. And if you want more detail, he provides links to many others of his column inventory, all of which are designed to make you a better blogger.

We particularly liked his recommendation that bloggers need to make sure that you write blog posts that "don't suck." While defining "not sucking" posts may be a little tricky, Brooks emphasizes that people who write vanity posts—posts that brag about their achievements or talents or posts that rave about the products they make and sell—that kind of thing—will end up writing for just one reader, themselves.

Blogging Resource 2-18: 101 Ways to Make Your Blog More Popular and Successful
http://seo2.0.onreact.com/101-ways-to-make-your-blog-more-popular-and-successful

This SEO 2.0 "Search and Social Media Survival Guide" lists more different ways that you could ever imagine to make a blog more successful, more than 100, in fact.

We suppose we could eventually figure out who the author "The Monnie" is, but he or she apparently wants a certain level of anonymity, and we'll respect that. But we are really impressed by this extremely useful list of ways to create a more powerful blog.

Advice in this post focuses on such topics as how to use Twitter, what effective copy writing is, finding and using smart images, and the all-important subject of getting and keeping blog subscribers.

Blogging Resource 2-19: 12 Things Every Business Blogger Should Know
http://www.prdaily.com/Main/Articles/8293.aspx

Susan Young's Ragan PR Daily post is both useful and entertaining. She lays out everything from why you should make up your own rules to how to identify your key audiences.

Rule seven encourages potential business bloggers to use video.

"Video continues to be a hot trend in social media. Not everyone is a writer, and not everyone is a reader," Young says.

"We all learn through different communication modalities. Some of us are more visual; others are more auditory. Enter video blogs (vlogs). Young describes one business blogging bonus as recording your own video and transcribing it "so you can repurpose it" for your blog.

Blogging Resource 2-20: 6 Ways to Optimize Your Blog for Search Engines

http://www.socialmediaexaminer.com/6-ways-to-optimize-your-blog-for-search-engines/

In the blogosphere, being findable is "where it's at." Author Jim Ludico begins this important article with this question: "Are you looking to get your blog highly ranked on Google?"

The answer begins with making sure you are starting with high-quality content, he says. We think he's right.

The selection and use of keywords is also a big part of the drill, and you'll benefit by looking at all six tips and trying to figure out imaginative ways to get them incorporated into your blog.

Jim's tip #3 is to "Write Strong Meta Titles and Descriptions." So, we ask, just exactly what does that mean?

> Meta titles and descriptions tell both the search engines and the reader what's on the page. The Meta title and description also show in the search engine results, so they need to convince readers to click through to the website. Good content management systems and blogging programs include a place for meta information.

That's the kind of crisp, clear response that caused us (and our students) to list this SocialMediaExaminer.com post as among our favorites.

Blogging Resource 2-21:
Is Commenting on Blogs a Smart Traffic Strategy?

http://www.copyblogger.com/blog-comment-traffic/

We'll give a number of kudos to CopyBlogger.com during our presentation of key resources. We hope they appreciate the plug. This particular post speaks to the important topic of when and how you might effectively comment on blogs in order to get more traffic back to your site or blog. You need to be careful of this one.

As Brian Clark points out in his recent post that has, as of this writing, already produced nearly 500 comments: "If one of your primary traffic strategies is to leave fast comments on the posts of larger blogs in your niche just to get a few clicks from the passing traffic, stop. You could get more traffic from one piece of stellar content than months of that type of comment strategy.

"And without good content, there's no reason to attract a few 'curiosity clicks' under any circumstance. What's going to make them stick around after the click if your content sucks?"

"Nothing," Clark says, and we think he's right.

"Plus," he says, "the root motivation for those curiosity clicks is often bad to begin with. The nature of the game makes it that way."

This is just the kind of advice we wrote this book to provide. But don't stop here. Go to Brian Clark's post, and then check out some of the hundreds of comments that it has generated so far.

Don't be bashful in letting him know you appreciate his advice, but don't you dare use this as a way of trying to *crap-trap* big-shot bloggers back to your site.

Blogging Resource 2-22: Best Practices for Blogger Outreach

http://samirbalwani.com/social-media-marketing/best-practices-blog-outreach-online-pr/

Here's a wonderful resource by digital marketing strategist, Samir Balwani. He describes himself as a passionate and innovative marketer helping businesses create holistic marketing solutions. And from the looks of it, he's capable of doing a good job.

In the true spirit of the Internet, Samir offers many tips, not only for dressing up your blog, but also for making sure you have a solid blogger outreach program.

Some of his advice seems like basic common sense. For example, the first step in reaching out to bloggers is to get familiar with the specific blog to which you are going to reach out. Read it, Samir says.

He also recommends going to "PostRank.com to see if the blog has been included there, so you can read the most popular articles."

His advice then moves from creating a blog template to figuring out a way to "Let the bloggers then decide they want to be part of the campaign." You can read the rest, and we strongly recommend you do, by going to Samir's blog through the link provided above.

Blogging Resource 2-23: Blogger Relations and How to Get Links and Relationships, and Not Get Murdered

http://netvantagemarketing.com/blog/blogger-outreach-how-to-get-links-build-relationships-and-not-get-murdered

Mallory Woodrow epitomizes a phenomenon in public relations that has yet to be documented, much less written about in any detail. Not too many years ago, journalists were a dominant force in public relations. Drawn to big dollar consultancies, ex-journalists saw their role as schmoozing editors to cover their client's business in the daily papers. Somewhat ironically, today it's the PR practitioners who are becoming journalists, writing client-oriented stories for niche blogs.

Clients seem to be catching on to the notion that the "R" in PR is relationships and that relationships are built through the kind of authentic dialog facilitated by social media—especially through blogs. But finding the right blogs remains a challenge.

"We use tools http://ontolo.com/ in the office to locate guest blog opportunities and places to review products, but sometimes I use other methods. Obviously, you can take a look at your competition and see where they are getting links and blog reviews or you can just go in blind. I like Google Blogs for this particular task," Mallory says.

Blogging Resource 2-24: 5 Ways to Keep Your Blog Fresh: A Series Inspired by 150 Posts

http://www.jeffkorhan.com/stand_out_in_your_market_/2010/01/5-tips-to-keep-your-blog-fresh-a-series-inspired-by-150-posts-.html—

Here's more advice from a guy, Jeff Korhan, who appears to be deeply interested in providing useful and important ideas about blogging with anyone who shares his interest. Jeff's first principle is hardly novel, but that doesn't make it any less important to be said:

> Frequency sets expectations. "I put this one at the top for a reason. Very few bloggers are consistent. Therefore, frequency is an approach that creates new expectations that are—well—unexpected. This keeps your blog fresh and your readers engaged.

Great point, simply stated: To stay fresh, you have to be sure your blog stays fresh. Everything important flows from that.

Make sure the stories you share on your blog are original, or at least uniquely told, and, by all means, avoid ranting.

"There is nothing fresh about the rant," Jeff says. He's right.

Blogging Resource 2-25: Blogger Relation Blunders to Avoid

http://www.prdaily.com/mediarelations/Articles/7751.aspx

Blogs are media and dealing with bloggers requires the same attention to media relations as PR practitioners paid, and still pay, to traditional reporters, editors, and publishers.

London-based fashion journalist, Sasha Wilkins, runs LLG Media, which (as she says) encompasses LibertyLondonGirl, her award-winning blog. In this post, Sasha speaks specifically to the approach you may want to take to promote an event on the blog.

Her advice, however, opens the door to a much more detailed conversation, some of which we'll have in the PR section of this book, on the importance of realizing that "bloggers are a lot more sophisticated these days, and can smell blog-sploitation a mile away.

Blogging for Business

Blogging Resource 2-26: Blogging For Business—5 Steps to Success

http://www.theglobeandmail.com/news/technology/digital-culture/
trending-tech/blogging-for-business-5-steps-to-success/article1761450/

Now comes one of North America's most respectable traditional news operations, *The Toronto Globe and Mail*, with some of the best advice for business bloggers our students have been able to find.

> Trendy online services (like Facebook and Twitter) are increasingly keeping us away from in-depth conversations and compelling content, and a business blog is the perfect resource to give your company an official and authoritative voice on the web.
> Moreover, with a blog as an important part of your overall site, you will give your customers or clients reason to discover more about what you offer.

The Globe and Mail recommends, for example, choosing your blogging platform carefully.

Here is what it says on that score: While services such as Blogger have been around for years, two of today's most popular platforms are Word-Press.com and SquareSpace.com. Both provide hosting, a number of attractive templates (if you don't have a designer on hand), and easy integration with other social media services.

We think their advice is wonderful, and strongly suggest that you take a look at it if you have any interest in using a blog to support a business platform of any kind.

Blogging Resource 2-27: Blogging for Your Business Success

http://ezonlineoptions.com/2011/03/27/blogging_for_your_business_success/

Like so many of the other "dress for success" articles about blogging, it's all about the content.

"Showcasing new content keeps customers interested in your business," post author Etty Fhima says. An expert in drop-ship business—marketers make the sale before ordering the product shipped from the supplier—Fhima says there's plenty of material to keep a blog hot:

Choose from all sorts of topic related to your drop-ship business—new products, a new brand you're carrying, the history of your business or one of your signature brands, company information, employees, industry news, and so forth. There are always subjects to write about that will interest customers.

Blogging Resource 2-28: Business Blogging Success through Facebook

http://business.ezinemark.com/business-blogging-success-through-facebook-16b4f803bdd.html

Doing this book project makes our heads feel like they are going to explode. It seems every single time we turn around we come face to face with another spectacular resource. Take Ezine.com for example. You simply have to be prepared to spend some quality time with this site.

Go to the link directly above and you will find an article by Michelle Salater. She's an award-winning writer and president of Sumèr, LLC, a company that specializes in web copywriting, SEO copywriting, and the promotion and marketing of websites after they launch.

According to Salater, "Expanding the reach of a blog has become increasingly easy thanks to growing social media platforms. Not only do social media sites allow you to share content that isn't necessarily appropriate for a blog, but they also enable you to reach various markets that your blog might not reach."

So rather than seeing Facebook as a competitor to blogs, Michelle sees an evolution occurring that is a harbinger of good things to come for social media.

"In particular, Facebook is one of the most powerful ways to extend the reach of your blog."

We agree.

Blogging Resource 2-29: How to Choose a Blog Platform

http://www.youtube.com/watch?v=IRh2oM5jiOI

This post takes you to a YouTube Mahalo.com "Learn Anything" video in which you can learn about the "big three" blog platforms, and you can also experience a great variety of other information about blogging. You can learn, as their slogan says, about just about anything on this site. Mahalo.com has become a favorite of ours for lots of reasons.

The brief tutorial opens with a brief description of WordPress. Mahalo tech wiz Sean Percival also describes Google's Blogger/ Video that gives viewers advice on choosing the right blogging platform.

Blogging Resource 2-30: 10 Benefits of Hosting Your Own Blog
http://www.blogtrafficexchange.com/10-benefits-of-hosting-your-own-blog

BlogTrafficExchange.com features a post arguing that in order to get a competitive edge in the competition for bloggers, you should consider hosting your own blog. With arguments ranging from "professional appearance" to "recall ability" to increasing your ability to generate revenue, this subscription service provides a seemingly endless string of tips for successful blogging.

We think there may be a point for most folks to set up their own blog, but you probably ought to make sure you have the expertise and the time to support it first.

We have some former students who started an amazing web business only a couple of years ago. The business, called Texts From Last Night http://textsfromlastnight.com/About-Texts-From-Last-Night.html is as close to an "overnight sensation" as any business we've ever seen.

If you're not afraid to read some stuff you'd not want your mother to see, have at it. Our point in mentioning TFLN is because it began as a simple blog that Ben and Lauren started on one of the free blog hosting sites. As they tell it, their little experiment got so big so fast that one Friday afternoon they got word from the free blog host that they were going to be shut down within a couple of days.

So literally overnight, they had to build the TFLN website. Fortunately, they had the funds and friends at their disposal to pull this off. But the record will show that they were quite vulnerable, finding themselves at the mercy of a free service that proved incapable of keeping up with their growth.

Blogging Resource 2-31: *New York Times* Gets Its First Tumblr
http://mashable.com/2011/04/06/nytimes-tumblr/

In this Mashable.com account, writer Jolie O'Dell applauds the *New York Times T Magazine* move to the Tumblr platform. The new *Times* account—*T on Tumblr*—covers the domain of *T Magazine*, the style and culture magazine of *The New York Times*.

In an earlier account, http://mashable.com/2011/02/06/fashion-tumblr-kate-spade/ writer Lauren Indvik described Tumblr's appeal: "Fashion brands are creating increasing amounts of visually rich, branded content to share via their websites, blogs and social networks like Facebook, Twitter, YouTube and Flickr. Tumblr provides, among other things, another outlet for distributing that material. And, best of all, the native fashion community on Tumblr is highly receptive to it."

According to Jolie O'Dell the "subject matter is a perfect fit for the arts- and community-focused mini-blogging platform." Tumblr sources say nearly 200 of the top 1000 Tumblr blogs are fashion related.

Blogging Resource 2-32: How to Blog for a Living

http://howtoblog.org/

Tenacity: That's the first requirement for getting your blog into a position where it can make some money for you. You have to be tenacious as all get out.

Robin started his blog in November 2009. The domain name "How to Blog" pretty much sums up his blog's focus by showing bloggers how to make money off of blogging. His blog, which he describes as being turned into a website as we write, includes a great inventory of news, tips, and other information on blogs.

And if you like what you read, Robin has even set up a simple and convenient donation page, and, yes, he accepts most major credit cards.

But be careful. We once heard that there's a surefire way to make a small fortune blogging for a living: *Start out with a large fortune.*

Blogging Resource 2-33: Naming Your Blog:
How to Create Catchy Blog Names

http://www.chrisg.com/catchy-blog-names

Chris Garrett, a blogging and Internet marketing consultant, tells readers and fellow bloggers how to create a catchy and memorable blog name:

> Naming your blog is an important aspect of blog branding, or blog success for that matter. It seems very important to my visitors too. Ever since my original 'What's In a Name?' post, "people have been asking for advice on how to select the best name for their blog.

So here are a couple of his tips. And like most of the websites we reference, you're smart to check Chris's blog out for yourselves:

> When choosing a domain name there are some factors to consider:
> - How original and unique is it?
> - How descriptive is it?
> - What image does it convey?
> - Would you remember it after seeing it once?
> - Could you spell it after hearing it once?

Blogging Resource 2-34: What You Should Include in Your Blog Bio

http://sethgodin.typepad.com/seths_blog/2010/09/five-rules-for-your-about-page.html?utm_source=feedburner&utm_medium=feed&utm_campaign=Feed%3A+typepad%2Fsethsmainblog+%28Seth%27s+Blog%29&utm_content=Google+Reader

Here's some advice from one of the Internet's true wizards, Seth Godin, about the five things you need to include in your bio.

By the way, if you wanted to learn as much as there is to know about social media and could only go to one source, Seth Godin would be a pretty good choice.

He says you should avoid jargon and stock photos. Humanize your bio and use lots of third-party testimonials to establish your credibility. And don't forget to make it easy for someone who finds you to get in touch.

Remember, the trick to success on the Internet may be as simple as making yourself the most findable source within your niche.

Study guys like Seth Godin, David Meerman Scott, and Eric Swartzman if you really want to know how that's done.

Blogging Resource 2-35: The 7 Deadly Sins of Blogging

http://www.copyblogger.com/blogging-sins/

One common list of the seven deadly sins is anger, greed, sloth, pride, lust, envy, and gluttony. If somebody just took this list and translated it into stupid things people do on blogs, you'd come up with a pretty useful list of things you could do if you wanted to see your blog fail.

Our friends at CopyBlogger.com came up with a great list. It's another one of our students' favorites.

Here is the kind of useful information you'll get from checking out this post:

> It's lovely to put your heart into your content, to infuse it with your personality, to come across as a real and likable human being, but...
>> The game still ain't about you, baby.
>> Some people are naturally attracted to topics that other people care about. Others aren't. Don't try to sell broccoli ice cream, even if that's your favorite.

Blogging Resource 2-36: The Concise List of Must-Have SEO Plugins for Wordpress

http://lornali.com/social-media/concise-list-seo-plugins-wordpress

Lorni Li describes herself as an "expert in social SEO -- the art of leveraging the social web to increase your web rankings.

"I can help you with buzz marketing and online reputation management. And I know a great deal about blogging," Lorni says as she tells a story about how she figured out how to identify and install the best plug-ins as a result of some "fortuitous tweeting."

In the true spirit of social media, the aforementioned Joost DeValk volunteered to thin down her original list of 30 recommended plugins.

You can see his picks by linking into to Lorni Li, and then, she says, "You ought to mosey on down to Joost's site and read his WordPress SEO Bible. Good stuff."

Blogging Resource 2-37: Is Your Blog the Unpopular Kid?

http://www.cnn.com/2010/TECH/web/06/29/your.blog.unpopular/index.html

The most anthropomorphic resource we came upon is also one of the most useful, falling under the category of "how to make sure your blog doesn't suck."

This post got big-time play with CNN as high flying news editors Andrea Bartz (*Psychology Today*) and Brenna Erlich (Mashable.com) team up to show you how to make sure your blog doesn't end up being taken to the prom by her stepbrother.

"Why?" they ask.

"Last year the total tally of blogs hit 126 million, according to BlogPulse. That's a big class to climb to the top of. We're not saying you have to be head cheerleader, but it would be nice to be noticed among the digital masses."

Among their best advice—and there's lots of it in this column—is to pick a narrow niche—one you can own—and own it.

"You're a jock? Write all things jock-related. You dig D&D? There are scads of kids out there just waiting at their computers to read your stuff.

"A narrow subject is best. If your theme is, say, 'mental health,' you're competing with gazillions of more-established blogs. But 'bizarre psychological conditions,' you can totally own."

The Best of the Best Blogs

One of the amazing things about the world of social media is that there are truly so many wonderful people putting out great information—caring and sharing and showing us all what it means to "pay it forward" as Jeremy Porter says in one of his notes about the best PR blogs out there.

We are just providing a few examples of the "best of the best blog" lists in a couple of the categories we are chiefly interested in—public relations and social media marketing. Looking these lists over, and taking the time to explore some of the "picks" will give you a good sense of what's going right and, maybe, what's going wrong in the social media space.

What's going right is that the public relations community is demonstrating how blogs—actually, social media in general—is helping build better relationships between organizations and audiences because of one thing and one thing alone. The thing is dialog. And perhaps nowhere than social media is there a better example of how dialog is creating and strengthening relationships.

And don't forget that you have to imitate before you innovate. Many of the most competitive people in the world recognize that imitation is the highest form of flattery, and they are more than willing to help a future competitor get started.

Blogging Resource 2-38:
What Can You Learn from 7 Awesome Corporate Blogs?

http://blog.kissmetrics.com/7-awesome-corporate-blogs/

One of the wonderful things about the world that the Internet has opened up to us has to do with corporate names.

In this link you'll find the blog of an outfit called KissMetrics.com introducing you to a way that you can have a conversation with, for example, the CEO and COO of Zappos.com, one of the countries hot on-line shoe and apparel retailers (Go to http://blogs.zappos.com/blogs/ceo-and-coo-blog).

What sets this blog apart is the transparency it offers to Zappos.com customers. Internal emails, memos, and other corporate news are all shared.

The fact that internal emails are copied in their entirety and shared with the general public is something a lot of corporations would scoff at. But it's all about building trust. Zappos, for instance, recently posted an extensive internal email that marked the one-year anniversary of their deal with Amazon, and included the original email they sent out when the deal with Amazon was announced.

But Zappos' CEO and COO blog is just one of the blogs that you can go to get a sense of what KissMetrics.com says is corporate state of the art. To see the rest, just go to the link we provided, and make sure let them know you heard about their blog from KissMetrics.com, which you can say you read about first in this book.

Blogging Resource 2-39: Technorati Top 100 Blogs

http://technorati.com/blogs/top100/

Here's a list that is updated once a day of the top 100 blogs. And this is a great way to see what the big guns are doing.

As of the day of this writing, although certainly subject to change, one of our favorite blogs—Huffington Post—ruled as number one. One of the things we wonder is just how long Huffington Post is going to be considered a blog and not an on-line magazine? The differences between on-line magazines and blogs are certainly blurring and Huffington Post is contributing greatly to that.

On-line giant AOL recently bought Huffington Post to become part of its growing inventory of content.

Second on the Technorati list on the day we were putting this section together was another AOL acquisition, TechCrunch. This is a blog that began in 2005 to provide profiles of startup companies, products and websites.

Blogger Resource 2-40: The Social Media Marketing Blog

http://www.scottmonty.com/

There are people who can talk about or write about things, and there are people who are the actual doers—people who get things done and done well. Scott Monty is both, as his The Social Media Marketing Blog at ScottMonty.com proves beyond any question of a doubt.

Scott is the head of social media for Ford Motor Company, which is increasingly known as a social media marketing leader. His blog covers a wide range of services involving social media as applied to both marketing and building public relationships.

While you are at it, poke around the *Google Translate* gadget Scott has on the blog's landing page.

> Il 31 maggio, Cinch ha annunciato ai propri clienti via e-mail che sarebbe cambiare l'URL del servizio da http://www.cinchcast.com al più breve http://icin.ch. Più facile da ricordare, giusto? E poiché hanno un applicazione per iPhone, iCinch sembrava logico.

Which, in Italian, means: On May 31, Cinch announced to its customers via email that it would be changing the service's URL from http://www.cinch cast.com to the shorter http://icin.ch. And since they have an iPhone app, iCinch seemed logical.

Ciao.

Blogger Resource 2-41: 10 Ways to Find Blogs You'll Love

http://mashable.com/2011/04/11/blog-discovery/

The first thing to do to find some good blogs to investigate and, maybe, imitate is to go to the blog-a-logs—the blog catalogs.

"Alltop.com is the granddaddy of all blog discovery tools," according to Mashable.com. Alltop.com allows you to customize the service "allowing you to save blogs (or feeds) you like to a home dashboard. . . ."

One of our favorites, Technorati, allows you to "search by keyword for specific posts on a topic or by entire blogs devoted to that topic. . . ."

Other sources for blog identification include Blog Catalog, Guzzle.it, YourVersion and five other Mashable.com favorites.

Blogger Resource 2-42: Jeremy Porter's Favorite PR Blogs

http://blog.journalistics.com/2010/the-best-pr-blogs-out-there

Jeremy Porter puts out a great list of his favorite PR blogs. One of the things we like about this listing is that he's a PR guy who covers PR blogs like a good journalist would. He seems to be very objective covering everything from blogs operated by major public relations firms to PR blogs operated by individual authors like one of our favorites Deidre Breakenridge.

Of Breakenridge, Porter says she exhibits "great insight on PR 2.0 strategies" (personally, we think her stuff is more like PR 3.1)."

Also on Porter's list is Brian Solis. He says:

> Brian offers so much more than "PR" knowledge these days, it's almost unfair to put him on this list. That said, he's one of the leading innovators in our industry and is somebody you should pay attention to when he posts (he's also a pretty nice guy). If you want to know what people will be talking about next year, just read Brian's blog today.

We like Brian so much we track him on Google Reader.

We didn't put links to these blogs listed by Jeremy Porter. We want you to check them out though. Just connect through the "journalistics" blog link above so Jeremy Porter will get credit for his hard work, and let him know where you read about him.

Blogging Resource 2-43: Social Media Marketing Blogs on the Web

http://www.fridaytrafficreport.com/top-142-social-marketing-blogs-on-the-web/

Here's the grand kahuna of lists—142 top social marketing blogs put together by another real expert. The only problem here is that these are social media marketing blogs, not social media blogs—a common mistake.

Jack Humphrey, writing on FridayTrafficReport.com, put together what he calls "this big resource" more than a year ago, but the information is still mostly fresh and very valuable. How valuable is it?

Well, as Jack says: "If you could put a dollar value on the information shared across all these sites it would be impossible for most people to afford. Luckily, you can access all these sites and keep up on social marketing trends and news for free."

He's right. One of the things we like about the list is that you can do something so simple as make your own word document out of the list, and simply click and view these blogs one at a time. Come up with your own ranking system based on your wants and needs and tastes.

"The sites are not ranked in any particular order, nor did I come up with a complicated algorithm to sort and sift them into any order of importance. They all have something to share and they are all popular sites with their own following, large and small."

Once you figure out your favorite blogs, you'll have to figure out how to follow them. This has always been a problem of ours. It was, that is, until we read what follows.

Blogging Resource 2-44: Official Google Blog—Follow Your Favorite Blogs

http://googleblog.blogspot.com/2008/09/follow-your-favorite-blogs.html

Here's an important posting from Mendel Chuang, Product Marketing Manager at Google Blogspot:

> At Blogger we're passionate about helping communities form around blogs. To further that goal, we've introduced a new feature that lets you easily follow your favorite blogs and tell the world that you're a fan.
>
> To follow a blog with the Followers' Gadget, simply click the 'Follow This Blog' link. You can show your support for the blog by following it right from your Blogger Dashboard or in Google Reader.

Perfect Practice Makes Perfect—

Five tasks that will help you understand the concepts and ideas talked about in Part II.

Exercise 1: Find blogs to follow. Go to www.technorati.com or Google Blog Search http://blogsearch.google.com/ and find some blogs that interest you. When you find a blog you like, subscribe to their RSS feed. Here's a guide of how to do that: http://rss-tutorial.com/rss-how-to-subscribe-to-feeds.htm Then you can read these blogs and keep up on topics that relate to your interests or industry.

Exercise 2: Start commenting. The best way to get into blogging is to comment on other people's blogs. This will give you an understanding of how the blog community works. And it will help you build some relationships with other bloggers. Comment, share your thoughts and give praise or constructive criticism. Try it on for size. After a few weeks of commenting, you will be ready to start your own blog.

Exercise 3: Start your own blog. Now it's your turn. Pick a topic you like, and one that you can write about consistently. Choose a blogging platform (Typepad, Wordpress, Blogger, Tumblr). Think of a name for your blog. Build your blog. Add a blog roll of other blogs you like. Write your first post. Customize the look and feel of your blog. Starting a blog is not easy. You will need to decide if you want your blog to be hosted so your web address looks like this: www.yourblog.wordpress.com or if you want your blog to have its own URL like this: www.yourblog.com. If you choose the latter, you may want to ask for some help in setting up your hosting to get your blog launched. Or you can read or watch one of the many online tutorials on starting a blog.

Exercise 4: Post once a week. Pick a day that works for you and commit to it. Sure you can post daily to your blog, but if you commit to posting at least once a week, you will get good results. When you write your blog posts, it's always good to include some visual impact by adding a photo or video. Also, you can link from your blog to relevant outside resources that will give credibility and show your sources if you used any. Posting once a week will give you some content, and help your blog get going. Now it's time to take the last step.

Exercise 5: Promote your blog. Submit your blog to Technorati or other blog directories. When you comment on people's blogs, now you can leave a link to your blog, so they can find you and comment on your blog. Promote your blog on Facebook, Twitter and LinkedIn if appropriate. You can even email a link to your blog to your friends or business colleagues and ask them to give it a read. You are now a blogger. Tell the world, and build your audience.

Part III

SOCIAL
NETWORKING

CHAPTER 3

Everyone's Friend: Facebook

If you are not a current Facebook user, all we can say is, "What are you waiting for?" Everyone is on Facebook. Well, not exactly everyone, but almost.

If you really want to get into the analytics of who is and who is not using Facebook, a great place to start is with a website called Ghacks Technology News and specifically with this article—http://www.ghacks.net/2011/02/15/who-really-uses-facebook-twitter/

Ghacks Technology News is a daily update website chock full of wonderful software reviews, Windows, and Linux tutorials as well as general Internet news.

In February 2011, they reported on what they called some "amazing" charts that were released by a group called Digital Surgeons. You might want to look at these charts. http://www.digitalsurgeons.com/facebook-vs-twitter-infographic/

The digital surgeons chart "the demographic breakdown of who was actually using the social networking sites Facebook and Twitter at that time. It reveals some extremely interesting data. This includes the fact that of Facebook's 500 million users, a massive 41% log in every single day and that 12%, that's 60 million people update their status every day.

According to Ghacks:

> The gender spread is broadly equal with 54% of Facebook users being men and 46% women. The largest groups when it comes to income are people earning between $26k and $75k. People earning less than this make up 13% of its user base.
>
> General awareness of the services in the minds of the general public is excellent with 88% of people aware of Facebook and 87% of people aware of Twitter.
>
> On Twitter 27% of users log in every day and over half of all users, 52% update their status every day. Again the income levels of users are the same as for Facebook.

No matter how the history on this subject is written, it's very clear to both of us that one name will surface as one of the two or three greatest toolmakers of this new era of marketing and public relations. And, ironically, if you read what he has to say anyway, influencing marketing and public relations was the furthest thing from his mind when Mark Zuckerberg created Facebook.

If you want to know what he had in mind, go to Mark's Facebook page http://www.facebook.com/markzuckerberg where you'll find these words: "I'm trying to make the world a more open place by helping people connect and share." We believe Zuckerberg is sincere.

So, let's see how well he's doing.

About Facebook: The Big Kid on the Block

Ad advertisement by Internet Strategies Group (of Richfield, Ohio –received via email June 24, 2011) promises leads, loyalty, and revenue by implementing a Facebook advertising campaign:

> Got Facebook Ad Strategy?
>   The ad line, a takeoff on the "Got Milk?" tagline, tells potential advertisers that the "behavior of your prospective customers has changed. Are you adapting your marketing strategy to be where your customers are?
>   Facebook numbers are off the charts! Are you building strategies to take advantage of these?
>
> - Approaching 700 million world- wide users (some now say 1 billion)
> - 12 million NEW users in May, 2011!
> - 770 BILLION page views each month
> - Average user visits the site 40 times per month
> - Spends an average of 23 minutes per visit
> - 200 billion users access Facebook via mobile app
> - Average user create 90 pieces of content each month
> - 30 billion pieces of content are shared each month
> - More than 2.5 million websites are using Facebook Social Plugins"

Facebook Resource 3-1: How Facebook Really Won the Social Media War: Viral Marketing Lessons from "The Social Network"

http://www.huffingtonpost.com/sean-smith/how-facebook-really-won-t_b_828629.html

If you haven't yet subscribed to Huffington Post, were not going to convince you to do that. You'd just think we're soft-headed liberals if we were to promote Huffington. But even if you're not a subscriber, check this post out by InfoDesk marketing director Sean Smith. We've been trying to figure out how we could plug "The Social Network" film without appearing too commercial. Huffington's Smith takes care of that for us.

Smith's position, to which we heartily subscribe, is that the film offers wonderful insights into some of the brilliant, however accidental, marketing decisions Facebook co-founders Mark Zuckerberg and Eduardo Saverin made at critical points in the network's development.

For example, there's this tidbit: "They (Zuckerberg and Saverin) didn't bother trying to get every email address at Harvard; they knew they didn't need to. Somehow they understood that it was better to reach the trendsetters or influencers. The rest would follow."

Facebook Resource 3-2: Facebook Page Statistics

http://statistics.allfacebook.com/pages

Here's a statement about American culture, if not about Facebook itself. Texas Hold'em Poker, which as of this writing boasts nearly 43 million fans, has a larger fan base than Facebook itself. And if her fan-base growth rate of more than a half-million fans per week continues, Rihanna may catch numbers three and four, Eminem and Lady Gaga.

You can find these "Facebook Page Statistics" and more on the link we show above.

The statistics pages at All Facebook, which describes itself as "The Unofficial Facebook Resource," also links to mediabistro.com and its "Social Times" job listing as well as to an "Application Statistics" scoreboard that shows top applications and hot, and not-so-hot developers.

So, let's back up one step and look at the source of all these numbers.

Facebook Resource 3-3: All Facebook All the Time

http://www.allfacebook.com/

"AllFacebook.com is the online guide for everything related to Facebook. We provide everything from tips to how-tos, and the latest news for Facebook users as well as brands, marketers, and anybody else looking to take advantage of Facebook."

Describing itself as an "insightful blog to learn more about Facebook," it's not exactly easy to understand who officially owns and operates the site, but it is clear that it's loaded with useful information.

For example, in a post that we'll be using in our New Media Driver's License® classes, we're enchanted with these 10 Facebook features we'd love to see. http://www.allfacebook.com/10-facebook-features-wed-love-to-see-2011-05

Here's one feature that would be sure to generate significant attention. "Who wouldn't want to know if anyone has been peeking at their profile information or looking at their pics?"

The post goes on: "It would be heaven-sent to receive a notification every time a social media snoop was sniffing around your account—potential employers, an old flame, a *frenemy*, or even the FBI! Intel-gathering from whatever source is oftentimes never a good thing."

In reality, not everyone agrees that a stalking-the-stalker service would be the best idea. Nor do they agree with some of the other 10 ideas in this post, as you'll find out if you check out the comments.

Facebook Resource 3-4: The Biggest Brands on Facebook
http://mashable.com/2010/11/15/biggest-facebook-brands/

This post is a few months old now, and there are other sites that can tell you some of the same type information, maybe even more current information; but we think this Mashable resource is well worth your time. In it, Mashable's Shane Snow tells us that 20 million people "like" brands on Facebook every day.

So far the leader of the brand pack is Starbucks with well over 16 million Facebook likes. Coke follows closely behind Starbucks, with Oreo cookies in third place. Skittles is in fourth place as of this writing.

The average brand "liker" is 31 years old with more than 20% of the "liker" population being unemployed—roughly double the current US unemployment rate, suggesting, perhaps, that people who spend time "liking" brands might be better off spending just a bit more time liking the idea of trying to get jobs. We'll talk more about how people can use Facebook to help find jobs.

By the way, the advertising agencies might "like" to tell their paying clients that, whatever its worth, more than 75% of all "likes" are generated from Internet advertising.

Facebook Resource 3-5: How Facebook
Learned from MySpace's Mistakes
http://tech.fortune.cnn.com/2010/11/19/how-facebook-learned-from-myspaces-mistakes

Kyle James, writing in doteduguru.com (http://doteduguru.com/id3701-social-network-failure-what-happened-to-myspace.html) said he had once described MySpace as "the wild west or Las Vegas of social media, dirty and ghetto."

"Yup," James said. "That quote pretty much summed up MySpace a year and a half ago and now it's even worse."

How does Facebook avoid a fate similar to the once popular MySpace?

First, CNN Money contributor Kevin Kelleher, says Facebook is not, as MySpace, going to let its user decide its business mission or what it's going to look like.

"In other words, MySpace, like everyone else in 2004, wasn't sure what would make a social network click," Kelleher says.

"So it let its members figure it out, offering them to design their own pages with widgets, songs, videos, and whatever design they pleased. The result was a wasteland of cluttered and annoying pages that were as garish as the self-designed home pages on MySpace's 1.0 predecessor, Geocities.

"Facebook, meanwhile, opted for a cleaner, Google-like interface that resonated with a broader audience," which allowed it to connect with a much broader audience than MySpace.

The second reason had to do with the failure of MySpace to capitalize on its potential to deliver product—its members—to advertisers. They had the right idea of favoring advertising over the earlier proposed subscription model they rejected. But MySpacers didn't want to click through to advertising.

"The only information anyone seemed to want on MySpace was what their friends were up to," says Kelleher. "MySpace responded by putting multiple banner ads on pages, making the poorly designed pages even more unbearably cluttered."

Facebook Resource 3-6: Social Media Marketing— 5 Benefits of a Facebook Page—Do I Really Need One?

http://business.ezinemark.com/social-media-marketing-facebook-page-5-benefits-do-i-really-need-one-16bf1d4de31.html

We suppose there are some people out there who are really wondering whether or not they really need to get engaged in Facebook.

We had a bit of trouble sorting out just what five benefits, Ezinemark.com—the free content article directory—was referring to with its key words, but its logarithm led us to a virtually endless stream (35,649) of articles that speak to everything from generally why a small Brooklyn storeowner should consider using social media as a marketing tool to Berkle George's recommendations on how to use videos in social marketing.

By the way, here is the story within the story. You must be interested in how social media can be a vehicle to create and sustain relationships between your organization and the audiences upon which your organization depends in some way or another. If you were not concerned about this, then why in the world would you be reading this resource book?

So, if you really care about this subject, go to this site now http://business.ezinemark.com/Public-Relations/ where you will experience a great example of the new way business is done on the web. You are going to find more than 40 articles about public relations, most of them associated in one way or another with social media and many of them excellent examples of the kinds of great resources available to anyone who might want to look for them. We're giving you a short cut here.

Facebook Resource 3-7: How to Use Facebook: 5 Tips for Better Social Networking

http://www.readwriteweb.com/archives/how_to_use_facebook_5_tips_for_better_social_networking.php

It's been a couple of years since Richard McManus posted this great starter kit for better Facebook networking. His recommendations are not rocket science, but then we're not building rockets here, are we?

"Update your status regularly," McManus stresses. OK. Time out while we go update our Facebook statuses.

Facebook Resource 3-8: Facebook Accounts for 25% of All U.S. Pageviews

http://mashable.com/2010/11/19/facebook-traffic-stats/

Mashable writer Jolie O'Dell discusses the huge audience that Facebook had as of year-end 2010, an audience that is growing by leaps and bounds each year.

"Facebook is putting up some big numbers in terms of U.S. web traffic. Right now, the site accounts for one out of every four page viewed in the United States—that's 10% of all Internet visits."

ComScore (the Internet-based marketing research company) placed Facebook's unique monthly visitors, in 2010, only slightly behind Google.

How Business Exploits Facebook's Potential

Facebook Resource 3-9: 32 Ways to Use Facebook for Business

http://gigaom.com/collaboration/32-ways-to-use-facebook-for-business/

Meryl K. Evans, brings us 32 excellent tips on how to use Facebook for business. Read the rules first, Evans says, so you can "stay out of trouble."

"Start a group or fan page http://romcartridge.blogspot.com/2010/01/how-to-create-fan-page-on-facebook.html for product, brand or business. Unless you or your business is already a household name, a group is usually the better choice."

Demonstrating the beauty of a blog post, you can see how others—everyone from students to professional marketers—reacted to Evans's advice. For example, Mickmel "disagrees with # 27. What I tell clients is that groups are better for events/seasons and pages are better for long-term things."

Facebook Resource 3-10: 25 Tips for Killer Facebook Marketing

http://web.appstorm.net/roundups/social-media-roundups/25-tips-for-killer-facebook-marketing/

Justin Stravarius does a masterful job of doing exactly what the title of his post suggests. Not only are the tips well thought out, they are beautifully presented. This is a "how-to" mini-manual for anyone with a product or service to sell.

His "Design a Custom Facebook Page" tip, for example, shows the Dunkin' Donuts page that includes free offers, a fan of the week feature showing a couple of over-caffeinated fans jumping for joy and compelling photos of latte.

We also liked his "Keep the Conversation Going" tip:

> Conversations help foster the sense of being a community and that will do wonders for your brand.

Facebook Resource 3-11: The Facebook Marketing Bible

http://gold.insidenetwork.com/facebook-marketing-bible/

This isn't a free service, and it's not even particularly cheap as Internet services go. But given the likelihood that many of our readers are dead serious about using Facebook to "get the most out of the rich opportunities present in the Facebook ecosystem," we want make sure you know about this resource.

Put together by the publishers of Inside Facebook, we're sure many of the tips and tactics are available for free on line, but we're equally sure that this Bible is a most direct way to get the complete rundown on Facebook marketing.

Katie Adams, head of interactive marketing at 1-800-Flowers, isn't bashful in her endorsement:

> The Facebook Marketing Bible and Inside Facebook are my lifelines! As the head of social media for my company, I rely on it to keep me up to date on what's going on with Facebook. Complete dependency!

Facebook Resource 3-12: Facebook Advertising Basics

http://www.websitemagazine.com/content/blogs/posts/archive/2009/05/19/facebook-advertising-basics-social-promotions.aspx

The world of social media is full of wonderful tips on how to promote yourself, your company, and anything else on Facebook. In this post, *WebSite Magazine* lays out the basics of advertising on Facebook.

There's no shortage of cyber advice available regarding this subject or almost any other one we cover. And as is often the case, there are two sides to the story about the effectiveness of Facebook advertising. So before you embark on a major Facebook ad campaign, you'd better do more than just read a few of the many tip columns out there.

You'll have to decide for yourself if Facebook advertising fits the marketing model that will work for your business. But be sure to read the next column before you commit.

Facebook Resource 3-13:
How Effective Is Advertising on Facebook?

http://www.labnol.org/internet/are-facebook-ads-effective/13957/

Here's a handy column in which market researcher Amit Agarwal set up a quick study to see just how effective Facebook advertising could be.

He begins by expressing his love of the Facebook advertising system.

"It's extremely easy to set up ads, and yet I can target the exact audience that might be interested in reading my blog."

But the results produced by the Facebook advertising campaign he describes in the article were certainly much less than stunning.

What is interesting about this post is not so much Agarwal's report of the study, but the string of more than 30 comments this post generated.

Facebook Resource 3-14: 5 Killer Tips for Facebook Ad Ownage

http://www.nickycakes.com/5-killer-tips-for-facebook-ad-ownage/

I love the phrase "ad ownage" even if my spellchecker doesn't. Nickycakes is on fire. He's a shameless entrepreneur, and I'd be a bit careful taking absolutely everything he says as gospel. But isn't that true about everything you read?

Nickycakes is really into selling stuff through Facebook, and this column on his website links you back to a couple of other advertising tutorials. And while some of his material is a bit dated, there are lots of interesting comments that constitute a great way to learn more . . . and fast.

Some of his tips make us a bit squeamish; we're not certain we'd advocate selling everything that he would, but much of his advice seems very solid.

You'll find a link on his website, for example, to a recent webinar in which lawyers describe what the FTC is letting advertisers get away with. http://www.nickycakes.com/ftc-2011-crackdown-and-you/ We'll call this "required reading" for any social media marketer, as long as you understand its probably also required reading for the regulators.

Facebook Resource 3-15: 5 Ways to Instantly Boost
Your Facebook Page Traffic

http://www.allfacebook.com/5-ways-to-instantly-boost-your-facebook-page-traffic-2009-10-

Jackie Cohen tells us: "Every brand and business wants to know the secret of how to increase the number of fans to their Facebook fan page. While there is no one stop shop to success, there are some sure-fire ways to grow your fan base organically."

And in this post, Jackie promises that if you take the 5 steps outlined in this post, you will increase your fan base by 100 within a week—no mean feat. We don't agree that each one of these tips will produce the promised results, but we found this one quite intriguing, and it's worth a try. Jackie says:

> Create a *simple* and *direct* landing page that makes it very clear what you want people to do. Look at the WooMe fan page http://www.facebook.com/WooMe?sk=app_4949752878 for example—originally we created a very dynamic and interactive fan page that would allow people to view and rate fan photos, sign up for the company blog and watch videos from WooMe TV.
>
> However, we revised our strategy and decided to focus on one thing—get people to click the "become fan" button. We also added an "invite friend" box that supports the first goal by encouraging new fans to invite their friends to become fans of the brand as well. By doing this we saw our visitor to fan ratio double.

Facebook Resources 3-16: Increase Facebook Engagement: Tips For Brands

http://www.huffingtonpost.com/2011/04/06/increase-facebook-engagement-tips_n_845597.html

This HuffPost Tech posting by Bianca Bosker provides several tips for brand managers on how to increase Facebook engagement.

It's not just blog content that connects your brand to potential customers in the blogosphere. At least, that's Bianca's reading of research presented by Buddy Media in April, 2011 http://www.buddymedia.com/:

> Posts that were made before or after the workday had an engagement rate 20% higher than the average. The research, done on 200 of Buddy Media's clients over several weeks, also found that shorter posts connect better.

Facebook Resources 3-17: Facebook SEO 101

http://www.clickz.com/clickz/column/1896009/facebook-seo-101

This is definitely a must read if you are interested in getting the very basics on Facebook SEO. In fact, the author Ron Jones, posting in ClickZ Marketing News and Expert Advice, gives the basics on how to make it easy to help people find your Facebook page.

Jones, President of Symetri Internet Marketing, calls his article "Facebook SEO 101," as if to imply that he's providing basic training. He is. He begins by showing you how to set up a vanity URL, and why.

We particularly like his description of the "autocomplete box" and why it's so important that you pay attention to this. Ron is obviously big into cycling, and his article pays dividends by explaining "the list of things that rank when you do a search in the autocomplete box."

Facebook Resource 3-18: Top 5 Facebook SEO Tips

http://business.ezinemark.com/top-five-facebook-seo-tips-16bf186dde3.html

This post at EzineMark.com is (as is the case on a huge variety of subjects) an almost overwhelming list of separate columns, which provide insights from a large number of authors talking about social media Search Engine Optimization.

Kitty Cooper's article is another take on basic SEO training. It's a useful stream of consciousness piece (excuse the typographical errors) by a writer who uses her SEO skills to market "retro bar stools."

Dario Montes de Oca takes SEO directly to Facebook:

> You can, very simply, use SEO on your fan page so that new traffic will be sent to your search engines every day.
>
> The best part about this method is that the people who go to your page from the search engines will actually be interested in what you have to offer.

Facebook Resource 3-19: 5 Rules of Facebook That Companies Should Be Thinking About

http://www.mlive.com/business/west-michigan/index.ssf/2010/08/column_5_rules_of_facebook_tha.html

Here's business reporter Candace Beeke's take on Facebook, published first in August, 2010, in our home state's Booth newspaper chain Internet service—mlive.com. This is a little more basic than some of our previous recommendations—it is, after all, written for a newspaper audience.

Here's what Beeke calls her first rule:

> Thou shalt focus on Facebook. Otherwise, you'll find yourself writing on someone else's wall things you meant to write on your own, posting information publicly that you meant to keep between certain friends, and other social media faux pas.

In other words, you really need to understand this new media, including the consequences of acting without thinking, before you venture into Facebook as a business tool.

Now that you are much better versed on how businesses are using Facebook, we'd recommend you use this article from mlive.com as a brief summary review.

Facebook Resources 3-20: Facebook Ad Prices Rise 40%

http://technorati.com/business/advertising/article/facebook-ad-prices-rise-401/

As competition increases for Facebook ad space and the ads are more tailored to the users specific interests, advertising costs increase—around 40% during the most recent year.

The bloggers at Technorati.com (who follow these kinds of things for a living, obviously) are upbeat. "Facebook's advertising product is picking up speed as online marketers begin to get a grip on it. They allocate larger budgets on the social network to benefit from the scarily precise targeting options. With an audience of around 500 million active users across an increasing demographic range the potential becomes obvious to most."

Some Important Information about Facebook Users

Facebook Resource 3-21: 3 Tips for Maximizing Engagement with Facebook "Likes" and Shares

http://mashable.com/2010/11/08/facebook-like-share/

Now we go back to one of our favorite sources, Mashable.com, for this simple but profound reminder that there are some basic things we need to do to "maximize engagement."

Engagement has been a pretty big concept in public relations during the past decade, in no small part because of the influence of the Internet. Generally, we think of someone being engaged with us if they are interacting with us, and if they increasingly show signs of being dependent on us to fulfill some aspect, however small it might seem, of their professional or personal lives.

In this post, David A. Yovanno, CEO of Gigya, Inc., takes us back to the basics:

> When it comes to Facebook, if you're uncertain where and when to place a 'Like' button on your site and when to use 'Share,' you're not alone. Social sharing technologies have evolved significantly in the past several months, but it's not as complicated as it may seem.

Yovanno's column told us of a new Facebook post on the value of a "liker."
http://www.facebook.com/notes/facebook-media/value-of-a-liker/150630 338305797
Check this out. It will make you feel smarter than you think you are.

Facebook Resource 3-22: 21 Creative Ways to Increase Your Facebook Fan Base

http://www.socialmediaexaminer.com/21-creative-ways-to-increase-your-facebook-fanbase/?doing_wp_cron

It's pretty difficult to overstate the value of Mari Smith's 21 great tips on getting people to become a fan of your page on Facebook. And if you look at the comments from others—there should be more than 400 by now—you'll see that we are not the only ones who appreciate these suggestions.

Again, some of the material is not new—it would be crazy to think that it could be—and almost all of it is useful.

> Create an attractive landing tab (canvas page) with http://www.marismith.com/how-to-add-a-custom-landing-tab-to-your-facebook-fan-page/—a video that explains exactly (a) what your fan page is about, (b) who it's for and (c) why they should become members.
> The result: you'll increase your conversion rate from visitors to fans. One of my favorite fan page welcome videos is by Steve Spangler, the Science Guy! After watching his video, http://www.facebook.com/stevespangler, you can't help but want to join!

Facebook Resource 3-24: When Are Facebook Users Most Active?
http://mashable.com/2010/10/28/facebook-activity-study/

Cristina Warren gives an excellent overview of a three-year study by Vitrue that shows us exactly when Facebook channel users are most active.

Warren reports:

> Here are some of the big takeaways:
> - The three biggest usage spikes tend to occur on weekdays at 11:00 a.m., 3:00 p.m. and 8:00 p.m. ET.
> - The biggest spike occurs at 3:00 p.m. ET on weekdays.
> - Weekday usage is pretty steady, however Wednesday at 3:00 pm ET is consistently the busiest period.
> - Fans are less active on Sunday compared to all other days of the week.

Facebook Resource 3-24: What's a Facebook Fan Page Really Worth to Marketers?
http://latimesblogs.latimes.com/technology/2010/05/facebook-page-value.html

So we know when Facebook users seem to be most (and least) active, but how much is fan page worth in dollars and cents to a marketer? And again, we turn to Vitrue, via the *L.A. Times*, for an insight. This is an important question, after all, especially to anyone who has tried to make the case to a client that their business may depend upon a little more activity in this department. Here's one example from the *Times*:

> Starbucks . . . has one of the most highly valued fan pages. According to Vitrue's tool, the Starbucks fan page is currently valued at more than $20 million in annual worth to the company. But because the company doesn't post enough and it typically posts text content, rather than video or audio, it loses significant value. In fact, Vitrue's tool contends that Starbucks' page could be worth more than $76 million if the company optimized its page.

New Facebook Tools

Facebook Resource 3-25: Facebook Lets Users Interact in Small Groups

http://www.nytimes.com/2010/10/07/technology/07facebook.html

Here we go again, relying on traditional media—*The New York Times*—to get us up to speed on an aspect of social media. In this case, we're reading about Facebook's 2010 announcement of a feature that "allows users to interact with small groups of people, like their family, high school friends or colleagues."

"The move is an effort to address a longstanding problem: Facebook friends often span a broad range of relationships that include relatives, classmates, casual professional acquaintances or jogging partners—and not everyone wants all of them to see his or her information."

So, how's it working?

In May 2011, Facebook users began reporting getting this message:

> Over the next few months, Facebook will be archiving all groups created using the old groups format. Moving forward, you can create groups using the new groups format, which makes it easy to share with the important groups in your life.

You can get deeper into the discussion at All Facebook. http://www.allfacebook.com/news-flash-the-end-is-near-for-old-facebook-group-2011-05

But suffice it to say that the evolution of Facebook Groups is occurring at a speed consistent with the breathtaking speed at which the word "Facebook" has become almost a synonym for social media.

Facebook Resource 3-26: Facebook Messages Takes Aim at Email Leaders

http://www.nytimes.com/2010/11/16/technology/16facebook.html?_r=2&scp=2&sq=facebook&st=cse

What better way to document the rapid evolution of Facebook than with a *New York Times* article from November 2010 predicting that Facebook Messages may be the next big thing on the Internet—so big, in fact, that email may go the way of cursive writing. according to NYT writer Miguel Helft (November 15):

> Facebook Messages is a bold move by Facebook to expand from a social network into a full-fledged communications system. It could help the company chip away even more at Internet portals like Google, Yahoo, MSN and AOL, which have used e-mail as one of their main draws with consumers.
>
> The new service, which will encourage users to sign up for an e-mail

address ending in @Facebook.com, has the immediacy of instant messaging and chat built in," according to Facebook founder Mark Zuckerberg.

Despite the hype, Facebook Messages has not taken off at the speed Zuckerberg and others may have expected.

Commenting on Axleration.com blog http://www.axleration.com/what-happened-to-facebook-mail-everything-explained/

Ganesh Babu said: "Recently there was a lot of buzz around the new Facebook mail. Many techies blogged that Facebook mail will sweep off Gmail. When we expected Facebook mail to roar today, it came out with a small meow."

"But Facebook mail is not totally false, but it is not as big as we expected."

Facebook Resource 3-27: Don't Drink and Facebook— New Plugin Mitigates the Fallout

http://mashable.com/2010/11/07/social-media-sobriety-test/

Maybe America needs a new organization—MADF (Mothers Against Drunk Facebooking). There's little doubt of the effect Mothers Against Drunk Driving has had. Deaths on the highway related to simultaneous alcohol and vehicle use are down. But what about career deaths related to simultaneous alcohol and Facebook use?

Make sure you read Brenna Erlich's sobering post if you have any doubts about the serious nature of this advice:

> Raise your hand if you made a mistake this weekend. Maybe sent a scathing Facebook message to an ex who broke your heart? Told everyone—via Twitter—how much you hate your boss? Uploaded something scandalous to YouTube? Well, it's too bad we waited until Sunday afternoon to tell you about the Social Media Sobriety Test, now isn't it?
>
> Firefox has created a plugin that requires users to pass a "social media sobriety test" before they are allowed to post on their profiles.

Brenna's column will take you to the Firefox site.

Facebook Resource 3-28: 10 Privacy Settings Every Facebook User Should Know

http://www.allfacebook.com/facebook-privacy-2009-02

This AllFacebook.com post of Nick O'Neill will take you to the Facebook privacy guide. It's cool.

Nick says that everyday he receives an email from somebody about how his or her account had been hacked, "how a friend tagged them in the photo and they want a way to avoid it, as well as number of complications related to their privacy on Facebook."

We followed Nick's lead and found the Facebook advice very, very useful indeed. The first tip reiterates what Facebook had said in an earlier privacy guide—understand your friend list, and take the time to configure it properly.

You can read the rest. And if you really want to increase your Facebook security, take a look at this advice from CNN.

Facebook Resource 3-29: New Facebook Privacy Tip: "Super Log-Off"
http://www.cnn.com/2010/TECH/social.media/11/12/facebook.superlogoff/index.html

Time after time we find traditional news sources—newspapers, radio, television—contributing to information about social media. Here, CNN correspondent John D. Sutter tips us off on Facebook privacy.

He tells us "Some young, privacy-concerned users are simply deactivating their Facebook accounts each time they leave the site."

Then they reactivate their accounts to log back on.

"Why go to all this trouble?" Sutter asks.

His column will send you off to visit the advice of Microsoft researcher and social media expert danah boyd (she doesn't capitalize her name), "who identified the trend . . . on her blog, (and who) believes young people may have good reasons for deactivating and reactivating their accounts frequently.

"In many ways, deactivation is a way of not letting the digital body stick around when the person is not present. . . ."

Facebook Resource 3-30: 10 Cool Facebook Status Tips and Tricks
http://mashable.com/2010/07/10/facebook-status-tips-tricks/

For the Facebook fanatics, Amy-Mae Elliot shows us a variety of what she calls "tips and tricks" that can put you at the front of the Facebook merit badge line.

This is a classic Mashable "How-to" column—tremendous advice stated in very simple terms that "will help you get the most out of your status update, from official features to apps, Easter eggs, jokes and more."

Facebook and Personal Finances

Facebook Resource 3-31: Using Facebook to Make Money
http://www.blogstash.com/12-ways-to-make-money-on-facebook/

Our lawyers would remind us from time to time to point out that we are not endorsing any specific advice that you may get from any of the wonderful, or even not-so-wonderful, resources we are leading you to. And this makes especially good sense when we're talking about ways to make money. But it is happening—some people are making money through Facebook (other than Mark Zuckerberg, that is.) And in this post, the folks at Blogstash.com show you 10 different ways you can do that. Better than that, go to their site and let them take you on a tour.

One of their recommendations was a Facebook site called "my merch store." The storekeeper was offering a wide array of items from t-shirts to coffee cups.

But hey—this is only 1 of 10 tips. You can spend hours just cross tracking through this post alone and who knows, by the end of your trip here you may have figured out a way to use Facebook to get you that Ferrari.

Facebook Resource 3-32: Facebook Deals Could Make You Want to Check Into

http://www.pcworld.com/article/209745/facebook_deals_could_make_you_want_to_check_in.html

PCWorld writer Jared Newman broke the story about a year ago about Facebook Deals "as part of the sites new push into mobile."

Newman's article leads us to a recent study from the Pew Internet and American Life Project that found that only 4 percent of online adult Americans are using location-based services like Facebook Places and Foursquare. "What's the point?"

Facebook Deals might be the best answer to this question, Newman says. "It'll save you money."

Facebook Resource 3-34: How to Score a Job through Facebook

http://mashable.com/2010/10/30/facebook-jobs/

Look. You need to understand that we're not shilling for Mashable.com, but we have to admit we love it. And since it's an advertising-based service, we have to assume they don't mind us referring to them as often as we do.

If you go to the "About" page at Mashable.com you'll find out they have been around since way back in 2005. Here's how they describe themselves: "*Mashable* is the top source for news in social and digital media, technology and web culture. With more than 40 million monthly pageviews, *Mashable* is the most prolific news site reporting breaking web news, providing analysis of trends, reviewing new websites and services, and offering social media resources and guides."

Here's one reason we're "Mashablephiles." Stephanie Marcus provides some wonderful advice we're sharing with our students (and our children, by the way).

While Facebook is better known for helping people lose their jobs, it's largely an untapped resource when it comes to job hunting. With 500 million users, it has the potential to be one of the largest. But finding a job through Facebook isn't about pestering your friends and junking up their news feeds with status updates like "Unemployed and Looking For Work—Help A Dude Out." It's about making the most of your network in a positive way, not by being a nuisance.

Stephanie lays out six major steps that you can take to use Facebook to help you get that job of your dreams. Each step provides wonderful advice and practical examples that just might do the trick for you. And as soon as we complete our Facebook section, we'll take you on a guided trip through a social network—LinkedIn—that's increasingly known for finding jobs.

Facebook Resource 3-34: Just How Offensive Is Your Facebook Profile?

http://mashable.com/2011/02/18/socioclean/

This is one of those throwaway resources. If you don't care about whether you ever get a decent job or whether you'll be promoted in the job you have, throw this resource away. If, on the other hand, you don't want to be in that category of almost hired or almost promoted (but for the fact that the employer used social networks to screen candidates and employees), you might consider getting into Socioclean.

This is also not a free service, but it may be more than worth your while. According to their sign up page http://www.socioclean.com/Sign-up.aspx "Socioclean crawls through your Facebook profile photos, groups and wall posts, and alerts you to anything inappropriate."

Enhancing Your Facebook Page

Facebook Resource 3-35: Enhance Your Facebook Fan Page with 11 Quick Tips

http://socialmediatoday.com/index.php?q=frankbarry/186134/enhance-your-facebook-fan-page-11-quick-tips

Thank you socialmediatoday.com. We are big boosters of a number of nonprofit organizations in the Mid-Michigan area. And when we saw the work that Frank Berry and Jeff Patrick had done last fall, we just couldn't wait to send it off to the Children's Trust Fund. Here are some of Frank Barry's words:

Because of Facebook's large user base and incredible popularity businesses and nonprofits are using the services in increasingly effective ways. Nonprofits specifically are figuring out how to connect with their supporters, donors, volunteers and advocates in new and interesting ways. Some are even using Facebook to successfully raise money.

Jeff Patrick and I had a chance to speak to over 350 nonprofits a while back. We shared a Facebook 101 for Nonprofits type of presentation that was focused on highlighting what a few nonprofits are doing well in hopes that others would see the possibilities and be inspired to take action. Here's the presentation followed by 11 useful tips to get you moving in the right direction with your Facebook presence.

Facebook Resource 3-36: 10 Ways to Grow Your Facebook Page Following

http://www.socialmediaexaminer.com/10-ways-to-grow-your-facebook-page-following/?doing_wp_cron

Not everyone cares how many followers they have on their Facebook page. If that's you, skip to the next section. But we love Ching Ya's post last summer because he answers, for us, a question that he gets from his clients on a regular basis.

> From the day you set up a Facebook page, it does require an ongoing commitment to brand, monitor, and network with people who find interest in your product. Besides quality service, it's important to build close-knit relationships with visitors.

Like we said, it takes work, and it is certainly not something you should do unless you intend to do it well. But if you're looking for some great tips on how to get people to like your Facebook page, take Ching Ya's advice. The common theme throughout his tips is fan engagement. And if you're really interested in this, dig the next Ching Ya post.

Facebook Resource 3-37: 9 Ways to Enhance Your Facebook Page

http://www.socialmediaexaminer.com/9-ways-to-enhance-your-facebook-fan-page/?doing_wp_cron

"To create an important hub to reach out to millions of potential supporters, you need to up your game and optimize your fan page to meet its ultimate purpose." Ching Ya doesn't mince words. And neither should you if you want to be a Facebook high flyer. Check his Tip #3, for a good example:

> When it comes to service providers and professionals, nothing is more convincing than a testimonial page. You can have a static page with testimonials or have a designer create a catchy layout to attract peoples' attention. How you decide to showcase your testimonial page is only limited by its relevancy and your creativity.

Facebook Resource 3-38:
Top Marketing Tips for Updated Facebook Pages

http://www.socialmediaexaminer.com/top-marketing-tips-for-updated-facebook-pages/

In one of our favorite free resources, SocialMediaExaminer.com, the inquiring mind of Michal Stelzner wants to know if you are "struggling to understand how to get the most out of your Facebook Page . . . ?" Never fear, the answer to your problem, he says, is in a video from Social Media TV host Mari Smith. It's embedded in the post, and believe us when we say it's worth watching.

The tutorial is sponsored by the Social Media Examiner Social Media Success Summit 2011. One of the neat things about this ad is that you can see a sample class from the 2010 summit.

Facebook Resource 3-39: 10 SEO Tips for
Maximizing Facebook Visibility

http://searchengineland.com/10-seo-tips-for-maximizing-facebook-visibility-24477

Putting your face on milk cartons is no longer the premier way of being found in America. How about the possibility that making yourself findable to the search engines might be a better way to get your brand out there?

This post may be a couple of years old now, but its still among the most useful we've found. Marty Weintraub, writing in SearchEngineLand.com, admonishes readers to think beyond Google and other mainstream engines, and to start thinking about Facebook:

> There are more than 45 million (more today) active user groups. Little-to-none of Facebook's activity is indexed by Google and other mainstream engines. It's easy to see why Facebook's members-only organic search results deserve attention!
>
> At the root of this new consideration is the reality that Facebook is now allowing users to search the last 30 days of their news feed for status updates, photos, links, videos and notes being shared by friends and the Facebook pages of which they're fans.

Some of the specific data may have changed since Marty's 2009 post, but the principle remains the same. Facebook is quickly becoming a massive walled-garden parallel organic internet.

Facebook Resource 3-40: Anatomy of a Shared Link on Facebook

http://socialmediatoday.com/mattsullivan/284714/anatomy-shared-link-facebook

Matt Sullivan, client services manager at MoonToast, used this post in Social MediaToday.com to show us how he nearly doubled click-throughs to his client stores by properly promoting sharing to a Facebook Fan Page. His advice is thorough:

> Needless to say, giving our clients the ability to customize the title, message, and image specifically for sharing to their Facebook Fan Pages made a huge impact, and drove even more qualified leads to their stores.

Facebook Resource 3-41: 10 Reasons to Delete Your Facebook Account

http://www.businessinsider.com/10-reasons-to-delete-your-facebook-account-2010-5

Let's wrap up the Facebook love fest with an alternate point of view. Dan Yoder, writing in businessinsider.com, is mad as hell, and he just isn't going to take it any more.

Yoder ticks through a list of objections ranging from (10) Facebook's "completely one-sided" terms of service to (9) the ethics of Mark Zuckerberg all the way to objection number one—"The Facebook application itself sucks." He leaves no stone unturned or should we say "un-thrown"?

But all is not lost. As he is signing off this column advocating deleting your Facebook account, he sends us to a second column "10 Reasons You Will Never Quit Facebook (Even If You Think You Want To)."

"You may feel a slight twinge of anxiety," Yoder says. "But you'll stay on Facebook forever."

Facebook Resource 3-42: Breaking Dawn Attack: What You Need to Know to Avoid Getting Bit

http://www.pcworld.com/businesscenter/article/224915/breaking_dawn_attack_what_you_need_to_know_to_avoid_getting_bit.html

Tony Bradley's April 2011 *PC World* article is well worth the read, showing how fans of the vampire series Twilight are being infected with malware. You can click through to an earlier article by Carrie-Ann Skinner to read how a security firm helped university students fight Facebook status jacking, called "clickjacking."

The latest Facebook jam (at the time of this writing) appears as a link to a fake promotional game for the upcoming Twilight movie "Breaking Dawn." Once tricked, the user clicks on to something that leads to a number of unintended actions being taken on behalf of the user without his or her knowledge. Bradley includes a number of links to similar articles relating to security scams and Facebook—definitely worth the look.

Extra Point: Facebook in the Future

Facebook Resource 3-43: How Facebook Can Become Bigger in Five Years than Google Is Today

http://techcrunch.com/2010/10/02/facebook-bigger-google/

Sporting an image of a blue Pac man with a Facebook "f" gobbling Google, PayPal, Skype, and Groupon, Adam Rifkin's TechCrunch.com post makes a bold prediction:

> I have been mulling over data from both companies, and I'm ready to declare in public my belief that Facebook will be bigger in five years than Google is right now, barring some drastic action or accident.

Perhaps that reveals why Google at the time we wrote this seems to be putting all their vast resources behind their new social media platform called Google+. Google may see the writing on the wall and realize that they need social media if they want to truly become *too big to fail.*

> How could this be?
>   Facebook will inexorably grow as big as Google is today and maybe bigger, because Madison Avenue's brands are less interested in targeting than they are in broadcasting to vast mother-loving buckets of demographically correct eyeballs, and Facebook has become the perfect platform for that.

A couple of paragraphs can't do this tremendously detailed and documented article justice. But if you have any interest in the advertising implications of social media and what might just happen in the future (and if you didn't, why would you use this resource?), you need to go to Rifkin's column now.

Facebook Resource 3-44: Facebook for Journalists: More Work than Twitter, But with a Bigger Payout

http://www.insidefacebook.com/2011/04/10/facebook-for-journalists-twitter/

In April 2011, Facebook launched a page called "Journalists on Facebook" http://www.facebook.com/journalists in what post author Josh Constine (InsideFacebook.com) says was "an effort to encourage the news community to use the sites' Page feature as a distribution and research tool."

With Facebook sporting as many as 10 times more active users (than Twitter,) journalists should still be focused on mastering the social network, even if it takes more work than just tweeting copy and pasted URLs.

Constine's comparison of the journalistic value of Facebook to Twitter is compelling and convincing. Facebook holds the upper hand, despite some obvious disadvantages.

Facebook Resource 3-45: What Facebook Mail Will Mean for Marketing?

http://www.utalkmarketing.com/pages/Article.aspx?ArticleID=19642&Title=What_Fac
ebook_Mail_will_mean_for_marketing

Facebook continuously changes. New features, privacy settings and display options regularly evolve.

An UTalkMarketing.com article by ecommerce product manager and SEO specialist at Actinic, Bruce Townsend, provides an interesting perspective on Facebook's email feature.

Townsend says: "Facebook email will obey the same privacy settings as the current Messages. This means that users can choose to share their message stream with their friends—potentially drawing messages to the attention of many more people."

Fairly new advancements permit open settings and less privacy restrictions leaving an opening for marketers to creep in early and begin e-mailing, messaging and texting information to Facebook users. The article warns marketers to be cautious when using Facebook messaging due to the threat of spammers who will ultimately determine the fate of the new messaging innovations.

Facebook Resource 3-46: Measuring Facebook: 5 Key Indices the Folks at PR Daily Watch

http://www.prdaily.com/Main/Articles/7886.aspx

OK—here's the key question. So how do I know it works?

All that glitters is not gold, we know, and yet we're all smitten with shiny objects from time to time. But when we're dealing with client money, we have to be sure what we are doing for them on Facebook is paying off.

The folks at Ragan PR had Arik Hanson post his thought on the subject. He says we should be looking at five key indicators of Facebook performance.

Arik says begin with tab views. "Just like reviewing Google Analytics on your blog, one of the first things you should know is where people are going on your site. Which tabs are fans viewing? On Insight, 'Tab Views' is where you find out."

The thing we especially like about Arik's column is that he not only tells us what numbers to look at, but he also tells us how and why they are important. This resource is a must read.

By the way of an unsolicited testimonial, if you are interested at all in the use of social media in PR (why in the world would you have read this far if you are not?), we strongly recommend you subscribe to Ragan's free enewsletter, the Daily News Feed. http://www.prdaily.com/Main/Home.aspx

CHAPTER 4

LinkedIn to Business Connections

The ultimate business social networking tool, LinkedIn is a 100 million member website—all about making business connections. Put your resume online, and you are on your way to connecting on LinkedIn.

Building your LinkedIn profile is your first step. Be sure to follow the guide and build it to completion. A few things to consider when building your LinkedIn profile:

1. Your custom URL—LinkedIn.com/in/yourname—is an important marketing tool for you. So go to your custom URL and change it from the standard URL that every LinkedIn user gets. Having your name as part of your LinkedIn URL will make it easier to find you.

2. Write a keyword rich description of yourself in your professional headline at the top of your profile. Be clear and impactful. Avoid the simple and short description like Accountant. Because people will have a hard time finding you for that phrase. Use a long tail approach with some specific keywords based on expertise, location, awards, title, and the like.

3. Add all your connections. This is easy with Gmail or Yahoo mail to upload all your contacts and see who is on LinkedIn. Then if they are there, you can select them and invite them to connect with you. Invite all business connections, and even friends who you could do business with.

4. Ask for recommendations. One of the best things you can do is to get recommendations from your peers. Past bosses, colleagues, clients. Ask them all for a recommendation and when you get it display it proudly in your profile. Remember, the best way to get a recommendation is to give a recommendation first.

5. Build links to your profile. Use your profile URL in your email signatures. Link to it from your website. And when you comment on blog posts or news articles online, use your LinkedIn URL as your web address. This will help your profile rank higher for searches on your name.

Building your company page on LinkedIn is a smart investment of time and energy—and it allows your employees to all connect under the same umbrella. It also allows people to follow the updates of your company, and spread the good news about what your company is doing. Derek's company, Ingenex Digital, created a resource guide of how to build a company profile on LinkedIn. You can view it here: http://ingenexdigital.com/how-create-LinkedIn-company-page.

Typically a network for business professionals, LinkedIn lately has been working to get more students on board by letting them talk about extracurricular activities and affiliations at their universities. Read about that change here: http://newmediadl.com/blog/LinkedIn-reaches-out-students

Since you are taking this journey with our book, building and maintaining a strong LinkedIn presence is a good first step and a great way to build your personal and company brand.

LinkedIn Resource 4-1: Why LinkedIn Works

http://www.psychologytoday.com/blog/positively-media/200903/why-LinkedIn-works-the-strength-weak-ties

If you're interested in understanding why LinkedIn works as a professional social networking website then this *Psychology Today* article is a must read.

Dr. Pamela Brown Rutledge uses the work of network theorists like Mark Granovetter and Albert-Laszlo Barbasi to get into the heads of the LinkedIn crowd. She uses these theorists to examine why social media networks, mainly LinkedIn, have attained to much power and attention.

"LinkedIn isn't the only network for professionals, but it has managed to gather critical mass which means you are potentially connected to a vast network of people," says Rutledge. "Personally, I like that people have figured out how to connect to and help each other."

"Not only does LinkedIn demonstrate the power of social media, it shows the broader reframing of how social media has changed the way people think about accessing information and the world. People have moved from hunting for 'jobs' to connecting with people. And for good reason."

LinkedIn Resource 4-2: 10 Ways to Use LinkedIn

http://blog.guykawasaki.com/2007/01/ten_ways_to_use.html#axzz161dzv3Yf

According to Guy Kawasaki, "Most people use LinkedIn to 'get to someone' in order to make a sale, form a partnership, or get a job."

Kawasaki is a founding partner and entrepreneur-in-residence at Garage Technology Ventures. He is also the co-founder of Alltop.com and was an Apple Fellow at Apple Computer, Inc. His blog, "How to Change the World," provides readers with useful tips to help them become more successful.

The Blog.GuyKawasaki.com post explains, "It is a tool that is underutilized, so I've compiled a top-ten list of ways to increase the value of LinkedIn."

Kawasaki's post provides tips streaming from years of experience in the business and technology industry and is a great resource if you want to differentiate yourself from the millions of other LinkedIn users.

Using LinkedIn for Business

LinkedIn Resource 4-3: 33 Ways to Use LinkedIn For Business
http://gigaom.com/collaboration/33-ways-to-use-LinkedIn-for-business/

Want a quick resource guide to help you understand and capitalize on the power of LinkedIn in your professional life? Then check this link out.

Gigaom.com blogger Meryl K Evans post provides 33 different ways to use LinkedIn. Evans says, "You can do so much more with it than simply look up contacts: find gigs, sell products, expand your networks, grow your business and gain free publicity."

LinkedIn Resource 4-4: 8 Areas Where You Have to Pay Closer Attention
http://www.prdaily.com/Main/Articles/8780.aspx

Social networking tools like LinkedIn offer users the ability to connect and communicate with other industry professionals. In this *PRDaily* post, Pete Codella explains how LinkedIn became the first social media company to be taken to the street in an initial public offering (IPO).

"The recent investor acceptance of LinkedIn has once again focused my attention on the usefulness of this social network," says Codella.

Codella conducts a webinar series for *PRDaily*.com on social media tools for PR professionals. In his webinar series, Codella spells out 8 areas you should pay a little more attention to on LinkedIn.

His LinkedIn guide will aid you in completing your business profile to attract the right connections and help your career in public relations or any other industry.

LinkedIn Resource 4-5: Advertise on LinkedIn
http://www.LinkedIn.com/advertising?src=en-all-el-
lihb_tab_ads&utm_medium=el&utm_source=li&utm_campaign=hb_tab_ads&trk=
hb_tab_ads

Are you interested in advertising on LinkedIn? The company has many tools to help begin advertising on LinkedIn, and this link is the official word on that. "LinkedIn Ads is a self-service advertising solution that allows you to create and place ads on prominent pages on the LinkedIn.com website."

If you want to target your audience, connect with and attract customers, and be in control of advertising costs then LinkedIn Ads is an option to consider.

This resource will get you started, help you identify advertising goals and teach you how to easily create an advertisement on LinkedIn.

LinkedIn Resource 4-6: How Connecting Your LinkedIn Contacts Builds Social Influence

http://www.socialmediaexaminer.com/how-connecting-your-LinkedIn-contacts-builds-social-influence/?doing_wp_cron—Tips on how you can leverage your presence on LinkedIn to build social influence

There are many ways to connect with people online. LinkedIn is unique in that it allows you and others to view valuable work experience information that can help you build a relationship with potential employers.

Stephanie Sammons is founder and CEO of Wired Advisor, a turnkey blogging and social media platform consultancy advising financial practitioners.

"There are also a number of ways to build deeper relationships with your connections on LinkedIn," Sammons says in this SocialMediaExaminer post:

> Working to *connect your connections* on LinkedIn not only helps you become a more influential person, you'll also benefit from triggering the rule of reciprocity. The power of the LinkedIn network provides a compelling opportunity to grow your business.

LinkedIn Resource 4-7: How-To Create a LinkedIn Company Page

http://ingenexdigital.com/how-create-LinkedIn-company-page

Here's one from Derek's company blog at IngenexDigital.com.

LinkedIn, like many other social networking websites, has space for a business to post its profile.

"A company profile on LinkedIn is a powerful resource for any company to have. A LinkedIn Company Profile helps users find potential companies to do business with or to work for," Derek says.

In the company profile you display "an overview of the company, people you may know at the company and worthwhile data about the company that LinkedIn can provide."

Take it from the horse's mouth—or in this case, the co-author's mouth—these straightforward steps will help you setup a perfect company page to connect with employees, potential customers and other business connections on LinkedIn.

LinkedIn for Personal Growth

LinkedIn Resource 4-8: 5 Clever Ways to Get a Job Using Social Media

http://mashable.com/2011/06/19/get-job-using-social-media/

Social media allows us to connect with friends, family and find jobs. If you want to use social media to your advantage then you'll want to pay attention to this article by Dan Schawbel.

Schawbel is the founder of Millennial Branding, a full-service personal branding agency. His advice in this Mashable.com article could help you get the job you want.

Schwabel insists that "by understanding who you are, what differentiates you in the marketplace and establishing your personal branding online, you can compete. . . ."

LinkedIn Resource 4-9: 8 Tips to Get More Out of LinkedIn

http://www.socialmediatoday.com/justinlevy/240281/8-tips-get-more-out-LinkedIn –

It's very common to get sucked into social media networks other than LinkedIn. And (SocialMediaToday.com) Justin Levy is concerned that we may be losing focus on the one that is most closely linked to our professional futures.

Levy asks, "Have you kept your LinkedIn profile updated? When was the last time you provided a recommendation for someone? Are you taking time to explore Groups and Answers?"

In the post Levy reminds us that just because we're on LinkedIn doesn't mean it's doing us any favors. "What you get out of LinkedIn will only be as good as what you put in."

The SocialMediaToday.com article suggests 8 tips that will help you use LinkedIn to its fullest.

LinkedIn Resource 4-10: LinkedIn—
What It Is and Why You Need to Be on It

http://www.job-hunt.org/executive-job-search/LinkedIn-for-executives.shtml

Here's a great resource that doesn't look so great when you first go it. But remember *you can't judge a book by its cover*, or a website by its landing page, for that matter.

This is an executive job hunting website, and we didn't dig deep enough into it to be sure about what its business model is, but hidden within this landing page is some pretty good advice for execs seeking jobs on how to use LinkedIn.

"If you're an executive, and you don't have a presence on Google, recruiters and employers are likely to dismiss you as a lightweight. Increasingly," the site proclaims, "if you're not on LinkedIn, the same thing happens."

There's a wonderful segment in this column about the importance of building a serious profile, starting to invite participation and get endorsements, and using the variety of other available LinkedIn features.

LinkedIn Resource 4-11: 4 LinkedIn Tips to Help You Stand Out

http://www.socialmediaexaminer.com/4-LinkedIn-tips-to-help-you-stand-out—
Tips on how to stand out above everyone else on LinkedIn

Once you've made a connection on LinkedIn what do you do? If you've answered this question with "nothing," then you are going to want to read this article by Linda Coles.

Coles, of Blue Banana, is a sought-after speaker who also runs various workshops and seminars on how to use social media tools effectively and productively. In this SocialMediaExaminer.com post she asks: "So how can you use social etiquette to really make your LinkedIn connections valuable and stand out from the crowd at the same time?"

Coles provides four different tips to help you develop new connections.

> View LinkedIn as your own boardroom of connections versus your coffee shop connections on Twitter or Facebook. They tend to be managers, directors, business owners, CEOs and the like.

These are very important people who are using LinkedIn daily, many CEOs and business owners view LinkedIn as a more valid form of connection. Learn how to make the most out of new and potential connections to build your network and stand out against everyone else.

LinkedIn Resource 4-12: Building Online Credibility on LinkedIn

http://www.socialmediatoday.com/charlottebritton/198623/building-online-
credibility-LinkedIn

I'm sure you're sick of hearing about how important LinkedIn is. This resource will tell you why it's important and suggest the places where you should invest your time on LinkedIn, and will help save you time.

The blog post on SocialMediaToday.com by Charlotte Britton provides information to help build your credibility online in the post, which links to a Slide Share presentation expanding on the articles main points.

Britton works at Optimum Exposure, a company that works with you to build trust and integrity in your brand in the online environment. The Slide Share presentation hosts more detailed information about building credibility and tips of where to invest LinkedIn usage time.

In the post Britton explains:

Your online credibility is an increasingly important way of showcasing your specialized knowledge and expertise, which will build your online credibility. As more people engage with the social web, differentiating yourself become imperative.

Most people understand the basics to setting up the profile, but beyond that they do not understand the potential of how they can use this online networking.

LinkedIn Resource 4-13: Are You Making the Top 3 LinkedIn Profile Errors

http://www.careerealism.com/top-LinkedIn-profile-errors/?goback=.gde_3393675_member_30998483

There is little, if any room for error in your professional career. There are a lot of ways to make mistakes on various social networking websites, but above all LinkedIn is one where the errors should definitely be avoided.

Laura Smith-Proulx is a resume expert and former recruiter. She posted an article on Careerealism.com to help LinkedIn users avoid common profile errors:

> . . . using it [LinkedIn] incorrectly can actually reduce your chances of being hired. Here are 3 common pitfalls to avoid when setting up and using a LinkedIn profile for your job search.

This resource will help you avoid common mistakes and maintain your online credibility and impress potential employers and/or customers.

CHAPTER 5

Becoming a Master of Your Twitterverse

One of the things that made it difficult for some people to take Twitter seriously is the language—Twitter, Tweeting and the latest, Tweeple, a word being used to characterize those who are increasingly relying on Twitter to give and get messages out to increasingly large circles of Twends.

But regardless of what you may think of the wordplay—it's thought that Twitter was named to mimic the sound birds use to communicate with one another—tweeting has had a huge impact in the world of social media.

In July, 2011, traditional and new media was abuzz with talk about the first "Obama White House Twitter" town hall, called a Tweet-up.

As of that date, the White House Twitter account—@whitehouse—had more than two million followers. "Obama team members use Twitter all the time to chat, break news or take the temperature of their Twitterverse." (http://commpro.biz/news/corpcomm/5906)

Now it's time for you to fire up your Twitter account, choose your handle wisely, and begin tweeting. You may discover that Twitter is loads of fun. But surely after reading this chapter, and trying it for yourself, you will see that Twitter is an important component to social media marketing. Enjoy, and Happy Tweeting.

Twitter Twends

Twitter Resource 5-1: 27 Twitter-Ready Consumer Trends You Need to Know
http://adage.com/adagestat/post?article_id=146612

Twitter-ready is the key phrase here because none of these stats are "about Twitter." But don't let that put you off.

If you're interested in predicting the future of this media, you need to have a clear picture of the kind of people who will be using Twitter, or won't.

This resource really could have been placed almost anywhere in this resource guide. We have sections on Social Media, Internet Marketing and PR. All of these sections, as well as this one on Twitter, benefit from the kinds of basic demographic trends Matt Carmichael first put forth in this AdAge.com blog.

Twitter Resource 5-2: What The Trend—Find Out Why Terms Are Trending on Twitter
http://www.whatthetrend.com/

What's hot on Twitter? WhatTheTrend.com can tell you what is trending in America and everywhere else across the globe. The website allows users to participate and discuss why certain hash tags are trending on the website. Join in on the trending conversation and interact with the Twitter community.

"We are the front page of the real-time web," the FAQ for WhatThe Trend.com boasts. "Our contributors are people from all over the world, people just like you, who are interested in providing a little context around what's currently trending."

Twitter Resource 5-3: How Twitter Will Change the Way We Live
http://www.time.com/time/business/article/0,8599,1902604,00.html

Here is one of the reasons that *Time* magazine is still around and reportedly profitable. Despite their storied role in traditional media, many folks think that the only way magazines of *Time*'s stature can survive is to not only be delivered in a new media format, but to make sure it's covering new media.

Time writer Steven Johnson, was on top of Twitter more than two years ago when he reported that Twitter's success was helping him overcome his earlier skepticism:

> I think there is something . . . profound in what has happened to Twitter over the past two years, something that says more about the culture that embraced and expanded Twitter at such extraordinary speed.
>
> In short, the most fascinating thing about Twitter is not what it's doing to us. It's what we're doing to it.

You should take the time to read this, and a companion piece— http://www.time.com/time/specials/packages/0,28757,1901188,00.html— focusing on the impact of Twitter on business.

Twitter Resource 5-4: Twitter Search—Twitter's Way to Show You What's Happening Now
http://search.twitter.com/

This is Twitter's way to allow you to see what is happening on Twitter right now.

Twitter is constantly being updated, and its open nature allows people to view tweets from just about everyone. Search.Twitter.com allows you to search a keyword or term on Twitter will show you instantaneous tweets from users everywhere right now. It's a good tool to search hot and trending terms.

Twitter Resource 5-5: Twitter: 3 Out of 4 Tweets Are Ignored

http://www.onlinesocialmedia.net/20101017/twitter-3-out-of-4-tweets-are-ignored/

Reading this Gary Johnson post in OnlineSocialMedia.net might not seem like its worth the effort, but actually, he provides good food for thought.

We won't restate the basic finding that Johnson reports from the Sysomos and *PCWorld* studies he's examined, except that a cynic might conclude that most Tweets are getting just exactly the amount of attention that they deserve.

And that ain't much, for sure, but it also doesn't mean you need to throw the baby out with the bathwater. Make sure your Tweets are worth reading. I'm not sure I care that much that you're at the beach with the kids, unless of course, I thought you'd be home working on this resource guide.

That Tweet Smell of Successful Strategies

Twitter Resource 5-6 and 5-7: How To Use Twitter: (Two) Tips for Bloggers

http://www.problogger.net/archives/2008/01/23/9-benefits-of-twitter-for-bloggers/
http://www.problogger.net/archives/2008/01/25/how-to-use-twitter-tips-for-bloggers

Here are two great posts. Both from the same writer, the second post is referenced in the first, so we decided to list them both.

The author of this post on ProBlogger, Darren Rowse, admits (like one of your authors does) to being kind of slow in adopting Twitter because "I didn't think it had much to offer me." However, Rowse says, "I'm beginning to see how wrong I was."

Rowse uses Twitter to improve the quality of his blogs, network, expand his subscriber base, and "grow my profile."

In the first post, Rowse will give you a number of what he calls Twitter Tips and to demonstrate how committed he is to using Twitter to improve his blogging, he has developed a new blog that he will happily connect you to.

One of the best pieces of advice applies to so much more than blogging. Darren Rowse warns us against the kind of creeping scope that can ruin almost any project—including a simple resource book like this.

Stay disciplined with your objectives," he says, while recommending that you take your list of objectives and put them where you'll see them regularly. If the tweet that you are about to put out there doesn't advance your objectives for using Twitter, then *distweet* it.

Twitter Resource 5-8: How to Gain Attention on Twitter

http://www.cnn.com/2011/TECH/social.media/04/07/twitter.influence/index.html

Focusing your Twitter account on one subject may be your key to success.

Twitter is a popularity contest, but Twitter accounts with a large following aren't necessarily the most influential.

Amy Gahran, writing for CNN.com, explains what it means to be influential and successful on Twitter. She cites results of a study from the Association for the Advancement of Artificial Intelligence.

An international research team examined the metrics of about 55 million Twitter accounts. The article suggests different tactics to help point your Twitter account in the right direction and become more influential and gain attention.

Twitter Resource 5-9: Seven Great Strategies for Growing a Great Following

http://www.socialmediaexaminer.com/7-twitter-strategies-for-reaching-critical-mass

For some reason, SocialMediaExaminer.com seems to be a little slower to load than the average resource. But this might just be our anticipation showing because we know that their guides into the "social media jungle" are normally quite rewarding. In this case, the book *Twitter Power* by Joel Comm inspired Dino Doran's Post in SME.

Unless you're a Kardashian cast member or what a jaundiced TV viewer might call a more a "legitimate" celebrity, generating a following on Twitter is hard work.

To get on with it, Doran encourages Twitter users to search for the people you already know. He describes a clever method for using a free Gmail account to use your existing contact list to find Twitter friends.

Integrating social networks with each other and joining in conversation are two of the many suggestions Doran suggests to help define your Twitter account as a credible source.

Twitter Resource 5-10: Who Are All of These Tweeple?

http://www.briansolis.com/2010/11/who-are-all-of-these-tweeple/

Gives demographics of Twitter users who are developing a social media strategy. BrianSolis.com posted an overview of research conducted by Ad-ology Research: "Twitter Users in The United States."

Solis summarizes U.S. Twitter demographics. The Ad-ology research covers usage beyond gender, education, and age. Psychographic data imputes goals of various Twitter users categories.

Business Twips, Tactics, Tools and Tricks of the Trade

Twitter Resource 5-11: The Twitter Guide Book

http://mashable.com/guidebook/twitter/

PDF VERSION: http://www.slideshare.net/AmitRanjan/mashable-twitter-guide-book-2009

The "Twitter Guide Book" from Mashable.com will rock your world. It is the most complete all-in-one resource we have found for the social network. Mashable organized the Twitter Guide for a simplified search system. Credible resource articles and links are divided into like-minded subjects, saving you valuable time to make search easy.

Resources are available for beginners, business owners, and marketers to help anyone build a community through their Twitter account. This guidebook will teach you how to develop and manage an account for a number of purposes. Reference the "Twitter Guide Book" from Mashable anytime by downloading the free PDF version.

Twitter Resource 5-12: Quick Twitter Tips:
A Twitter Guide For Beginners

http://www.huffingtonpost.com/2011/03/31/quick-twitter-tips-a-twitter-guide-for-beginners_n_843351.html - slide_image

Beginners have no fear and prepare to jump into the Twitter game head first with confidence. The information you need to get started is here and in nine easy-to-understand tips. Bianca Bosker from the HuffingtonPost.com put together a list to help. The article, "Quick Twitter Tips: A Twitter Guide For Beginners," will give you the tool to get started.

Learn basic Twitter terminology and how to share pictures instantly on Twitter. The article also discusses options for URL shortening and how to correctly use hash tags. Create your Twitter account with the basic understanding of the differences between @replies, @mentions, and direct messaging and be on your way to becoming a Twitter star.

Twitter Resource 5-13: Tweeting 101: A Twitter Cheat Sheet

http://gigaom.com/collaboration/tweeting-101-a-twitter-cheat-sheet/

Thanks to Aliza Sherman for putting this cheat sheet together, and we love the graphic of the student who has his test answers written on the inside of his wrist. Must have been a short test.

The advice in this Gigaom.com post is pretty basic, for sure, but it's also very useful. We always appreciate the step-by-step approach, and this is sure it. Step 1: "Check @ messages. First check to see who has publicly referenced you in their tweets and acknowledge, answer or respond."

There's more. If you're looking for a cheat sheet, this one will almost fit on the inside of your wrist.

Twitter Resource 5-14: What Are Hashtags in Twitter?

http://www.dailytut.com/social-networking/twitter-hash-tags.html

Hash out the confusion and learn how to get the most out of #Hashtags on Twitter. The article on DailyTut.com by "Lenin" will help you learn how important hash tags are on Twitter and how to use them to stay out of the Gulag (or was that Stalin?)

Lenin begins by describing the function of hash tags on Twitter as a system to organize tweets. Credibility is essential and learning the proper hash tag etiquette will contribute to credibility.

Using hash tags is a great way to create conversation via Twitter and will help build your brand on Twitter.

Twitter Resource 5-15: 11 Twitter Tools You Probably Don't Know About

http://www.prdaily.com/Main/Articles/8282.aspx

Despite the dangling preposition (Does anybody care anymore?), this excellent post by Lauren Fisher does exactly what it says, although any regular Tweeter knows, for sure, about many of these. Consider it a refresher.

Here's the kind of information Fisher catches:

> Many people use the advanced search function on Twitter, and the same search operators apply when searching on TweetDeck. TweetDeck offers a more efficient and streamlined search if, for example, you want to filter by location or exclude certain keywords from your search.
>
> First, load up the search bar as you normally would (select *add column* then *search*), then apply the search operators. You can even save your searches for instant updates.

Twitter Resource 5-16: Calculating and Improving Your Twitter Click-Through Rate

http://www.seomoz.org/blog/calculating-and-improving-your-twitter-click-throughrate

Most business people want to see the numbers, whether that means the ROI, increase in sales, or whatever for a social media marketing campaign. This is sometimes hard to do and the reason analytics are extremely important.

Rand Fishkin, SEOMoz CEO and co-founder says, "Not many of us spend time thinking about how or taking action to improve the CTR [click through rate] we get from the links we tweet."

Fishkin's SEOmoz.com article will teach you how to calculate the click through rate for a Twitter account.

"As analytics junkies, we're well aware that we can only improve things that we measure, analyze and test," Fishkin says explaining the importance of analytics.

In this article Fishkin takes you through the process, "For measuring our tweets, analyzing the data and testing our hypotheses about bettering our click-through-rates." He adds, "If we do it right, we could increase the value Twitter brings us as a marketing and traffic channel."

Twitter Resource 5-17: Use Twitter for Your Business the Right Way
http://www.twitip.com/use-twitter-for-your-business-the-right-way/

Twitter is a great tool for business; if used correctly it can help establish your brand as an industry leader. The article, "Use Twitter for Your Business the Right Way," from TwitTip.com instructs you on the proper practices for using Twitter in your organization.

Twitter for Business is all about building relationships and interaction with the community. This article can teach you how to create good karma by re-tweeting certain posts of people you follow and how to incorporate your business/product into the conversation at the right time to be successful.

Twitter Resource 5-18: Benefits of Using Twitter Infographic
http://blog.hudsonhorizons.com/Article/Benefits-of-Using-Twitter-for-your-Business-Infographic.htm –

Twitter bird is busier than a bee. A simple tweet, depending on who sees it and retweets can skyrocket your business's success, help you land a job, and

create a public image. This HudsonHorizons.com blog post by Rania Eldekki delineates the magnitude of Twitter's influential place on the web and in society.

The graphic portrays the benefits of Twitter for different users, how much time people spend using Twitter, and even displays famous Twitter scandals.

Twitter Resource 5-19: How to Use Twitter Hashtags for Business
http://mashable.com/2009/09/04/twitter-hashtags-business/

This Mashable.com post is replayed from a post that originally appeared on the American Express Open Forum—http://www.openforum.com/. It's a great resource that will show you how to use hashtags to promote your business. But first you'll need to know what a hashtag is:

> Hashtags are essentially a simple way to catalog and connect tweets about a specific topic. They make it easier for users to find additional tweets on a particular subject, while filtering out the incidental tweets that may just coincidentally contain the same keyword.
>
> Conference and event organizers often use hashtags as a method of keeping all tweets about the event in a single stream, and they've even been used to coordinate updates during emergencies. In fact, hashtags were first popularized during the 2007 San Diego wildfire, when the tag #sandiegofires was used to identify tweets about the natural disaster.

Twitter Resource 5-20: 35 Conversation Starters to Share on Twitter
http://www.marketlikeachick.com/35-conversation-starters-to-share-on-twitter/
Lists 35 ways to spark up conversation on Twitter.

Here's another great resource for businesses to use to market themselves

You've set up a Twitter account and made a super-optimized bio. Now comes the hard part. Tweeting, at least posting tweets that will generate conversation and in turn grow your audience and increase your brands presence on the Twitter channel.

Posting funny photos, blog posts, and tips are just a few of the ideas from the article "35 Conversation Starters to Share on Twitter," from MarketLikeAChick.com. The article suggests combining conversation starters and to be yourself and respond to your followers.

Twitter Resource 5-21: Twitter Tools to Organize Your Tweeps
http://mashable.com/2009/06/09/organize-twitter/

It might be time for some Spring cleaning, at least with the people you follow on Twitter. The more you use Twitter, the more people are going to follow you, and all of these people can get confusing, especially if you are following thousands of people. Not to mention the stress it could bring to your psyche if out of the blue you got an email that said @massmurder is now following you on Twitter.

Mashable.com Features editor, Josh Catone, posted an article to help you manage your "tweeples":

> Twitter's own tools for managing followers are subpar. It's nearly impossible to figure out who among your followers are following you back, and the interface for paging through followers is clumsy and difficult to use.

Catone's post describes different tools that will help you easily manage your followers/following lists on Twitter. You'll be introduced to different tools that allow you to figure out who you're following, manage lists to help you better organize your Twitter.

Twitter Resource 5-22: Top 10 Twitter Tools for WordPress Blogs

http://www.mediabistro.com/alltwitter/top-10-twitter-tools-for-wordpress-blogs_b40

Integrating various social media platforms is key when creating your online web presence. This can be time consuming and tedious from creating a blog post to disseminating it across all of your other platforms.

Co-editor at MediaBistro.com Lauren Dugan explains how you can easily integrate Twitter with the popular blogging and Web design platform WordPress:

> There are dozens of different ways you can integrate Twitter into Word-Press, like showing your latest Tweets, displaying your followers, or adding a button for your readers to easily Tweet your articles.

She explains 10 different tools that will make tweeting for yourself and others easy and will ultimately increase the viewership of your web page. Learn about different Twitter widgets and comment tools that will help you communicate with readers and make tweeting and blogging easier and more beneficial.

Twitter Resource 5-23: 25 Case Studies Using Twitter to Increase Business and Sales

http://kylelacy.com/25-case-studies-using-twitter-to-increase-business-and-sales/

It's okay if you are struggling to comprehend just how to go about incorporating Twitter into your marketing strategy. You're not alone.

Reviewing KyleLacy.com's 25 post can give you the confidence to start a Twitter campaign of your own. Lacy demonstrates how businesses like Jet-Blue and Comcast used Twitter to connect with customers about customer service issues instantly and directly.

The case studies also look at how companies like the outdoor apparel company The North Face used Twitter to extend their brand's identity by providing customers with outdoor tips that subtly promote products.

Twitter Resource 5-24: 3 Ways to Get a Twitter User's Attention

http://askaaronlee.com/3-ways-to-get-a-twitter-users-attention/

Here Aaron Lee lays out some more basic advice about using Retweets, for example, to get other Twitter users reading her 140s:

> I know everyone been telling you that retweets get attention from other Twitter users. Truth is they DO get attention from them. Some of the stuff that I say to everyone is that retweet someone once, and they will notice you. Retweet them a few times and they will remember you. Why? This is because your avatar is appearing on their timeline more often than usual.

It doesn't get much more basic than that.

Twitter Resource 5-25: 8 Ways to Not Get Retweeted

http://blog.hubspot.com/blog/tabid/6307/bid/6972/8-Ways-to-Not-Get-
ReTweeted.aspx#ixzz1ToL8tH4f

We're particularly fond of this post. Dan Zarella's in blog.hubspot.com should be a must read before you move on to the next chapter.

He's got data—lots and lots of data—and he presents them in Tweet-talk:

> There is nothing that will keep you from getting ReTweeted like talking about yourself constantly. It will probably also prevent you from getting many followers.
>
> Like any form of marketing, calls-to-action matter in social media. So if you don't want ReTweets, don't ask for them, and especially don't ask for them politely.

And our personal Zarella favorite: "Twitter is a fairly literate, intelligent audience. When you're avoiding ReTweets, you need to avoid saying anything too smart, so use only small, simple words." That may be kind of counterintuitive.

Do not-so-smart people often think they have to use big words to impress others they fear may be smarter than them?

To that we reply: "Indubitably."

Tweeting Your Personal Brand

Twitter Resource 5-26: Twitter 101: What to Tweet?

Twitter and Your Personal Brand

http://windmillnetworking.com/2010/11/03/twitter-101-what-should-i-tweet-about-
understanding-why-personal-branding-on-twitter-matters/

Hello? Is anyone there? Is anyone listening? Does anyone even read my tweets? You may be asking these questions, and/or feel like your Twitter isn't important. Well, maybe they aren't.

Neal Schaffer, a leader in helping businesses and professionals embrace and strategically leverage social media, posted a blog regarding his opinion on the importance of Twitter to the image of your brand or personal brand image: "In short, the world is watching you on Twitter. So what better place to share your expertise with the world?"

Neal's point is that when using Twitter, you'll learn how to leverage this media to help make your personal brand stand out. In this economy and changing communication landscape it important to establish yourself as some kind of expert or industry leader. So think of that the next time you're complaining about the heat.

Twitter Resource 5-27: How Twitter Makes You a Better Writer

http://www.copyblogger.com/twitter-writing/

Don't write so pretty good?

Twitter can help. Twitter supports business marketing tactics and creates more effect writers. Or it can make your company (and you) look stupid.

That's Jennifer Blanchard's opinion posted on CopyBlogger.com.

A 140-character limit means every word must count, and every message must be concise.

Businesses should demand Twitter users are also Webster users.

Twitter Resource 5-28: Tips for Writing a Killer Twitter Bio to Get Targeted Follower

http://www.mediabistro.com/alltwitter/3-tips-for-writing-a-killer-twitter-bio-to-get-
targeted-followers_b133

Lauren Dugan, posting in MediaBistro.com, reminded us that Twitter biographies shouldn't tell your life story. You have 160 characters to tell the world about yourself, make them count.

What do you want the world to know about you? Dugan's mission is to help Twitter users set up your bio for one purpose: to attract the followers you want.

Quality, not quantity, is the goal with Twitter Followers, since these are the people who will share your content. Learn the do's and don'ts for biographies. The article will help you convey the correct image of who you are, your accomplishments and goals through strategic key word choices to help get your Twitter account found, followed and shared by like-minded people.

Twitter Resource 5-29: 10 Tips to Be Effective on Twitter

http://www.twitip.com/10-tips-to-be-effective-at-marketing-on-twitter/

Spam alert! Marketing on Twitter is often mistaken for spam. There are certain things a marketer must do in order to use Twitter successfully.

In an article in TwitTip.com, blogger and web designer "Salwa M" explains the importance of using Twitter for marketing:

> Anyone who knows how to benefit from regular blogging formats can also find advantages in using Twitter, which offers the same benefits of blogging but in a quicker and more bite sized format.

This resource is excellent for anyone using Twitter for a marketing campaign. In his article Salwa expresses the importance of sending the right message. You'll learn how to avoid spam-like comments and execute a legitimate marketing campaign.

Twitter Resource 5-30: How Twitter Can Help at Work

http://shiftingcareers.blogs.nytimes.com/2008/09/07/how-twitter-can-help-at-work/

Sarah Milstein, in this early Twitter post in a *New York Times* blog for job hunters, shares her advice to get you out of a jam with your boss if you get caught tweeting.

There is a timeless nature to this piece that comes out of her advice regarding using Twitter to share ideas, show respect for your co-workers or competitors, or build your brand.

Twitter Resource 5-31: How to Use Twitter to Land a Job

http://money.usnews.com/money/blogs/outside-voices-careers/2010/11/4/how-to-use-twitter-to-land-a-job.html

If used wisely, Twitter can score you a job. If you're still a skeptic about the value of Twitter, check out this article from Money.USNews.com.

Lindsay Olson, founding partner and recruiter with Paradigm Staffing—a national search firm that specializes in placing public relations practitioners—put up this post. She'll show you how to customize your profile when searching for a job. If you don't think it matters, it does:

> Recruiters, HR representatives, hiring managers, and executives all use Twitter on a daily basis. Unlike an online job posting where you can only apply via the information provided, Twitter allows you to interact with these people directly by sending them an @ reply or a direct message.

Twitter Resource 5-32: 7 Steps to Successful Twitter Interviews
http://www.socialmediaexaminer.com/7-steps-to-successful-twitter-interviews/

What!? A Twitter interview? You may be asking yourself if this is even practical? According to the Managing Editor of *Social Media Examiner*, Cindy King, Twitter interviews are extremely valuable.

You can, ". . . expand your Twitter business network and get to know someone before connecting with them outside of Twitter," says King.

This SocialMediaExaminer.com article teaches you different kinds of Twitter interviews, the type of language to use while conducting a Twitter interview and much more.

You'll be interested to see how this new style of interviewing can be beneficial to your personal development as well as encourage business expansion.

Twitter Resources 5-33: Fired Over Twitter— 13 Tweets That Got People Canned
http://www.huffingtonpost.com/2010/07/15/fired-over-twitter-tweets_n_645884.html - s112801&title=Cisco_Fatty_Loses

The Wiener-gate Twitter congressional scandal is in a league of its own on the scale of career-ruining tweets.

The HuffingtonPost.com has compiled a list of the worst Twitter-related PR fiascos to show how you can get fired in 140 characters or less.

Examples illustrate how serious employers take tweets, even if they may seem harmless in a social setting. Some of the examples include violating HIPPA (health information privacy) laws and bigoted and hurtful remarks.

Twitter Resource 5-34: Twitter for PR Students—Free Guide
http://oneforty.com/blog/twitter-for-pr-students-free-guide/

Here's a piece in which a recent college student, now PR practitioner, Janet Aronica shares her Twitter experience in the oneforty.com blog.

Basic stuff, perhaps, but once you click through to some of Janet's source documents, you'll find a very simple outline to help you get started, PR student or not.

Monitoring, Evaluation and Security

Twitter Resource 5-35: 75% Use Same Password for Twitter and Email, Study Finds
http://www.twitip.com/

If you want to keep up with what's happening in the Twitterverse, you might consider signing on to a blog like twitip.com, which offers everything from twitorials to twools for long-time twitterers. (All right, we'll stop that.)

One recent tip that we found extremely valuable resulted from research done by the Internet security company BitDefender that revealed that "over 250,000 user names, email addresses and passwords for Twitter sites can easily be found online.

"The study also revealed that 75 percent of Twitter username and password samples collected online were identical to those used for email accounts." (http://www.twitip.com/75-use-same-password-for-twitter-and-email-study-finds/#more-4263)

Twitter Resource 5-36: 8 Easy Twitter Monitoring Ideas
http://www.socialmediaexaminer.com/8-easy-twitter-monitoring-ideas/

Listen to your Twitter. Take a time to listen (i.e., read) what people are posting. This means monitoring your brand, your competitors and yourself. Cindy King posted in SocialMediaExaminer.com to help Twitter users learn the value of listening and how to do it.

Monitoring your Twitter means determining what and who to follow and the value this has for your brand. King shows us how to find the right marketing monitoring tools to increase help increase the amount of information that can be monitored.

Twitter Resource 5-37: What Not to Post on Twitter: 11 Things Your Tweeps Don't Need to Know
http://www.huffingtonpost.com/2011/03/07/what-not-to-post-on-twitter_n_829903.html - s247718&title=Every_Detail_Of—

Security is what this resource is about, and we are talking more than job security here. Whether you are tweeting from a personal account or for a business, there are certain things that shouldn't be posted. If you haven't figured this out yet, well. . . .

Here's a great HuffingtonPost.com post that can protect (somewhat) you and family members from criminals and, in some cases, from your employer. A slideshow of photographs and real tweets illustrates the list of what not to do.

- Tweeting about your personal life issues is not advisable. That's what a diary is for.
- Listing exact locations and photos of children and their names is too inviting for criminals and child molesters.

Remember, a misguided tweet you make could cost you your job and compromise your safety.

Twitter Resource 5-38: Obama Loses 36,000+ Twitter Followers in #Compromise Campaign [STATS]

http://mashable.com/2011/07/29/obama-compromise-campaign-stats/

Here's another Mashable.com contribution on the use of social media measurement and how messaging is interpreted.

For those that don't follow politics all that closely, the word *compromise* is kind of a dirty word to many who do. We tend to be drawn into political action because of our ideals. And, despite the fact that most of us understand that democratic processes require some level of compromise, we often want our leaders to hold on to their principles, or ours, and put up a good fight before compromising them. One way of looking at the drop off of Obama Twitter followers is many of those who signed on to be social media followers are sick and tired of seeing their leader compromising.

Extra Point

Resource 5:39: How Twitter Could Unleash World Peace

http://www.businessweek.com/technology/content/apr2011/tc20110411_512316.htm

This Bobbie Johnson piece we have linked to its Bloomberg *Businessweek* reprint is worth thinking about. More detailed and, in some senses perhaps, more interesting is the source document from which the Johnson summary is taken. http://www.cl.cam.ac.uk/~jac22/out/twitter-diverse.pdf

This article, written by four scholars for presentation at a conference associated with the American Association for the Advancement of Artificial Intelligence www.aaai.org, analyzed "links and tweets of 80 popular media sources and their 14 million audience members in late 2009."

Realizing that this academic article was written and submitted for publication long before the Twitter-assisted, if not inspired, uprisings in the Middle East in the spring of 2011, reminds you how important occasionally scanning the academic literature, however painful at times, can be.

For example, the authors of the source document that provided the basis of the Johnson post remind us that much of what is happening on Twitter is essentially old media. "Established media outlets retain the role of publishing (or presenting) the news and stories without much interaction with readers."

Twitter, on the other hand, activates audiences that mostly are political. "Just over half of all Twitter users studied showed a distinct interest in the media outlets and individuals they followed."

"Most of those lean to the left of the political spectrum, accounting for 61 percent of users who demonstrated some bias. Thirty-seven percent were doggedly biases. Just one percent of Twitter users who showed a political preference were right wing," according to Johnson's take on the data.

CHAPTER 6

Location, Location and Foursquare

An October 2010 Mashable.com post projected Foursquare would hit 4 million members that week, and that was less than two months after the August date when the fledgling location-based network hit the 3 million mark.

Mashable contributor Jennifer Van Grove (with an assist from Flickr photographer Mari Sheibley) attributes Foursquare's impressive growth "most notably" to "the release of version 2.0 for iPhone and Android, a Symbian release, and celebrity attention from the likes of Conan O"Brien and hip-hop artist Big Boi." She projected Foursquare additions of roughly 20,000 members per day—an annual rate of roughly 7 million. http://mashable.com/2010/10/18/foursquare-4-million-users

This kind of growth would have put the total number of users at nearly 10 million members by June, 2011. And, guess what? At this writing, the most recent *AdWeek* report on Foursquare usage places the number at roughly 10 million, right on track. http://www.adweek.com/news/technology/foursquare-says-10-million-members-have-embraced-check-132736.

Not all the news is happy talk for Foursquare, however, as Anthony Ha, in the *Adweek* cover announcing Foursquare's milestone, asked the question: "But how many will stick around?"

"But Foursquare's news doesn't really address the biggest criticism heard about the service, that most people will quickly tire of checkins that serve very little purpose," Ha says.

"As any Foursquare fan can attest, first-time users frequently ask, 'Okay, I've checked in. Now what?' And they know as many people who have signed up for and then abandoned Foursquare as they do people who've stuck with it. The real question, then, isn't how many people have signed up for Foursquare, but how many are still active in a given month. And a Foursquare spokesperson declined to provide that number."

That's not such an optimistic report for a network that saw nearly a tenfold increase in nearly a year. Nor is it an optimistic report for a network that was being talked about at its introduction as possibly the next Twitter.

As Jennifer Van Grove said in the summer of 2009, upon Foursquare's introduction a couple of months earlier, "We instantly saw the potential of a location-based service based on your Twitter network with an added layer of social gameplay."

"Now," Van Grove said, "we're starting to see the app get adopted by more and more of our friends, finding traction in San Francisco, New York, Los Angeles, Atlanta, Chicago, San Diego, and several other hyper-local metro hubs."

Van Grove reminds us that Foursquare "is by no means the first location-based social network to help you connect with friends using GPS via your mobile device."

And in speaking to the demise of Brightkite, an earlier location-based social network, Van Grove's comment sounds eerily prophetic: "In fact, it may have taught us all one big bright lesson—that even though the technology and the idea are fantastic, we don't really want to know where other people are in the world unless they are our friends, or we're at an event. Strangers meeting up with strangers is just strange." http://www.facebook.com/note.php?note_id=136144759732158

Understanding Foursquare

Location-Based Resource 6-1: Foursquare

http://www.crunchbase.com/company/foursqualt

If you want to understand location-based social networking, start with Foursquare. This crunchbase.com resource takes you through a basic explanation and a neat chronology of the talent Foursquare has added in the past year and a half or so.

Watch a Gillmor Gang YouTube post of an interview with leader Foursquare co-founder Denis Crowly. It appears as the second in the video stack. In it, Crowly talks about the history of his new network and tries to explain its problems and potential.

Learn more about Foursquare from the source. https://foursquare.com/

Location-Based Resource 6-2: What is Foursquare?
An Introductory Guide

http://publicrelationsblogger.com/2010/03/what-is-foursquare-introductory-guide.html

If you haven't jumped on the Foursquare bandwagon yet and if you can accept the possibility that you don't really use it because of a lack of understanding, today is your lucky day.

"With foursquare, your friends can follow your entire day on their phones, knowing your every move," according to this Public Relations Blogger.com blog post.

Follow these simple instructions, and you can do everything from creating an account to making Foursquare an instrumental aspect of your online brand identity. Anyone can learn how to upload photos of different locations, receive discounts, and benefits from checking in, how to get badges, points, and friends.

This post also discusses the benefits of using Foursquare to help develop a business: "For a company looking to increase their presence in the real world and the online world, monitor whether or not people are checking in at your location."

Location-Based Resource 6-3: A World in Which You Can Be Mayor

http://online.wsj.com/article/SB10001424052748704462704575590260880867750.html

So, maybe you can't be king, but you can be the mayor . . . of your office, the local coffee shop, or gas station.

"Many Foursquare players are dedicated and competitive. They use it to see where friends are hanging out and to avail themselves of special deals," Katherine Rosman explains.

Rosman's *Wall Street Journal* article describes why location-based services offering virtual rankings are popular and why you should take note, even if you don't become a pawn on their chessboard.

"Advertising executives are keeping an eye on Foursquare's potential as an avenue for targeted marketing," says Rosman.

The game-like geo-location services offer businesses new advertising opportunities.

Tips, Tactics and Foursquare Tricks of the Trade

Location-Based Resource 6-4: How to Unlock Your World with Foursquare

http://www.howcast.com/videos/386406-How-To-Unlock-Your-World-With-Foursquare

"Wish you were more aware of all the incredible things around you?" asks HowCast.com's Foursquare tutorial. HowCast.com staffer Dave Bourla created this user-friendly instructional video to show you how to "unlock your world and find happiness just around the corner." That's a big promise, and the language is somewhat hyperbolic, but. . . .

Check out this post. It's designed to show you how to use Foursquare without even reading—kind of like an amateur's perfect set of instructions. The only thing better is to plug it in and figure out how to play it later.

This step-by-step format is designed to remove the mystery of what Foursquare is and how to use it, but you'll still have to remember that practice makes perfect.

Location-Based Resource 6-5: 7 Quick Steps to Foursquare Marketing

http://realtimemarketer.com/7-quick-steps-to-foursquare-marketing/

Using Foursquare can be fun. People seem intrigued by the idea of letting your friends know where you are and being rewarded for multiple visits there. And this is where business applications to this new social networking begin to come into play.

Scott Bishop, Editor at RealTimeMarketer.com, RTM, and self-described marketing strategist, shows business owners reading this post how to exploit Foursquare's built-in marketing capabilities:

> Marketing using Foursquare is beneficial because although (it currently has) a small user base, they (members of the base) are loyal. It also takes up almost no time (to set up and use), so the ROI (return-on-investment) can be high. Anyone can take advantage of Foursquare.

This post plants idea seeds about how to get involved with Foursquare and recommends tips to users, who check into their business via Foursquare, or offer special promotions. For example, Bishop demonstrates how an event built around Foursquare can boost business and build customer relationships. "Because of the little time commitment, it is my opinion that the ROI is worth it."

Location-Based Resource 6-6: Social Media for Small Business

http://www.LinkedIn.com/news?actionBar=&articleID=574359181&ids=0PejkVe3sPdP-kIcjwNejkPd3sRb3kUd3oUe38TdiMQcj8Re3cQdPkIcPsOej0TczsR&aag=true&freq=weekly&trk=eml-tod-b-ttle-98

Oh. The world of social media! Here's a "CBS News" clip we got through LinkedIn about Foursquare. It's a CBS "Early Show" segment by correspondent Rebecca Jarvis, who showed how a young entrepreneur used money he made on his day job, and a little help from Foursquare, to corner the market on lobster rolls—or at least to market his corner, anyway:

Word of mouth from your friends is stronger than any other form of advertising, Luke says.

CBS's Rebecca to Luke: Do you think it's possible to do business as an entrepreneur without using these social tools?

Luke: I think it's possible, but I don't think it's smart.

Extra Point—Evaluation and Security

Location-Based Resource 6-7: How to Control Your Privacy with Foursquare and other Geolocation Services

https://foursquare.com/privacy/grid

Checking into places is a good way to network with people who are in the same area you are at the same time. It is also a good way to let everyone know where you are and when, and, theoretically at least, to come home and find someone has hauled off your plasma and laptop.

Privacy controls are important (ya think?), and Foursquare Labs US has put together a readable informational grid that organizes privacy and sharing options into, what they describe, as an easy to read and understand format. They do admit it's "detailed," however, and to some of us the word detailed seems perilously, semantically close to "complicated." You judge.

"We've put together this detailed table of information sharing on Foursquare for user accounts to show our default privacy settings and how they can be adjusted," according to the Foursquare.com's privacy grid web page.

Our Foursquare-user friends say this is as good a resource they know of to help you understand how to manipulate your Foursquare privacy settings to avoid unwanted recognition or attention. The grid displays different privacy and sharing options and how to adjust them according to what you want displayed to friends and to the public.

Location-Based Resource 6-8:
Who Won the 2010 World Series of Foursquare?

http://adage.com/adagestat/post?article_id=146851

You have to hand it to *Ad Age* for their ability to develop a timely marketing news story tied to an even larger event. The scene was the 2010 Major League Baseball World Series, and the news story was the idea of one of their readers. Develop an index that would fairly assess the penetration of Foursquare "check-ins" by persons attending the game.

The results were interesting. You'll have to read the cleverly written Matt Carmichael post to find out if the Giant fans were as successful in the stands as their team was on the field.

Perfect Practice Makes Perfect

Five tasks that will help you understand the concepts and ideas talked about in Part III.

Exercise 1: Practice, practice, practice. Add photos and videos to your Facebook profile. Tag some friends. Write a note and share it. Update your status daily and tell us something interesting. Now that you have a Facebook profile you need to use it. So find some interesting things from your life and share with your friends. You may just like it. Make lists. Turn your Facebook friends into lists so you can follow them, and communicate to them based on the topic. Share vacation photos with all your family members. Share some business advice with your business contacts. To make lists simply click on the Friends tab on the left side of your page, then click Manage Friends. You can then add your friends to specific lists you create.

Exercise 2: Pull in your other social media. By integrating your blog into your Facebook through RSS (real simple syndication) you can update your page with interesting content with little effort on your part. Apps like Twitterfeed or HootSuite allow you to pull in posts, and share across multiple platforms like Facebook and Twitter.

Exercise 3: LinkedIn—Join groups! Groups are one of the best ways to meet people who can help advance your career, and who you can help too. Search groups and find 10 that will impact your business and your career. Once you join them, you can post resources, respond to conversations, and connect with members. This will be a big boost to your LinkedIn experience and help you get more qualified connections.

Exercise 4: Twitter—Now that your Twitter account is setup, join a Twitter management site such as Hootsuite or CoTweet. These will allow you to setup Twitter lists and follow people based on industry or interests. You can also update multiple social media profiles from one place—a real time saver. We suggest you download the mobile version of any site you use, to make for each Twitter posting on the go.

Exercise 5: Location Based Services—Now that you have Foursquare on your phone, it's time to make it even more fun. First, add friends to your network, so you can see where they check in as well. Then, go after some badges! Here is a list of Foursquare badges:

http://thekruser.com/foursquare/badges/

You will find that checking in can be very addicting. And if you play the game, you will be ready when the marketing opportunity comes up. Have fun on the way!

Part IV

GOOGLE

CHAPTER 7

Google: Searching Out the Changes in Our World

You cannot even imagine the volume of hoots and howls that the opening line of the official Google overview page generated only a few years ago. http://www.google.com/about/corporate/company/

> Google's mission is to organize the world's information and make it universally accessible and usable.

Laugh if you will, but it's hard to argue that Google hasn't already, in the 15 short years of its existence, largely reached this goal. A great deal of the world's information has been organized, and it has been put within the reach of anyone with a hook-up to the Internet, thanks to Google. It's hard to imagine a world without Google. In fact, we think it's safe to say that if Google didn't exist, someone would have to invent it.

Take a few minutes and run through the abbreviated history of Google. http://www.google.com/about/corporate/company/history.html It begins in 1995 as 22 year-old East Lansing native with an Ann Arbor degree, Larry Page, visited Stanford to check it out as a potential place to attend graduate school. Upon his arrival, he was met by 21 year-old Moscovite-student Sergey Brin, who was assigned to show Larry around the Stanford campus. By the next year, Larry and Sergey were running a search engine they called Back-Rub, which evolved into Google.

They picked the name for their invention, Google, as "a play on the word 'googol,' a mathematical term for the number represented by the numeral 1 followed by 100 zeros. The use of the term reflects their mission to organize a seemingly infinite amount of information on the web."

The official Google history includes gag entries for nearly each of the past 10 April Fool's Days. My personal favorite: April 1st 2000 when Google announced MentalPlex: "Google's ability to read your mind as you visualize the search results you want." The question we have today is this: How far from reality can MentalPlex be today?

To ease your exploration of the resources identified in this book, please go to the Link Listing—www.NewMediaDriversLicenseResources.com

As we said, one great way to begin to get a sense of the immensity of Google—what it is, what it does, and how totally unprecedented in so many ways the emergence of Google has been—is to click through the history. It contains hundreds of links, which in some way chronicles more than just historical facts about Google. For example, the February 2010 historical overview contains a link to the first-ever Google Superbowl ad: "An American finds love in Paris." http://www.youtube.com/watch?v=nnsSU qgkDwU

If you are interested in getting a summary overview of Google from the business pages of one of the world's great newspapers, *The New York Times*, check out our first resource.

"It has built a powerful network of data centers around the globe in hopes of, among other things, connecting users instantly with high-resolution satellite pictures of every corner of the earth and sky; making the entire text of books, in and out of print, available online; and becoming the leading distributor of online video through YouTube, which it acquired in 2006.

Understanding Google

Google Resource 7-1: Google Inc. News

http://topics.nytimes.com/top/news/business/companies/google_inc/index.html?scp=1 -spot&sq=google&st=Search -

There's a reason why we refer to this collection of resources as a "sampler." Imagine, for a moment, how overwhelming the task would be to attempt to detail each and every Google tool, for example. These tools, most all of which are available at some level at no cost, are being developed every day.

We looked at one rather comprehensive list of Google tools and did a rough count of those tools that, to the best of our knowledge, are in current use. We counted nearly 200. And we certainly do not want to characterize this effort as comprehensive in any way.

Google Resource 7-2: 10 Fun Facts You Didn't Know about Google

http://mashable.com/2010/06/19/10-google-facts/

"Google is not a conventional company. We do not intend to become one." So began the "letter from the founders" penned by Sergey Brin and Larry Page in the company's securities registration form in 2004. Despite ever-increasing commercial success since that date, Brin and Page have kept to their word.

Here's Amy-Mae's sample number one.

1. The First Google Doodle

Google's famous homepage Doodles (the changing Google logo graphics) are well known and enjoyed by millions around the world as a way to mark an event or anniversary. But did you know that the very first Google Doodle was designed as a kind of "out of office" message?

In 1998 Brin and Page took the weekend off to go the Burning Man festival in Nevada. The Burning Man doodle (shown above), was designed by the Google guys and added to the home page to let their users know they were out of office and couldn't fix technical issues, such as a server crash.

Here's another personal favorite that emphasizes Google's tremendous sense of humor from its earliest state.

4. Google's First Ever Tweet

Google's first ever Twitter post was as satisfyingly geeky as you could hope for. The message, sent in February 2009, reads "I'm 01100110 01100101 01100101 01101100 01101001 01101110 01100111 00100000 01101100 01110101 01100011 01101011 01111001 00001010."

For anyone not fluent in binary, here's a hint: It's a well-known phrase from the company's homepage. Got it? Yep, it reads: "I'm feeling lucky."

Which got us thinking . . .

Google Resource 7-3: What Does the "I'm feeling lucky" Button mean anyway?

http://google.about.com/od/searchingtheweb/qt/imfeelingluckyq.htm

For the answer to this question, we went to About.com, one of the greatest sources of information in the big "I." This time it's Marziah Karch who comes to the rescue with this answer:

> The button may have been named as a play on the Clint Eastwood line in the movie "Dirty Harry":
> "Do you feel lucky, punk? Well, do you?"

Ordinarily when you type in a key phrase in a Google search, you press the **search** button, (you can also just press return or enter on your keyboard), and Google returns a results page that shows multiple Websites matching your search phrase. The I'm Feeling Lucky button skips the search results page and goes directly to the first ranked page for that search phrase."

There are a lot of different aphorisms regarding luck, and Google, through its corporate genius, and perhaps the good humor of its founders, provides a great demonstration for one of our favorites. The harder I work, the luckier I seem to get. We think the next resource shows you how to "get luckier."

Google Uses

Google Resource 7-4: Unknown and Unusual Uses of Google: Use Google for Other than Searching

http://dotgiri.com/2010/07/03/unknown-and-unusual-uses-of-google-use-google-for-other-than-searching/

The first time we read this post from Giridhar on the Internet "Information Yard," DotGirl.com, we tried to make way more out of it than the posting required. But there's nothing more to it than just "Googling." We use Google all the time, for example, for spell checking. Just type in the word "glossary" and you will be asked if you mean ". . .". It's as simple as that.

Want to find out what time it is in London? Google: London Time. What about current weather in Moscow, Russia? Google: Moscow weather. But wait, you're going to Moscow, Idaho? Google: weather Moscow Idaho (which today, by the way, is ten degrees F colder than Moscow, Russia).

How about converting US to Canadian dollars? Google: USD to Canadian.

Google Resource 7-5: Shortcuts in Google Search

http://www.googlearticles.com/google-search/shortcuts-in-google-search/

This article gives tips on how to make searching on Google more effective and efficient. For example, use quotation marks around the phrase if you are searching only for results with the exact phrase.

Or, on a slightly more exotic basis, if you want to search for keywords (phrase) like "child abuse prevention" only in a website's URL, Google the following: url:ChildAbusePrevention. We did and were somewhat over-whelmed at the number of organizations that seem to be organized specifi-cally around this great cause. We found this very useful as we were in the process of beginning a new blog designed to engage members of the millen-nial generation in the cause of fighting child abuse. What better way to find kindred websites, all of which have a tremendous amount of material on the subject?

In reporting on this resource regarding how to find and use shortcuts in Google searches, we reacquainted ourselves with an interesting general resource, Googlearticles.com.

Google Resource 7-6: More Search Help: Google Search Basics: Web Search Help

http://www.google.com/support/websearch/bin/answer.py?answer=136861

These search tips are right from the horse's mouth . . . from Google itself.

> The Basic Search Help article covers all the most common issues, but some-times you need a little bit more power. This document will highlight the more advanced features of Google Web Search.
>
> Have in mind though that even very advanced searchers, such as the members of the search group at Google, use these features less than 5% of the time. Basic simple search is often enough.

That having been said, I found advice in this resource to be very valuable. For example, take a look at the use of the asterisk (*):

> Fill in the blanks (*)
> The *, or wildcard, is a little-known feature that can be very powerful. If you include * within a query, it tells Google to try to treat the asterisk as a placeholder for any unknown term(s) and then find the best matches. For example, the search [Google *] will give you results about many of Google's products. The query [Obama voted * on the * bill] will give you stories about different votes on different bills. Note that the * operator works only on whole words, not on parts of words.

Google Resource 7-7: Google Now Lets You
Preview Search Results Before You Click Them
http://mashable.com/2010/11/09/google-instant-previews/

Ben Parr, writing in Mashable.com, told us in November 2010, about Google's new instant search feature that most of us didn't notice when it first appeared, and many of us take for granted today.

> Google Instant Previews . . . gives users the ability to see a website before they visit it. Google accomplishes this by taking a screenshot of every webpage in its index and giving users access to it via a magnifying glass icon that sits to the right of every search result.

That's one thing you may not have known about Google. Here are a few more, also brought to you through the generosity of Mashable.com and the good research and clever writing, this time, of Amy-Mae Elliot.

Google Resource 7-8: Google News Badges: Yawn, What's Next
http://www.zdnet.com/blog/gamification/google-news-badges-yawn-whats-next/561

Libe Goad, writing in ZdNet.com, either wasn't a Girl Scout or was and didn't like it. The New York-based Texan, an excellent video game journalist, wasn't knocked out by Google's announcement that it was climbing on the "gamification bandwagon, adding badges to its Google News service.

Here's how it works. Do you want to earn a Harry Potter badge? Spend about a week reading certain types of Harry Potter-related articles, and you'll earn a badge. Then, as Goad says, you'll "start the ramp-up process."

Google Resource 7-9: Google Gives Blogger a Dynamic New Look
http://mashable.com/2011/03/31/blogger-views/

In yet another Mashable post, by Ben Parr, we learn that Google isn't satisfied just improving the way blog posts appeal on Blogger, they want to "change the typical way people consume content on the web."

Blogger product manager Aril Sabharawal told Mashable these changes are much more than cosmetic, the changes are "really revolutionizing the blog consumption experience."

"To that end," Parr says, "Google has launched five views that harness the power of new web standards."

Google Tools and Apps

Google Resource 7-10: Google Scholar Changing Academic and Other Research

http://scholar.google.com/

Google's scholarly literature search engine has changed the way many academics and other researchers do their work. Again, we turn to Google for a brief explanation:

> Google Scholar provides a simple way to broadly search for scholarly literature. From one place, you can search across many disciplines and sources: articles, theses, books, abstracts and court opinions, from academic publishers, professional societies, online repositories, universities and other web sites. Google Scholar helps you find relevant work across the world of scholarly research.

Go to the Google Scholar home page and you can find everything from a help site to advanced search tips. Libraries and publishers also can get the scoop on how Google attempts to support them. We're particularly grateful for this Google acknowledgement:

> We recognize the debt we owe to scholars everywhere whose work has made Google itself a reality and we hope to make Google Scholar as useful to this community as possible.

Google Resource 7-11: Go to Google School and Learn How to Make the Most of These Great Google Tools

http://edutraining.googleapps.com/

This site is officially called the "Google Apps Education Training Center." If anyone would have told you 10 years ago that a profitable company, by some measures, among the world's biggest companies, was going to offer you free computer applications and then provide content modules to train you, again for free, you would have said they are absolutely nuts. But that's the truth.

For example, if you have ever felt like you are not getting the most out of your Gmail account, take a run at "Becoming A Gmail Ninja." The training starts with a one-hour video of a webinar run by Christopher Craft, a sixth-grade teacher. If you can't learn from him, you might consider yourself unteachable.

If you go to Craft's video, you'll see a link to a catalog of 381 videos, most of which are considerably shorter than this video.

Google Resource 7-12: 57 Useful Google Tools (for) Scholars, Students, and Hobbyists

http://www.collegeathome.com/blog/2008/06/18/57-useful-google-tools-youve-never-heard-of/

Again, we relied on a wide variety of resources in coming up with this resource sampler. This link will take you to a list of a great many useful Google tools and apps, some of which most people have never heard.

We got this list from College@Home. A great deal has happened since the post first went up in 2008, but this is still a great resource. By the way, if you're interested in off-campus learning, you might consider doing what they suggest by checking out their reviews of the 100 or so online schools and correspondence college programs.

About their post, they say this: "If you're like most people, you use Google's products several times a day to search for information or check email," they say:

> Most people don't know, however, how many useful tools Google has to make research and time management much easier. Here are just a few of the products Google offers that may be worth trying whether you're a scholar, student, or hobbyist.

Categories include "must haves," maps and travel, web browsing and developing, social networking and communication, custom search tools, third party tools and miscellaneous.

Like we said earlier, we counted nearly 200 Google tools and apps that are in current use. But you can get started becoming more Google proficient by focusing on College@Home's list of 57.

Google Resource 7-13: The Best Google Tools You Never Use

http://www.chinadaily.com.cn/life/2009-02/02/content_7438726.htm

If you ever had any questions about the international nature of the Internet, let alone Google, check out this post from *China Daily*:

> Google's headline applications—search, Chrome, and Gmail—get all the attention. But behind the scenes, the company has released an impressive array of applications that most people have never heard of—or used. As you might expect, they're all designed to make it easier for people to use today's Internet more efficiently—and they're all free.

At least those covered in this article are free.

China Daily highlights Google Docs (Google: Google Docs), Google's Blogger tool (Google: Blogger), and Picasa http://picasa.google.com/mac/

"You can spend a lot of money on software to organize and manipulate your digital photographs. Or you can use the free Picasa," says *China Daily*, which also promotes Google's Notebook, which we are sorry to say has been closed off to new users since 2009, and Alerts, http://www.google.com/alerts which "draws upon Google's main search engine to notify you when new entries for a particular news item, blog, Web page update, or video appears."

Google Resource 7-14: Google Products with "Notebook-like" Functionality

http://googlenotebookblog.blogspot.com/2009/01/stopping-development-on-google-notebook.html

This is the official 2009 announcement by Google that it was stopping development on Google notebook. Here's Google's position on this issue:

> If you haven't used Notebook in the past, we invite you to explore the other Google products that offer Notebook-like functionality. Here are a few examples, all of which are being actively improved and should meet your needs:
>
> - **SearchWiki**—We recently launched a feature on Search that will let you re-rank, comment, and personalize your search results. This is useful when you've found some results on Google Search that were really perfect for your query. You can read about how to use Search-Wiki here: http://googleblog.blogspot.com/2008/11/searchwiki-make-search-your-own.html
> - **Google Docs**—If you're trying to jot down some quick notes, or create a document that you can share with others, check out Google Docs. https://docs.google.com/?pli=1#home
> - **Tasks in Gmail**—For a lightweight way to generate a to do list or keep track of things, we recently launched http://gmailblog.blogspot.com/2008/12/new-in-labs-tasks.html
> - **Google Bookmarks**—For a tool that can help you remember web pages that you liked and access them easily, take a look at Google Bookmarks. https://www.google.com/bookmarks/l You can even add labels to your bookmarks to better organize and revisit them.

Not all the blog reaction was negative, but some of the reaction and conversation provides interesting non-Google alternatives for Notebook functions. Here's a brief sample:

> January 14, 2009 7:45 PM
>   Bah said: I take SnagIt http://www.techsmith.com/snagit/default.asp screenshots of important information, or copy and paste the text itself into a Gmail and send it to myself with key words so that I can search well. I was never able to use Notebook successfully, unfortunately.

> January 14, 2009 7:54 PM
>   Chris said: Very sad to see Google Notebook discontinued. It was something I used regularly. Now I'll have to use Zoho instead. Here's how to do just that: http://www.zoho.com/?gclid=CliQyJm0uKkCFcPrKgodXEq8AA

Google Resource 7-15: Top 15 Google Apps for Businesses

http://www.stumbleupon.com/su/1DBUEC/www.informationweek.com/news/gal-leries/smb/hardware_software/showArticle.jhtml%253FarticleID%253D226700188%2526cid%253Dsmb_ROS%2526wc%253D4 -

Here, Jake Widman, writing in *Information Week SMB—Technology for Small and Midsize Business*—describes the Google Apps marketplace as a "gold mine for businesses offering dozens, if not hundreds, of generally inexpensive, cloud-based software solutions for everything from project planning to invoicing." Here is Jake's list of 15 of the best.

First on the list is SlideRocket, which "lets you import presentations from Google or Microsoft PowerPoint or create them right within the program, and then access them from any PC, Mac, or Linux computers. You can add audio and share presentations with your Google Contacts. It also includes analytics for measuring audience engagement." And as Jake points out, the price is right for this app—it's free.

Google Resource 7-16: Ten Most Effective
Free Google Marketing Tools

http://www.buzzle.com/articles/effective-free-google-marketing-tools.html

Here's a list of 10 marketing tools that appeared on Buzzle.com thanks to the work of Titus Hoskins, who describes himself as a full-time online marketer who runs numerous web sites, including two sites on Internet marketing:

> Google has many effective free Internet marketing tools which every web master and marketer should be using to make their website or online business run more efficiently. These marketing tools will make any website or business run more efficiently.

We'll talk about some of these apps later, but here's Buzzle.com's top 10.

1. **Google Analytics,** which Buzzle describes as "perhaps the premier marketing tool offered by Google. Google Analytics is extremely valuable in analyzing your marketing funnel. It tracks all the steps leading up to your sales or checkout page, which is vital information for raising your conversion rate and ROI."

2. **Google Sitemaps,** which "webmasters can use . . . to almost instantly place newly created pages on their site into the Google Search index."

3. **Google Alerts** that allow you to be notified "when someone or another site lists your site or mentions your name."

4. **Google Froogle** "is Google's price directory! It simply lists all the cheapest prices for products on the web.

5. **Google Checkout**—"Not exactly free, but for those marketers who use AdWords, for every $1 spent on AdWords, you can process $10 for free."

6. **Google eBlogger**—"Creating a blog (online journal) on the topic of your web site or product will bring in extra traffic and target customers."

7. **Google Toolbar (Enterprise Version)**, the new business version of Toolbar that "integrates countless features with all you employee's or corporate network."

8. **Google Groups** for building contact lists.

9. **Google Adsense** is a "simple way to monetize your web content . . . Just place the Adsense code on your site and receive a check from Google each month."

10. **Google Writely**—"a full-featured online writing editor with spellcheck and great collaborating features."

Google Resource 7-17: Google Reader
http://www.google.com/reader/view/#overview-page

This is the free Google tool that puts content into an RSS feed and makes news easy for users to read and, more importantly, much easier to keep up with. Here's the gist of it:

Google Reader constantly checks your favorite news sites and blogs for new content.
Google Reader shows you all of your favorite sites in one convenient place.

We mentioned Brian Solis is one of the bloggers we read. Google Reader keeps us from having to leave our site and go directly to his to see what he's interested in these days. Google Reader creates our own personal newsletter, and Brian Solis is one of our personal columnists.

Google Resource 7-18: Google Alerts
http://www.google.com/alerts

Google Alerts are email updates of the latest relevant Google results based on choices you make. Here's how Google explains it:

Enter the topic you wish to monitor, then click preview to see the type of results you'll receive. Some handy uses of Google Alerts include:

- Monitoring a developing news story
- Keeping current on a competitor or industry
- Getting the latest on a celebrity or event
- Keeping tabs on your favorite sports teams.

Google Resource 7-19: Google Advertising Tools

http://www.ehow.com/list_6620255_google-advertising-tools.html

Here is a particularly good list of Google advertising tools put together by Rose Broyles, contributor to eHow.com. The list includes some advice on how to use the tools.

Each of the five primary advertising tools—Adsense, Adwords, Analytics, Feedburner, and Product Search—are explained in simple terms with links going to the official Google site.

The thing we like most about Broyles's work is that she also has related, and sometimes somewhat contrary, resources to which you are admonished to visit before you get too smitten with the Google solution. For example, while eHow does make its position clear the "Google Adsense is the most powerful Internet marketing tool . . . " it also describes Adsense competitors like AdBrite, Bidviser, Chitika, Clicksor, and Kontera.

Google Resource 7-20: 30 Essential Google Developer Tools

http://www.techradar.com/news/internet/30-essential-google-developer-tools-712506

This is a resource we debated including in this resource guide. Some might say that Karl Hodge, who wrote the post for TechRadar.com went a bit too deep for a novice new media driver, but then again Rick had a friend in high school who was racing dragsters by his 17th birthday, and he didn't learn this skill practicing parallel parking in the church parking lot.

Google tools for design, speed, coding, and teamwork are always a bit more complicated than they may look at first blush. The advent of Chrome, which we'll get to soon http://www.google.com/chrome/intl/en/make/download-mac.html?brand=CHKZ is certainly proving that one of their slogans—"The web is what you make of it"—is absolutely true.

As Hodge says "Google has an excellent repository of tools to help web developers get the most from their sites." You'd have to have just fallen off a load of pumpkins not to know that.

We'd say that Google has such an excellent repository of tools that, with a little patience and a sincere effort to experiment, even a relative novice can dress their website up so that it almost looks like it's been worked on by a real web developer

Google Resource 7-21: 10 Features of Google Chrome

http://www.youtube.com/watch?v=Xlh8gSF_hhE

Since we are on the subject of Google Chrome, here's a little video that provides you with some quick tips on how to exploit this wonderful Google Chrome feature. We love this tutorial. It's less than four minutes long and does exactly what it promises: It tells you about 10 features of Google Chrome.

Google Resource 7-22: Google Analytics Tutorial 1: Setup

http://www.youtube.com/watch?v=MYLyrOZSPGg -

Don't be fooled. Setting up Google Analytics might not be quite as simple as Mark Widawer seems to say it is. But it is pretty simple. Go to the YouTube link above, you'll find a number of different tutorials that should make it pretty easy for you to get started. But why should you care?

Google Resource 7-23: Why Is Google Analytics Important for Bloggers?

http://www.wpbeginner.com/beginners-guide/how-to-install-google-analytics-in-wordpress/

We turn to WordPress.com beginner's guide to help get us to the answer of why we should care enough to install Google Analytics.

As WordPress.com says, "The best way to know your audience is through your traffic stats and this is what Google Analytics provides for FREE."

You need to read the entire post to get a deeper meaning of what good, day-to-day analysis can do for you. Among the questions Google Analytics will answer for you is:

- Who visits your site?
- What do they do when they visit your site?
- When did they visit your website?
- Where were they immediately before arriving at your website?
- How did they interact with the content on your website?

Look, we know some of this may seem daunting at first. How about doing a little experiment?

You have a Facebook page. (We have ways of knowing these things.) Why don't you take a few minutes right now and add Google Analytics to your Facebook Fan page?

How do you do that? We thought you'd never ask. And thanks to Miriam John's article at SocialMediaExaminer.com, we're going to tell you.

Google Resource 7-24: How To Add Google Analytics to Your Facebook Fan Page

http://www.socialmediaexaminer.com/how-to-add-google-analytics-to-your-face-book-fan-page/?doing_wp_cron -

Miriam John advises:

Facebook Insights shows some demographic information on your page, but is limited to information about interactions with your fans. The free Google Analytics tool offers more sophisticated and comprehensive data. Adding

Google Analytics to your fan page can be done easily but requires some special steps.

One of the limitations of Facebook fan pages is they can only run limited JavaScript. Google Analytics needs JavaScript code included on a page to correctly track visitors in the traditional way. And running JavaScript won't work on your fan page . . . .

However, there is a new solution. Using free and open source FBGAT (Facebook Google Analytics Tracker), you can get Google Analytics working on your Facebook fan page. Now you can track visitor statistics, traffic sources, visitor countries, and keyword searches with all the other powerful reporting of Google Analytics.

Miriam takes you through the entire process, step-by-step including doing what, just a few months ago, would have been impossible: working around Facebook JavaScript's limitation by using FBGAT, the free tool that will generate the custom image code that you will need to keep tabs on all the visitors to your fan page.

Get tracking, now.

Google for Business

Google Resource 7-25: The Cheapest Way to Get to the Top of Google

http://blog.brightnewmedia.co.uk/seo/the-cheapest-way-to-get-to-the-top-of-google/ -

In this blog post, the team at Bright New Media offers their complimentary advice on getting found:

The first thing to do is to make sure your website has been prepped correctly, this should be a fairly straightforward task that you could do yourself if that way inclined. Make sure that keywords (search terms) appear in your page titles, in correctly tagged headers, and are emphasized in the content of your web pages. (Go to their website and you can find a neat article on 'How to Code a Good Link,' for example.)

Next you need to publish new content regularly. The easiest way to do this is with a blog. We can install and integrate (match the look and feel of your website) a WordPress blog for around £300.

[We Googled through the conversion to $487.80 USD on the day we were writing this section of the book. It's a modest outlay that's proven to work—we're testament to that—the more content you produce the more important your website becomes.]

Finally you have to drive traffic to your website and build incoming links, this is a measure of a website's popularity and relevance. It's an ongoing process that you can do yourself, so no worries there; List the website in directories, exchange links with related websites, make good use of social media sites and run on and offline promotions.

Okay. We get it, but how will we know it's working? We thought you'd never ask. For this, you have to begin by hitting the pause button on your iTunes.

Google Resource 7-26: Google Industry—Media/Publishing

http://www.google.com/submityourcontent/media.html#utm_source=CPFE&utm_medium=House%2BAds&utm_campaign=Media%2BPublishing -

This link is one of the most fascinating resources we have come across. It's essentially an inventory for media companies and publishing houses showing them how a variety of free Google services "can get your content in front of people. . . ."

Thirteen different categories of media—from websites, books and business information to events, gadgets and images, news, product listings, scholarship, videos, and blogs—Google lays out in clear detail how content is submitted and shared and how they are, in fact, much more than the media company *The New York Times*, and us, thought it was.

Google Resource 7-27: How to Get the Most out of Google Adwords

http://mashable.com/2011/03/27/google-adwords-tips/

Consider this an appetizer to the sample platter we have coming up on Google Adwords. But even though we are going to devote considerably more on that subject to this book, it's quite important that you read this article now, if only to whet your appetite for what's coming a few chapters from now.

Matt Silverman's article does not answer every question, but as the string of comments that follow Silverman's post indicates, he's done a nice job of laying out some Adwords pros and some cons.

The article gives some small business success stories that begin, as did the business, with Google ads. One of his sources, for example was "an engineering company that specializes in LED lighting and testing. Its customers are technically trained engineers," but consumers looking for Christmas lights were going to the ads, and the company was wasting money on useless impressions.

Quoting Timothy Thomas, a small business consultant whose specialty is developing Adword campaigns, Silverman's article goes on.

"The solution was eliminating 'broad matching' criteria," says Thomas. "We put our keywords into either Phrase Match or Exact Match. Each day we would look at what the company had paid for on the previous day and just started [adding] negative keywords. Words like 'Christmas,' 'automobile,' 'rope light,' 'Playstation,' and all the variants for 'television' were identified and blocked from matching."

Extra Point: Google+

Google Resource 7-28: The Evolving Mission of Google
http://www.nytimes.com/2011/03/21/business/media/21carr.html?src=busln-

Maybe you're starting to get the feeling that Google is a little bit more than you may have thought at the beginning of this section. You're in pretty good company. No heavier media source than *The New York Times* also just figured out that Google is much more than the media company they once thought it was.

Here's *Times* reporter David Carr's take on "The Evolving Mission of Google."

> What company derives 96 percent of its revenue from advertising, has a video platform that is currently negotiating with the National Basketball Association, a movie studio and various celebrities, and is developing a subscription service that would be plug-and-play for publishers and consumers the world over.
>
> Time Warner? News Corporation? Viacom?
>
> Nope. Google.
>
> Here's just one little tidbit to keep your interests in Google up, and perhaps to give you another insight into why this upstart company, which opened on the exchange in 2004 with a share price of $85, closed today at $502 and change.
>
> There have also been reports that Google has set aside $100 million for incentives for well-known celebrities to program their own 'channels' on YouTube to increase the amount of high-profile content on the platform.

What's new about this, you say? Google's connection to media companies, after all, reaches into some of the oldest and most traditional publishing houses. In fact, Cambridge University Press, the "world's oldest continuously operating printer and publisher uses Google Book Search to offer its extensive booklist to more scholars more efficiently, boosting sales."

Google Resource 7-29: I'm Having a Party. Here's $50. Bring Cool People—Or You Owe Me $100.
http://techcrunch.com/2011/04/09/google-party/

We call this kind of article "inside baseball." You really have to be in the dugout to either understand or appreciate much of what is being said, but if

Google: Searching Out the Changes in Our World   149

you want a little insight into how nervous Google is about Facebook's domination of "social," this is a great article to read.

MG Siegler, writing for TechCrunch.com lays out Google's springtime 2011 announcement that it is tying employee bonuses to the success of their social strategy. Siegler links you to a deeper read on the Google social strategy published in BusinessInsider.com, but you don't need to read that to get the gist of what Google is trying to do, or why Siegler seems relatively pessimistic about its likelihood of success.

Contrasting Google's strategy to rivals Facebook, Twitter and others, Siegler says this: ". . . Google has nearly 25,000 employees. It seems that will lead to an artificially and prematurely inflated re-creation of the launch environment described above. And that may only serve to create the type of paid-for party that I talked about at the beginning. It's a party that will attract a lot of people. But it's not one that anyone will likely remember—or want to go to again."

Since Siegler wrote this somewhat prescient piece, Google began talking about Google+ (Google Plus, if you will). Will Google+ be the app that changes the world of social media? We don't purport to know, but in any case, the well-orchestrated build up to Google+ appears has hit its next level. And Google may have Facebook in its sights.

For all the anticipation, however, it does seem some folks that Google+ is coming out of the blocks a bit more slowly than might be anticipated.

Google Resource 7-30: But what exactly is Google+?
A Wikipedia Entry
http://en.wikipedia.org/wiki/Google%2B

Google describes Google+ (sometimes spelled Google Plus) this way:

> Google+ integrates social services such as Google Profiles and Google Buzz, and introduces new services Circles, Hangouts, Sparks, and Huddles. Google+ will also be available as a desktop application and as a mobile application, but only on Android and iOS operating systems.
>
> Sources such as *The New York Times* have declared it Google's biggest attempt to rival the social network Facebook which had over 750 million users in 2011. On July 14, 2011, Google announced that Google+ had reached 10 million users just two weeks after it was launched in a 'limited' trial phase.

The social networking service cobbled together from several extant Google services is still officially in beta phase (testing), but this much we know from the official Google+ website:

You share different things with different people. So sharing the right stuff with the right peoples should be no hassle. Circles makes it easy to put your friends from Saturday night in one circle your parents in another and you boss in a circle by himself—just like real life." That's Google+ *Circles* product.

Hangouts, the unplanned meet-up comes to the web for the first time. Let specific buddies . . . know you're hanging out and then see who drops by for a face-to-face chat.

Taking photos is fun, sharing photos is fun, getting photos off your phone is pretty much the opposite. With *Instant Upload,* your photos and videos upload themselves automatically, to a private album. . . ."

Remember when your grandpa used to cut articles out of the paper and send them to you? That was nice. That's kind of what *Sparks* does: looks for videos and articles it thinks you'll like, so when you're free, there's always something to watch, read and share. Grandpa would approve. Tell Sparks what you're into and it will send you stuff it thinks you'll like . . .

Finally, "Texting is great, but not when you're trying to get six different people to decide on a movie. *Huddles* turns all those different conversations into one simple group chat, so everyone gets on the same page all at once."

Announced in late June, 2011, MG Siegler, posting for TechCrunch.com http://techcrunch.com/2011/06/28/google-plus/ said that the company had finally announced Google+ "the one (new product) Google has tried to downplay as much as humanly possible—even as we got leak after leak after leak of what they were working on. "Yes," Siegler said, "the one they weren't going to make a big deal about with pomp and circumstance. It's real. And it's here."

One reason Vic Gundotra and Bradley Horowitz, Google's Generals Patton and MacArthur, were so hush-hush about the project, Siegler speculates, is because what we have seen to date (with Google+) is just the tip of the iceberg.

"In their minds, Google+ is much more than a social product, or even a social strategy. It's an extension of Google itself. Hence, (the name) Google+," said Siegler.

It didn't take long for actor and pitchman, William Shatner, to get booted off Google+. Robin Wauters reported http://techcrunch.com/2011/07/18/illogical-william-shatner-gets-booted-from-google/ in TechCrunch.com that Shatner's account was "beamed up for 'violating standards,' according to a tweet posted earlier this morning. Shatner tweeted, 'My Google+ account was flagged for violating standards. Saying hello to everyone apparently is against the rules. Maybe I should say goodbye?'" Shatner said.

Denny Crain might say "Denny Crain doesn't want to be unceremoniously booted from Google +".

Google Plus, as we have said, is hot off the presses as we write. And as of this writing, it's way too early to estimate the true meaning of what this assembly of Google tools can do, and whether Google+ actually has the power to unseat Facebook in the world of social media. But the PR and marketing implications of this development are immense, as Shel Holz wrote in Ragan's PR Daily. http://www.prdaily.com/Main/Articles/8808.aspx

Whether or not Google+ gets traction as a competing social network, PR practitioners have a strong need to begin to "monitor (Google+) for brand references and other mentions."

And if you have any doubt about the potential of Google+ check out this chart, which you'll find all over the Internet. http://technorati.com/technology/article/the-incredible-run-of-google/

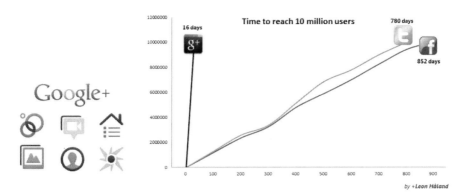

by +Leon Håland

Google Resource 7-31: Google+: The Complete Guide
http://mashable.com/2011/07/16/google-plus-guide/

This Mashable article bills itself as a definitive guide to the new social media platform called Google+. It walks one through how the system operates, provides a handy cheat sheet created by Simon Laustsen, and speculates on how Google+ might fit into the future of social media.

Google Resource 7-32: Google+: A Collaborative Document
https://docs.google.com/document/d/1cUjZ_7rlAmKRDVB6GXId73h_eUdXGKdjtSff0svbaz0/preview

The potential for Google+ to increase collaboration among formerly strangers, may be underscored in real life by a handy manual that 120 different users are helping to create. We doubt that they could have done this project without social media. The link above is the preview site for non-editors, because it frees the other site up for editors to be making real time changes. The guide is a working document, so it will be updated as Google unveils any new features. If you want to become a Google+ expert this is definitely your bible.

Google Resource 7-33: Google Plus Sparks Ideas for Causes
(Alan Stokes, New Media Coordinator for Prevent Child Abuse Michigan/Children's Trust Fund of Michigan).
http://alanstokes.blogspot.com/2011/07/google-plus-sparks-new-media-hope.html

Ray Kroc, the founder of McDonalds said, "The two most important requirements for major success are: first, being in the right place at the right time, and second, doing something about it." New media, especially the infant Google Plus, can help causes, like the one I am privileged to work for, raise awareness and rally support for diverse social issues by being visibly inspiring without tiring and creating a thriving social media environment with a variety of options to participate. Here's why I am sold on Google Plus for causes even though at the present time business accounts are under development. I thoroughly expect when they are released that the business accounts will be as good as personal accounts, if not better.

1. **Circles.** Being able to easily create and customize private names for *Circles*, place people in them, and then target messages to these specific groups are steps forward for personal and business imaging. Applicable messages can be sent to and received, for example, by clients/customers/supporters, legislative representatives, family, local community figures, or work colleagues. In addition, a message can be sent to a person's email address if they don't have a social account (we all have relatives that refuse to join social media, don't we?), assuring inclusivity.

2. **Spark.** The *Spark* feature that allows people to search for subjects reflecting their self-motivated interests and then easily share them with their *Circles* is seemingly the next generation of search. So when someone has an interest in my cause they can search for a spark on the information right through their Google Plus account.

3. **+1 and Google Search.** The +1 feature allows a public testimony for information as it goes viral and the groundbreaking feature is that +1's can be linked to a tab on one's Google Plus account and are visible by one's connections in the massive Google search system. After using Google Plus for several weeks, I was amazed at another feature. Anything shared by someone in one's circle is matched with Google Search results. So if someone in my circle Google searches for "child abuse" they will see my name under any website I have publically shared in Google Plus just like they can see my +1's. Wow!

4. **Hangouts.** Google Plus's *Hangout* feature provides free video conferencing for up to 10 people to collaborate and potentially do community organizing to help change the world. Ten really is a nice working number. I'm looking forward to the day when we can get partners and stakeholders into Hangouts focused on preventing child abuse and neglect.

Individuals and organizations have different types of relationships. Knowing they can separate people into *Circles* that represent those relationships means control over the content they share with them. Taking the open platform popularized by Twitter to the next level, this is encouraging the early adopters of Google Plus to meet new people with shared interests through social media that could birth relationships to change the world in unprecedented ways. Expect to hear more and more creative uses and positive results from Google Plus in the future as public officials, community leaders, businesses and nonprofit organizations start to use it to selectively and successfully communicate with the world through new media.

Alan Stokes. Children's Trust Fund of Michigan

Perfect Practice Makes Perfect

Five tasks that will help you understand the concepts and ideas talked about in Part IV

Exercise 1: Time to get a Gmail account. It all begins on Google with a Gmail account, and now is the time to get one. Sign up and work to get the best username you can. First Name. LastName@gmail.com is often a good choice. When you sign up you can import or invite all your contacts from your previous email. This is a good way to see who is there, and build your contact list on Gmail. Once you have an account you can chat with people, and access all that Google has to offer.

Exercise 2: Build your Google+ profile. The Google+ Project is a chance for you to have an enhanced online profile that is easily found on Google and can help you make connections in the digital world. Add keywords to your profile, add your location, add photos and videos, add links to your websites, and connect your Twitter account. Go through all the steps to build a profile that represents you and tells your audience what they need to know.

Exercise 3: Setup your Docs and Calendar. These are two of the most useful Google functions. With Docs you can write and share documents easily across the web and store them on your Google server for free. The calendar is a wonderful way to stay organized. You can import or integrate it with other calendars such as iCal or Microsoft Calendar. And you can follow other people's calendars and collaborate very easily. Set these up and you won't be sorry.

Exercise 4: Download Google Chrome. Why not use the browser from Google. Chrome will give you good insight into how Google works. It integrates easily with Google apps, and is a good browser choice. Chrome is built to load fast, and it's simple to use like Google. You can even get a Chrome Book—a laptop with a Chrome operating system, designed to give you easy web browsing using WiFi or a Verizon Wireless data plan. These new laptops are under $500 and with the Google cloud and web apps, it could be the only machine you need.

Exercise 5: Explore. Google is an ever changing company and offering that will keep you guessing and on your toes. Go to the Google Products page http://www.google.com/intl/en/about/products/ and see what you can find. With Google, you have to experiment to see what you really like and what will be useful in your personal life and professional career. With Google you can make free phone calls, chat with your friends, upload your entire photo albums, search online trends, build a new website, create groups for your friends, and much, much more. So learn Google and you will be on your way to greater Internet understanding.

Part V

ONLINE PUBLIC RELATIONS

CHAPTER 8

Online Public Relations: The *Dialog* We've Wanted

Before we go forward with this discussion of the *role of social media in Public Relations* and the *role of PR in social media*—two separate thoughts—we need to be aware that these issues involve both offense and defense.

The first point that needs to be made is to dispel the notion that PR practitioners are primarily engaged in dealing with "the media." PR practitioners (as opposed to publicists, one subset of PR) are involved with charting the course of the relationships between an organization and the broad list of individuals and groups that the organization needs in some way.

So, while we'll look at how PR practitioners use social media to implement relationship building and strengthening, it's wise to remember that social media are a long ways from being either the exclusive activity or within the exclusive domain of PR.

That having been said, PR practitioners are using social media in a variety of new ways everyday to take the offense in building relationships between their client organizations and key constituencies.

They use social media as the vehicles that carry the information that validates the authenticity of their client organization. They use social media to find new groups with which to "hook up" their client organization. These are only two examples of the many ways social media are being used to provide the *offense* for PR.

But we also need to think about social media in PR in terms of *defense*. Social media can also carry hand grenades that get lobbed into the central courtyard of our client's organization. The client will expect us to throw it back, or in the worst case, throw ourselves over the grenade protecting our client from the explosion. But most of all, PR clients will expect that the practitioner should have seen the grenade coming. That's the defense we are talking about.

PR practitioners are expected to be monitoring social media on a daily basis—looking for hand grenades. They are increasingly called upon to

---

To ease your exploration of the resources identified in this book, please go to the Link Listing—www.NewMediaDriversLicenseResources.com

demonstrate how they can use social media to help put out a fire. But often, by the time the fire spreads—especially across the Internet—it's too late. Social media are reminding clients, by daily example of Internet-spread crisis after crisis, of another important role. Besides serving as a listening post to warn of impending danger, PR personnel should be training clients to exercise caution in using social media.

In either case—offense or defense—it's hard to guess whether the social media have had a greater impact on the practice of public relations or that PR has, in fact, become the activity, more than any other that is shaping the social media.

We're not really sure what the answer to this question is. But we do believe it is important to understand several critical concepts and distinctions of PR before one proceeds on the rich trip through this section of this book.

The first distinction that needs to be made is, as we alluded earlier in this introduction, *the distinction between public relations and publicity.* There are, by the way dozens, if not hundreds, of definitions of PR. Some are quite complicated and others are quite simple. Rick has settled upon a definition that seems to work as well today as it did 25 years ago when he first used it:

> Public Relations is the art applied to the science of adjusting the behavior of a client organization to better conform to the values and aspirations of the audiences upon which the organization depends for survival.

That's a good start, but it turns out its only one part of the definition. This may be the most important part of the definition because it does no one any good to think you can change the way people look at an organization over the long haul without taking into account the way the organization behaves.

The word that is often used to describe PR is "spinning." The meaning is that through re-positioning, including the clever use of language, a PR pro can make a bad situation look good or at least not so bad. That's what we call trying to put ten pounds of crap into five-pound bags. Good PR really doesn't and can't work like that.

We have had the opportunity over the past few years of being in the same room with Richard Edelman and his brother John—the guys that run the international giant Edelman PR. Edelman has been stung a couple of times for engaging in practices on behalf of clients about which the firm was embarrassed later. But the Edelman firm stepped up, wrote about their mistake and spoke about it. I believe they learned some good lessons from those experiences.

In a recent interview in PRSA's *Tactics* magazine, Richard emphasized the need for PR to come to grips with the tarnished image of American business.

"We operate in a world without trust," Richard said. Talking about public perception of both the government and American business, he said: "There's no other word than dire. . . . People see everything as spin and lies."

So here's the lesson for the person trying to build the reputation of a business, or the PR person trying to help a client accomplish this. In the end, the truth is the truth. There is not other truth.

No matter what your client, or the marketing department, or the general public might think, PR should be far less concerned about getting publicity than it is about *helping your organization behave* in a manner worthy of positive attention—and doing your best to make sure the client doesn't misbehave. Some people define PR as "doing good and talking about it." We are OK with that. That's the right sequence.

Positive publicity is very important, but you must understand that in order for it to have a positive effect, publicity must be authentic.

If you are seen as a publicity hound, someone who is "seeking publicity," you will not be treated as a serious person. If you don't believe us, just ask Paris Hilton. People once said: "The press can say anything they want about me as long as they spell my name right." Those days are gone.

The point of publicity is this. First, you make sure the organization's behavior is aligned with audience expectations. Then you make sure the audience knows about it.

This leads to a second important distinction: the distinction between marketing and public relations.

In a posting by Apryl Duncan in About.com http://advertising.about.com/od/careersource/a/10advpr.htm the author attempts to highlight "10 Differences Between Advertising and Public Relations."

Essentially, what she does in this post, in some ways, makes worse the tendency many people have to think only of "publicity" when someone says the words "public relations." In fact, "PR" has been turned into a verb with an obviously negative connotation to mean getting publicity, as in "PRing" an issue.

Despite this narrow view of PR as a publicity generating function, Duncan's column is well thought out overall. It is very much worth reading as it does nicely differentiate between coverage from "earned" media and the attention that is "bought" through advertising.

We normally associate advertising with marketing. We should. Marketing is a process organizations use to help find potential customers and get them ready to make a purchase. Advertising is a persuasive enterprise designed to make the case.

We've said before and we'll probably say again that *nothing happens until someone sells something*. Generally, if an activity isn't associated with the process of making a sale, it's not marketing. But that doesn't mean that everything that might influence a purchase decision is marketing.

Public relations is not marketing. It has a different calling and has much more of a management than a marketing function. To get a clearer look at the *distinction between advertising and public relations*, especially as it involves social media from the perspective of a practitioner, check out this column in a recent issue of CommPro.Biz. http://blog.commpro.biz/?p=2567

Cheryl Gale is writing from the perspective of a principal in a technology-based PR company (that, by the way, *Bulldog Reporter* named boutique agency of the year in 2010). So you might expect that Gale's perspective would reflect a certain preference for *dialog* and conversation over *persuasion* and selling. And it does. And this is exactly the distinction we are making. Gale says:

> Social media has given customers a public platform to engage directly with companies."
>
> This is what public relations is in the truest, most literal, sense of the word. Social media sit on the very pillars that PR is built upon: an uncontrolled medium, conversations, and engagement. PR professionals are trained in the art of two-way conversation, unlike advertisers, who are accustomed to buying time and audiences.

PR's principal objective is, simply, to build and support relationships that the organization has, and needs to have, with a wide variety of individuals and audiences. Some of this activity may support the process of selling to the extent that there are fewer more important audiences to a business than its customers.

Customer satisfaction, in fact, is another function that is often in the domain of public relations. And social media are playing a larger role in customer satisfaction every day.

PR also can help other senior managers in the corporation anticipate and hopefully avoid, or if unavoidable, responsibly cope with a crisis that might otherwise damage the company brand. And, during the crisis, the PR team can be thinking about and interacting with all of the many audiences upon which their client organization depends for survival—from the shareholders and board, to the federal, state and local government, to the suppliers, dealers and individual customers.

Then there is the difference between *social marketing* and *commercial marketing* that we need to talk about.

One of the real geniuses in the world of new and social media just came out with a brilliant book. Eric Schwartzman, with co-author Paul Gillin, has done a complete job of showing how social media can facilitate business-to-business marketing.

"Listen to our B2B market, generate major account leads, and build client relationships," says the headline of the cover of the book. Almost everything is right about this book, in our opinion. Everything, that is, except the title which is oh-so wrong. The title of the book is *Social Marketing to the Business Customer*. Why is that wrong?

If the book had been written in order to describe and refine strategies to keep your business customer from drinking and driving, that would be *social marketing*. Social marketing is the well-established discipline in which the objective is to apply commercial marketing-like techniques to achieve behavioral change goals. And the target for the change in behavior is often thought of as entire segments of the population—heavy drinkers, smokers, or perhaps, promiscuous teenagers. The title of Schwartzman's book should have been "*Social Media Marketing* to the Business Customer" or words to that effect. Social media doesn't have anything to do with social marketing—except this.

The field of social marketing has been given a whole new set of tools to influence people to take actions that are in their interest or in the public interest, and the new tools are the tools we are looking at and learning about here.

The tools of social media are perfect for assisting social marketers in their efforts to change people's behavior, as they are proving to be equally perfect in a commercial marketing context in the sales of products. Social media provide wonderful tools for use in either commercial or social marketing context.

Out of this kind of discussion comes a better understanding about the differences between *social media* and *social marketing*, or between *social marketing* and *commercial marketing*, or—and this is very important—between *marketing* and *public relations*.

We need to understand these distinctions and keep them in mind as we go into this chapter on online PR.

Once you begin to get a feel for these distinctions, you can better understand how different communication theories and techniques and principles apply to different situations, and why if your approach to public relations begins to look like marketing, you might just get yourself and your client laughed right off your customer's radar screen.

PR's Role in Social Media and Vice Versa

Public Relations Resource 8-1: What is PR? Man on the Street Interviews

http://www.youtube.com/watch?v=aml6diAglb8

Here's a Marshall Thompson YouTube video designed to show that people don't know much about PR. It's pretty predictable in that it characterizes PR as a job for people who like people or for people who like to embellish the truth.

Going to this Google YouTube site gives you a good chance to relax for a while and see how the business of PR is characterized, but also to view a variety of other YouTube suggestions ranging from a 38-second word association clip on public relations http://www.youtube.com/watch?v=-Aa7aKJoTWc &feature=related to a 12-second definition of PR that focuses entirely on the use of publicity as the sole function of public relations http://www.youtube.com/watch?v=7zDGC2GujYI&NR=1 to a 5-minute diatribe on PR in Great Britain by great comedy actor John Cleese http://www.youtube.com/watch?v=NSUKMa1cYHk&feature=related which, after you view it, will become clear to you that the PR in this video doesn't have anything at all to do with public relations, but stands for "Proportional Representation."

Public Relations Resource 8-2: If You Really Want to Know about PR, Talk to a PR Job Placement Agency. We did.

http://www.wetfeet.com/careers-and-industries/careers/public-relations.aspx

This overview of the public relations field from Wetfeet.com will walk you through everything from what you might do on the job to who does well in the practice:

> Those who do well in PR have strong communication skills, are articulate both with the written and spoken word, are able to understand a variety of people, are confident and quick studies—you'll need to learn quickly what your clients do in order to communicate their messages effectively. PR professionals should also be quick thinkers and persuasive.

Public Relations Resource 8-3: The Changing World (& Responsibilities) of PR

http://publicrelationsblogger.com/2010/01/changing-world-responsibilities-of-pr.html

In this blog post, one of the most prolific and proficient PR sages with a "marketing orientation," Ashley Wirthlin, discusses five ways to take advantage of the changes Internet brings to the expanding world of PR:

> The Internet has made it easier to do PR, but it's also increased the responsibilities that a company has. While it is easier to release information, get in touch with the public, and address crises, there is an increased responsibility because the public knows how easy it is; with that ease comes a sort of expected response.
> If a crisis is underway, I expect a company to be responsive, available, and accountable because it *is* so easy to be these things online.

Public Relations Resource 8-4: Putting the Public Back in Public Relations (and, we are adding a few other great books on social media)

http://www.briansolis.com/2009/04/frank-gruber-on-putting-public-back-in/

This post, by Brian Solis, is essentially a promotion of his then-new book: *Putting the Public Back in Public Relations*. The book was co-authored with

Deirdre Breakenridge, another of our favorites, and, as Frank Gruber says, it sits at the intersection of the new and old public relations.

Of course, we also love David Meerman Scott's work—especially his newest book, *Real-Time Marketing and PR*, and we have used *New Rules of Marketing and PR* for several years in several classes at MSU. But you don't have to stop there. There is a world of David Meerman Scott material available to you, and like we said, we love it all.

David Meerman Scott—Links

blog—www.webinknow.com
twitter—http://twitter.com//dmscott

my FREE resources

iPhone / iPad app—http://bit.ly/fOxFXl

Marketing Strategy Planning Template http://www.webinknow.com/2010/07/free-marketing-strategy-planning-template.html

EBOOKS

Real-Time: How Marketing & PR at Speed Drives Measurable Success
Are you instantly engaging with your market?
http://www.davidmeermanscott.com/documents/Real_Time.pdf

Lose Control of your Marketing! Why marketing ROI measures lead to failure
Give this one to your boss, board, or investors
http://www.davidmeermanscott.com/documents/Marketing_ROI.pdf

The New Rules of Viral Marketing: How word-of-mouse spreads your ideas for free (2008)
Downloaded over one million times
http://www.davidmeermanscott.com/documents/Viral_Marketing.pdf

Amazon.com has a listing called "Amazon's Complete Selection of David Meerman Scott Books." If you follow Derek's Ingenex "Digital Bus" blog, you must know what a stark-raving *Phish* lunatic Derek is. Rick had a hard time breaking it to Derek that David Meerman Scott had a book out called *Marketing Lessons from the Grateful Dead: What Every Business Can Learn from the Most Iconic Band in History*.

Rick's also been a big fan of Eric Schwartzman for a long time and even attended one of his PRSA's seminars. You should do the same if you get the chance. And if you can get over the mistitling of his book about the use of social media in business-to-business marketing (*Social Marketing to the Business Customer*), you'll find the material in the book wonderful.

Public Relations Resource 8-5: The Future of Public Relations and Social Media

http://mashable.com/2010/08/16/pr-social-media-future/

In this Mashable.com post, Erica Swallow assesses the future of press releases, the evolving social platforms, and their limitations. She also addresses the importance of getting and staying connected with other PR professionals as the world of social media continues to grow.

Swallow observes: "

> Public relations specialists were some of the first people to embrace the power of social media, and as a result they are often the ones leading the way in the social space, whether they are consulting with clients from an agency point of view or strategizing on an in-house PR team.
>
> During the past few years, we've witnessed a shift towards what some are calling the *social media release.*
>
> Services like *PitchEngine, PressLift, PRX Builder,* and *MindTouch* are bringing the press release into the new millennium with embedded multimedia and easy distribution through various channels, including social media and e-mail.

Embedded in her column, Swallow provides a neat little video tutorial provided by PitchEngine.com.

PR Resource 8-6: Want to "Rock" in PR and Marketing? Everything (Actually 10 Principles) You Need to Know Can Be Learned from Rock Bands

http://blog.commpro.biz/marketinghq/?p=256

Aside from resembling David Meerman Scott's treatise about The Grateful Dead, this article may contribute to the cynic's view that PR people believe that exaggeration is a fundamental skill of the practice.

Otherwise however, this is a pretty useful and interesting article. Again, it points to a growing tendency—an outgrowth of how the electronic media is being used—to blend marketing with public relations. In fact, author Rodger Roeser is president of a firm he describes as "integrated buzz marketing."

His technique for making his point, though not unique, is certainly useful. Roeser uses a number of similes, metaphors and analogies to demonstrate and highlight some important principles in the modern practice of social and commercial marketing.

We are particularly grateful for his principle number eight: Practice:

> There is no substitute . . . amateurs practice until they get it right, but professionals practice until they get it wrong—it just becomes second nature. I can stand out on stage, play a killer bass line, belt out my song, jump up and down, press the button for the fog machine and point to a "fan" all at the same time without even thinking about it.

So, to, must business. You must work with your team over and over and over again. Rehearse your speech, your movements, your key messages, your interviews.

Our biggest concern with Rodger Roeser is that he may leave some of our readers with the impression that we believe turning on the fog machine is a critical PR skill.

Public Relations Resource 8-7: 13 Reasons Why PR Should Lead Social Media Efforts

http://www.prdaily.com/Main/Articles/8933.aspx

Ragan's *PR Daily* shared this post from Elizabeth Sosnow who acknowledges the irony that in this era of media defined as "social" anyone would hold such a territorial position on the ownership of social media:

> Our colleagues in sales, advertising, customer service, HR and IT all want control of the digital media PR budget. I understand why they would ask for it, but I just don't think they're as well equipped to head the effort as PR pros.
> We are storytellers. Thought leadership is already in our DNA.
> We begin—not end—every project with an analysis of how to approach influencers.
> We are already trained to empathize and converse with different audiences (at the same time).

We think that everyone is entitled to his or her own opinion, but we all should be striving to work from the same fact base. And we believe the fact base Sosnow presents in this post speaks volumes about the management role (as opposed to marketing role) that PR must hold in the organization to meet its promise of relationship building.

Going Social with Traditional Media Reporters and Editors

Public Relations Resource 8-8: Things to Check before Sending That Press Release

http://www.ereleases.com/prfuel/5-things-check-sending-press-release/

This post is a really "informative and useful" article for some public relations practitioners. "Amanda" commented on the article (comment 12).

> Having the ability to write publishable news releases is an asset to any PR pro. The format of the news release, the context of the news release, and the content of the news release all work together to make the release attractive to journalists and editors. This can seem like a difficult task at

first, but your tips have given great insights into writing the types of news releases that will stand out.

So what are these tips? Again, you'll have to go to the link to find out for yourself, and if you do, you'll have a shot at getting a great insight into a fairly traditional view of "press releases," as author Mickie Kennedy calls them. (We are calling out this reference to "press releases" because for more than two decades, many PR practitioners have been calling their bread-and-butter tool "news releases" so as to not offend radio and TV reporters who do not consider themselves part of the "press." Now, we have social media also in which the news is often going directly to various constituencies without the intermediation of the "press").

Mickie Kennedy is the founder of eReleases.com, which he describes as the "online leader in affordable press release distribution." Among the things he makes available is a 160-page book of sample news releases—something we find very valuable if only as a way of comparing to our writing.

Not everyone agreed with Amanda's assessment of the value of this article. For example, in comment number 5, Brad Brenner, gives a very clear illustration of how the marketing functions of a news releases is beginning to overtake, at least in some circles, the traditional role of a news release. He says:

> Wrong! This might have been true ten years ago but things change—and thinking marketers need to periodically reexamine the rules to make sure they are still relevant.
>
> There was a time when newsworthiness was critical to press release content. That was when editors were the gatekeepers of the news and a press release was used solely as a tool to gain their interest. Today, reporters no longer hold the keys to the city of distribution and press releases (our agency now calls them 'news releases') can serve a variety of purposes: show company momentum, increase visibility, grow market share, increase web traffic and page rankings and EVEN (heaven help us . . . here it comes . . .) sell stuff!
>
> Once a heresy in the old PR bible, we are now creating news releases that include links to 'special offers' and discounts . . . and they work (just ask WebEx and Cisco among others).
>
> Now would I send a marketing news release to a reporter? No. Would I send it to customers or post it on my website and send it out over an Internet distribution service? You bet.

PR Resource 8-9: Public Relations and Social Media: 10 Social Media Do's and Don'ts

http://publicrelationsblogger.com/2010/04/public-relations-social-media-10-social.html

Anyone very serious about understanding how the world of social media is changing the practice of public relations needs to become a regular reader of Ashley Wirthlin's PublicRelationsBlogger.com.

She describes her website as "a free, educational resource for public relations with hundreds of articles to browse on various PR topics including its role in social media (or social media's role in PR), PR and marketing, PR and advertising, and much more."

This post is an excellent example of the gift Wirthlin is giving all of us. By the way, if you want an opportunity to read Wirthlin's take on where the industry is and where its going, follow this link to get her free public relations book. http://www.publicrelationsbook.com/

We particularly like Wirthlin's description of the "Ten Social Media Do's and Don'ts" because it's a good characterization of the offense versus defense view of the role of social media in PR that we talked about in our introduction to this chapter.

"Connect with others in the industry and collaborate with them. Not only is it important to connect with them through social networking sites, it is crucial to the growth of your blog to connect with other bloggers and exchange links," Wirthlin says.

The moral of Wirthlin's story: "Use social media to connect, respond, and communicate with your audiences. Be personable and personal, making it more fun for your buyers to communicate with you. Moreover, measure results so you can impress upon the shareholders of your company the importance of PR, marketing, and social media. Advertising yourself is a somewhat necessary evil in PR and in social media, but do so tactfully and in moderation."

Pay Attention to the Blogger

Technically, a blogger is a blog author—someone who keeps and maintains a blog. So, what's a blog reader?

A couple of years ago, the Pew Internet and American Life project found that about a third of all regular Internet users (roughly a quarter of all American adults) say they read blogs, with 11% of all adult Internet users saying they read blogs on a typical day.

The word "blogger" is a bit trickier. It's a place as well as a person—a free blog publishing tool provided by Google. It's a great way, as Google says, for sharing text, photos and video. (Google: Blogger)

We picked just a handful of our many favorite resource entries to include in this section of the *New Media Driver's License*® resource guide.

Public Relations Resource 8-10: Blogger Outreach the Human Way

http://www.youtube.com/watch?v=TUg9AmEEu9g

Our New Media Driver's License® seminars focus to no small degree on public relations, as you must know by now. And if you have been paying attention to the evolution of public relations, you'll know that it's growing to no small degree in the direction of social media. Why is this, you say?

One simple word answers the question: *DIALOG*.

Dialog is a key, if not *the key*, to relationships at every level from the most singular, intimate, personal relationship to the relationship between an auto manufacturer and the financial analysts whose reports influence stock prices. Nothing ever invented has contributed more to dialog—people-to-people, people-to-business, business-to-business, and even country-to-country—than has social media.

In this post, YouTube video, chief programmer Phillip Rhodes—that's right, *programmer*—presents some of the best PR advice we've heard in a long time. Principally, he reminds us that blogging is all about conversations between and among people.

The way to get bloggers to have an emotional connection to your business, Rhodes says, is simple. Let your employees develop personal relationships with them, and the only way they can do that is by getting personal.

If your employee, Bob, is out there in the blogosphere making friends, answering questions, providing honest and sincere information, asking questions, perhaps, the people he connects with are going to want Bob to succeed.

Phillip's three-minute explanation of the importance of remembering "there are people behind the pixels" should be required viewing for anyone considering a formal blogger outreach program.

Public Relations Resource 8-11:
3 Ways to Get to Know Your Audience
http://blog.premiersocialmedia.com/2010/09/21/know-your-audience/

As "Ana RC" says in her well-read blog post, there are a number of free analytics tools at your disposal from "Google Analytics to Stat Counter and the demographic-oriented Facebook Insight. . . ."

She also emphasizes that these are all tools that "can help you with a lot of information on your visitor."

The information available ranges from "the type of content or pages they like best, the time they spend on your site and the number of pages they visit to the keywords that bring them to you, the operating system they are using and a few demographic insights, such as age and sex. There is plenty of information on your audience right at your finger tips."

Public Relations Resource 8-12: Introducing Blogger Stats
http://buzz.blogger.com/2010/08/introducing-blogger-stats.html

It's been a more than a year since Noah Fidel and Viktor Gore, Blogger software engineers, announced: "Just in time for our eleventh birthday, we are excited to introduce Stats for Blogger:

First launched to Blogger in draft (form) back in July, Blogger Stats is a cool real-time stats service that's fully integrated with Blogger; you don't need to do anything to enable it for your blog. You can find the new Stats tab on your blog's dashboard—go ahead and take it for a spin!

They describe Stats as "an important piece of the blogging puzzle, as it allows you to track your blog's traffic and find out exactly what your audience is looking for. As such, integrated, 'real-time stats' has been one of the most frequently requested features from our users."

Public Relations Resource 8-13:
How to Effectively Build Relationships with Bloggers

http://www.searchenginejournal.com/topic-hubs-how-to-effectively-build-relation-ships-with-bloggers/16209/

We really like this post by Dr. Tony Karrer, CEO of TechEmpower.com, who gives really important and down-to-earth tips on how to build effective, lasting relationships with bloggers. He begins his post by pointing to a variety of other posts offering advice on the subject. Then he adds one more piece to the puzzle. He calls it "Topic Hubs."

Let's let Tony explain what he means in his own words:

I've recently been finding myself building relationships with bloggers using a very different strategy that has worked very well for me. The key to this strategy is what I call "topic hubs." http://elearningtech.blogspot.com/2009/02/topic-hubs.html

A topic hub aggregates a collection of information sources (web pages and RSS feeds) to form a new information hub around a particular topic—hence the name "topic hub." For example, the B2B Marketing Zone http://www.b2bmarketingzone.com is a topic hub on B2B Marketing.

Relationships with bloggers naturally form when a topic hub is involved.

Public Relations Resource 8-14: 10 Tips for a Successful Blogger Outreach Campaign

http://thecaffeinatedblog.typepad.com/the_caffeinated_blog/2009/02/10-tips-for-a-successful-blogger-outreach-campaign.html

We've put a lot of focus on the *dialog* that powers public relationships, but we shouldn't forget that the marketing side of the house has a big stake in effective social media, especially blogging. With all this talk about dialog, the power and role of persuasion that drives marketing could get lost. It shouldn't.

In this post the anonymous, obviously over-caffeinated, blogger points out that "with more than half of blog readers saying that blogs influence their purchase decisions, it's no wonder that many companies are eager to generate some buzz about their products on blogs. Unfortunately, it doesn't happen magically."

"In order to get the attention of these influential bloggers, companies have to reach out to them and make themselves known—but in a meaningful way. This post provides tips on how to effectively reach out to bloggers. Some tips include actually reading the blog, being prepared for negative feedback, and making it personal," advice that is made easier through effective and self-less social media.

The Importance of Location, Location CONTENT

There seems to be an increasing feeling among those in the public relations business that their jobs are morphing into an interesting form of something that in another age might be called *journalism*. And they are right.

PR practitioners are required to spend an increasing amount of time writing. (And, as a study we did using Public Relations Society of America membership data proved, the seasoned practitioners in the PR agencies don't think universities are doing a very good job turning out competent writers. Email rcole1@ msu.edu for an electronic copy of this study.)

As we said earlier, the secret to good writing is: "Writer's write."

It's almost that simple. You can't expect to be a successful PR practitioner, especially in this day of instant opinions delivered through the Internet, without being a good "first-draft" writer.

Writer's write and that's increasingly what PR people are and do. So that's why this next resource resonated so clearly with us.

Public Relations Resource: 8-15 How to Write for the Web: 23 Useful Rules

http://econsultancy.com/us/blog/6771-how-to-write-for-the-web-23-useful-rules

With a tip of the hat to Chris Lake (and the 40 people who commented on the econsultancy.com blog) these tips on how to write effectively on the Internet are not terribly different from what others in traditional media advise. We especially liked the advice on writer's block.

Pour your thoughts out first, edit later. Write the opening paragraph last or, said another way, write the closing paragraph first. Begin with the end in mind, is how some might say it. Exercise the one-comma rule. More than one comma may mean the sentence is too long. Make sure you keep your sentences short.

If we tried to identify any more of the great rules that Lake lays out in this article, we'd violate his rule on brevity. Read it yourself.

Public Relations Resource 8-16: Social Media: Moving beyond the Wire to Real-Time PR

http://cindykimblog.wordpress.com/2010/10/05/social-media-moving-beyond-the-wire-to-real-time-pr/

Here's another great resource that demonstrates how the traditional lines between the management function of PR and marketing functions like advertising are blurring as a result of the emergence of social media.

"Don't get me wrong," Cindy Kim's says in her Wordpress blog she calls "The Marketing Journalist":

> For many, PR is still about how to provide content for reporters to repost or write a story based around a good pitch. Today, however, there is much more to it than that.
>
> PR professionals whose job functions involve media relations must learn the rules of real-time PR. The new face of media relations requires even more speed and agility to seize market opportunities, real-time engagement and creative out-of-the-box approaches to become the first market mover.

Public Relations Resource 8-17: Five-Step Process to Turn 30 Pages and 10 Hours into One Month of Social Media Content

http://blog.commpro.biz/socialmediazone/?p=1570

This is exactly what Rick has been looking for. He's deeply engaged in a project to attempt to get the attention of the Millennial generation (18 to 30 year olds) so that he can interest them in taking up child neglect and abuse as the major cause of their generation. It's a mobilization effort—social marketing using social media—through which young adults can make a huge difference, he says. And there is a huge amount of information out there that will be very compelling to this age group.

So, we've started a campaign in our region of the state to connect young adults to this issue through social media. We're planning on these folks stepping up and saying they want to be involved, and we'll lead them to an appropriate child and family related agency in our area that is looking for volunteers to help.

The issue from Rick's standpoint is that he's responsible for the initial content for the campaign—for the blog www.EveryChildIsYours.org—and he knows there's a ton of stuff out there that will be interesting for readers who care about kids.

This ComPro.biz/SocialMediaZone feature, written by Kris Austin, walks right through a wonderful strategy that begins with developing a white paper with relevant topics for the audience and breaking each chapter into individual articles:

You will use these stand alone articles, which are typically 800-1000 words, as promotional articles and on sites where longer material is preferred and accepted.

Of course, even though the CommPro.Biz article is not clear about this point, make sure you properly reference the material.

Next, break down each paragraph into individual blog posts. You can then grab quotes out of each paragraph. "These will become individual blurbs for LinkedIn, Twitter, and Facebook,' says Austin.

Step five is to pre-schedule all of the above material into your social media dashboard creating a roll out of the materials.

(One of the best "educators" we have come across in the world of social media, by the way, is CommPro.Biz. Virtually every day, they send out more than one piece of great advice. Consider signing up for this free resource.)

Social Media PR Tools, Tips, Tactics and Tricks

PR Resource 8-18: 10 of the Best Social Media Tools for PR Professionals and Journalists

http://mashable.com/2008/10/30/best-social-media-tools-for-pr-professionals-and-journalists/

When you go to this Mashable.com post by Sara Evans, take a minute to click through to the Google Ad (If it's still at the top of the article when you get to it) entitled "Submit a Press Release to Spread Your News to Reporters & More." Trusted by Warren Buffet.

This will take you to the explanation of the BusinessWire.com Press Release Distribution System. BusinessWire.com is one of the biggest and probably one of the best in this competitive field. And it is trusted by Warren Buffet, we're sure, but this might just have something to do with the fact that Business Wire is a Berkshire Hathaway Company, Warren Buffet's amazingly successful investment fund.

The first resource that Evans details is what she says, as a PR pro, is her favorite tool:

The brainchild of Peter Shankman, this is the only free resource I am aware of where reporters submit questions directly to PR professionals—no strings attached. Subscribers to the list serve received up to three daily emails, each with anywhere from 15-30 queries per email.

We're glad that Evans listed this as her favorite tool, since it helps us emphasize the "relationship-management" nature of the business of PR, rather than reinforcing its stereotype as simply a propaganda mill.

On press releases, Evans says: "The emergence of the social media release (SMR) will soon dominate interactions between journalists and PR people."

Her favorite tool to help on this aspect of her work is PitchEngine (still in beta testing stage.)

You'll have to read the wonderful post to get the rest of Evans's top 10 list—a very good one, indeed. She talks about ReportingOn, Journalisted, Wikis, Twitter and how it is being used by media people, Twello.com, Beat-Blogging.org, WiredJournalists.com and my personal favorite *YourPitchSucks* (YPS) in which you can submit your draft pitch to PR experts for a serious review.

Public Relations Resource 8-19: 100 Media Monitoring Tools for PR

http://www.pamil-visions.net/100-media-monitoring-tools/218947/

Borderline overboard, this is the most comprehensive list of media monitoring tools we, or our students in our New Media Driver's License® courses, could find to assist anyone who may be interested in going into one of the hottest new disciplines in public relations.

One of our students, Nick Lucido, became an employee of Edelman PR's Chicago main office while a junior at MSU. His job—one that he loved to talk about to other PR students about—was what he called operating a *listening post* for Edelman clients.

We're not sure what his preferred monitoring applications were, but we think that Liliana Dumitru-Steffens, writing an "Everything PR" column, has the waterfront covered. Liliana, by the way, is a PR consultant for Pamil Visions PR.

If you want to get a sense of the value of this post to the industry, read the comments that follow her post. Here's one we really liked:

> **Comment by James Godwin** on 20 September 2010:
> One good SEO tip is make sure your site is performing. Website performance monitoring is also key else you get unhappy visitors plus effects your Google Pagerank. These guys are profiling hosts and monitoring their performance. Get a free monitor at http://pagestatus.info and help them track hosting providers.

Besides expressing gratitude to Liliana for this great work, some of the comments include some links to additional resources.

Public Relations Resource 8-20: Paid and Free Press Release Submission Site List

http://www.pressreleasepoint.com/paid-and-free-press-release-site-list

You can be as skeptical as you want about this list of paid and free news release submission sites. It's put up, after all, by PressReleasePoints.com, an international free press release distribution website. But you must admit that it's a great list from which to do your own research. Although the direct links are somewhat difficult to use—you may have as hard a time as we did return-ing to the chart of more than 63 different services—we find the idea behind PressReleasePoint.com quite compelling.

They boast that their site will allow the user to post releases on more than 50 free international websites, and that they will send your release to more than 100 online publications.

We had a student who experimented with one of these websites to put out a "hypothetical" news release he had written about a major donation to a New York hospital that had been (hypothetically) made by an executive with the New York Giants football team. Needless to say, when this practice release accidentally hit the free services, it generated considerable attention in the Giants' team offices and required dropping the name of Hall of Fame great, former Giants defensive back, now broadcaster, Carl Banks (an MSU alumnus), to get us, and our student, off that hook.

PR Resource 8-21: Using Email and Analytics to Track Actions and Score Coverage

http://www.prdaily.com/Main/Articles/8425.aspx

Here is some pretty basic and pretty useful information that reminds us that we need to look at reporters, editors, and increasingly bloggers, as discrete audiences that can be researched in essentially the same way a marketing department researches customers or prospects.

Tom Johansmeyer, writing in Ragan's *PR Daily*, reminds us:

> You can use the same systems deployed elsewhere in the marketing depart-ment for customer intelligence to learn from the actions of your top media outlets. Use information from email marketing platforms, Web analytics, and other tools to refine your press releases, pitch smarter, and generate measurable results.

These four questions need to be asked to remove some of the guesswork about pitching articles to reporters:

- What gets the reporter's attention?
- What motivates a reporter or editor to move?
- What keeps them involved to continue on your corporate blog or in your media room?
- What keeps them coming back for more?

"Web jockeys like repeat visitors. Publishers crave repeat readers. Businesses live for repeat customers. PR is no different," Johansmeyer says.

Johansmeyer's fifth question is the kicker: "What keeps *you* from getting ahead?" He put the special emphasis on the word *you*. You have to quit mak-ing assumptions about your target markets, including editors and reporters and bloggers, and you have to do some research to find out what it is they want, and then give it to them.

Once you begin to assemble important intelligence about this audience—professional journalists (reporters, editors, bloggers)—you are going to need a good system for managing these important contacts. One of the tools we learned about in a recent Mashable.com post is Gist. http://gist.com/corp/why-gist/view-all-your-contacts

Gist isn't the only service of its kind, for sure, and before you spend your time or money on any contact management system, you should shop around. But we think starting your shopping by exploring Gist.com is a good start.

Public Relations Resource 8-22: What is the Field of Public Relations? Get into the PR Blogosphere.

http://www.invesp.com/blog-rank/PR

If you are interested in the application of social media to PR—whether its for the purpose of advancing a commercial enterprise or developing and running a social marketing campaign—we think a good thing to do is to get a fix on just exactly how you want to define public relations.

You know, from the introduction to this section of the book, that we feel that a good definition of PR involves adjusting organizational behavior to conform to the expectations of key audiences and then letting the audiences know about it. That's certainly one common concept of PR, but there are others.

A great way for you to get a fix on how you want to define PR is from getting active in the PR blogosphere. As we were putting the guide together, we went to Blogrank to get their rank of the hottest PR blogs, and here it is. Pick a couple to test and get involved. It will definitely be worth your time.

Public Relations Resource 8-23: Digital Marketing and PR Posts

http://thefuturebuzz.com/2010/04/30/friday-links/

Here's a composite post from one of the most active PR bloggers out there, Adam Singer. If you're a regular follower of TheFutureBuzz.com, you'll love this piece even more. These are posts that Singer calls "some of my latest ideas published external to The Future Buzz."

For example, his post in TopRankBlog.com, "How to Develop Great Content," lays out 10 tips from Byron White, Chief Idea Officer of ideaLaunch.

Public Relations Resource 8-24: PR Strategies: 3 Ways to Differentiate Yourself

http://publicrelationsblogger.com/2010/01/pr-strategies-3-ways-to-differentiate.html

This is one more important post by Ashley Wirthlin at PublicRelations Blogger.com.

We've said before and we'll say again that Wirthlin is one of our favorite

PR sources. While the title is somewhat misleading—the post, in our opinion, really doesn't give you three discrete activities or actions that will differentiate you in your marketplace—it does give you some solid advice on standing out from the crowd. And it gives you a good method to figure out what your best potential points of differentiation are.

Her second point—"Analyze the situation"—is a great example of the line that PR often crosses into marketing. This is not to say there is no role for public relations in marketing, nor does it suggest that we don't believe PR experts can't be in charge of marketing communications. The line is pretty thin here, at best.

But Wirthlin does give an example of the importance of honesty as part of the differentiation equation.

Two stores, side by side, tried to differentiate themselves by outdoing one another on the mark-offs it was offering. One had a 75% off sale. The store next door had an 80% off sale. It was a good example of how not to differentiate a business.

Wirthlin's example reminded us of the story of the Chicago butcher who "differentiated" his store from the other butcher shops in the neighborhood. "Best Butcher Shop in Chicago" one sign proclaimed. The shop next door immediately put up a sign that said "Best Butcher Shop in Cook County." Not to be outdone, a couple of days later and couple of doors down the street came this sign: "Best Butcher Shop on the Block."

Public Relations Resource 8-25: Flack Me, the Talent Zoo's Blog is Loaded with Tips

http://www.talentzoo.com/flack_me/

This is one of many very interesting PR-related blogs. Just today in Flack Me we were able to find a great PR case about Sears dropping another PR ball. Doug Bedell wrote this post. More than 400 of Bedell's articles are available in the Blog's user-friendly archives.

One other thing we like about Flack Me is that it posts some cool job openings.

Today, we were able to "social-eyes" a really cool PR internship opportunity at an Atlanta events marketing company.

Public Relations Resource 8-26: 10 Ways to Make Press Releases More SEO Friendly

http://mashable.com/2008/11/04/how-to-make-press-releases-seo-friendly/

"On an average business day, more than 2,000 press releases are distributed by the five leading wire services in the United States—Business Wire, Marketwire, PrimeNewswire, PR Newswire, and PRWeb," says Sarah Evans in this Mashable.com post.

Sarah's point is quite simple here. In order for releases (whether you call them press releases or news releases) to be of value in making you findable to potential customers, for example, you have to make sure you'll show up at the top of the search results.

You have to focus on search engine optimization (SEO). Effective SEO helps you in other ways also, and there are some keys to being able to deliver better results. (We get into SEO and search engine marketing in the Internet Marketing chapter of this book.)

Public Relations Resource 8-27: How to Handle a PR Crisis

http://www.entrepreneur.com/magazine/entrepreneur/2010/august/207530.html

Social media is fluttering with advice on various aspects of PR, and no shortage of this advice involves what is called crisis management.

Crises are when the PR consultant gets his or her chops, as they say. That's when everyone turns to the PR expert (unless the PR expert caused the crisis) and asks the following question: "Well, what do we do now." We like Ronn Torssian's advice in *Entrepreneur Magazine*. Drop everything and deal with it.

There is a tremendous amount written about crisis management. One of our favorite authors on the subject is Dr. Timothy Coombs from Purdue University. He's won national prizes from the Public Relations Society of America for his work in what he calls "Situational Crisis Communication Theory" http://www.instituteforpr.org/topics/crisis-communication-and-social-media/ which actually provides recommendations for what to do in various different kinds of crises.

Torrsian's advice is much more "street level": It's aimed at mostly small businesses facing big problems. He uses a variety of real-world examples that reinforce the importance of planning for the worst, even if you are hoping for the best. (By the way, unlike Torrsian, Coombs believes there are times when a quick apology for a crisis may not be the best action to take.)

The single truth about all crises is this: The most important work that PR people do isn't handing well the crises that arise. That's important, for sure, but the most important work PR people do in relation to crises is advising management on how to keep crises from happening in the first place. Unfortunately, most PR counselors never get any credit for that.

Public Relations Resource 8-28: 10 Free Social Media Tools Every PR Pro Should Master

http://www.socialmediatoday.com/SMC/187381

We're fascinated with graphics, so when we saw the plastic safety goggles next to the opening paragraph of a posting from Adam Vincenzini in SocialMediaToday.com, we said this must be for real.

Everyone who has ever done PR work knows the importance of having safety glasses at the ready so when you are standing in front of the fan when your client throws the excrement into it, you might get hit, but at least you won't go blind.

Actually Vincenzini's column doesn't go into this "hitting the fan" aspect of PR, but it does deliver on its promise reminding us of the importance of AllTop (we've talked about this resource in a couple of places in the book), Social Mention, Bing real-time Twitter search, Klout, Backtweets, Wordle, Google Trends, BlogPulse, Alexa and SWiX.

This is a powerful column with clear and common sense recommendations. For example, about SWiX, Vincenzini says: "If you only use one tool a day, try and make it this one. It is a really (really!) simple way of tracking activity across all of your social networks/platforms."

He describes its PR value: "At-a-glance intelligence, lovely."

Public Relations Resource 8-29:
6 Reasons Why Social Media Didn't Kill PR
http://www.sys-con.com/node/1554304

Apparently there was some chatter over the past few years that social media would be the death of PR. We're not sure who actually believed that, but we sure didn't. Andy Beaupre, posted on Sys-con.com, his reasons for why social media is actually a good thing for PR:

> Specialized social media experts (who were ahead of the curve in the early days) understandably trumpeted this view (that social media would kill PR), leveraging the opportunity to directly or indirectly de-position PR agencies and professionals. Similarly, some journalists said PR's traditional media relations centricity was a model for extinction."

This is one time that, had some of the prognosticators been reading the academic literature of public relations, they likely would have come to just the opposite conclusion. Over the past decade, more and more research has supported the notion that PR was moving away from the "persuasion model" and into a "dialogic model." And, as we have said, social media are all about dialog.

Given this expanded capacity for organizations to interact directly through the Internet with the audiences they depend upon, why would we expect social media to somehow damage the efficacy of PR? That is, why would we have expected that unless we had a *shallow, publicity-oriented view* of what is clearly a more sophisticated discipline?

Beaupre concludes his post with a graph showing "The Stakeholder Ecosystem" –15 or so separate audiences that generally constitute key stakeholders of any business organization.

"True public relations practice isn't publicity," Beaupre says. "It's much broader, taking into account every stakeholder (or 'public') with which an organization interacts.

Strategically practiced, PR takes on a wide-ranging role, focused on earning a trusted reputation by acting in the best interests of these publics—not the organization's own myopic agenda.

Public Relations Resource 8-30: 6 Reasons Why Social Media Sucks and You Have to Use it Anyway

http://www.business2community.com/social-media/6-reasons-social-media-sucks-but-you-need-to-use-it-anyway-039812

We tell our students, especially those that seem to have a knack for public relations, to tread lightly in the world of social media. Don't study social media, we say. Learn how to use it to do whatever it is you want to do with your life.

Many of our students want to be PR practitioners. They must understand social media, use it, and know how to track it. Increasingly they need to know how it is measured. They must become experts in the use of social media, not to be social media experts, but in their case, to be experts in PR.

How could someone become an expert in modern PR if he or she doesn't understand the most powerful tools ever invented to aid dialog with more and more members of critical audiences?

We can give you many reasons to be very careful about social media. But Tom Pick, posting on the B2C blog has done it better than we could. Each and every one of these objections should be understood and reckoned with from the inherent loss of privacy in social media to the tendency for it to suck talented people into an endless black hole time suck.

Public Relations Resource 8-31: PR Needs to Change

http://thefuturebuzz.com/2011/03/31/proactive-pr/

The Future Buzz is, by its own account, "a digital marketing and social media blog run by communications professional Adam Singer."

Singer is no withering flower. And his article calling for practitioners in PR to be more proactive has a great deal to commend it. But we think it also runs the risk of missing a very important point.

Singer calls upon the PR industry to "flip" the thinking and become more like media companies, which, he says, are far more proactive than reactive PR firms. It seems to us as if PR companies would be well served to spend more of their time helping their clients make news, and less of their time making news releases.

We're quite sure many PR companies will disagree with that characterization, However, we are absolutely sure, as David Meerman Scott and many others have been saying over the past few years, every organization, no matter its mission, must become a media company and every executive must become a publisher. In fact, some might say that is exactly what has happened the past few years, and as a result, a good many media middlemen (read: newspapers) have fallen by the wayside.

Others have said that in the old economy *the big devoured the small.* Today, however, *it is the fact that are devouring the slow.* How anyone, in any business, let alone PR, could make the case that they can afford to be reactive is a bit beyond us.

Public Relations Resource 8-32: Tips for Pitching Mashable

http://www.prdaily.com/mediarelations/Articles/7770.aspx

Two of our favorite sources—Ragan's *PR Daily* and Mashable—team up in this post (reprinting an interview by Heather Whaling in prtini.com) to answer a very important new media question. How do you pitch a story to a new media juggernaut like Mashable?

PRtini interviewed one of Mashable's editors, Erica Swallow. (We've referenced some of her other posts). This is an especially good read:

> A great pitch is succinct and targeted to Mashable's audience. That's all. It's as simple as that. The most successful PR peeps know how to get to the point in 2-3 sentences and they don't even feel the need to attach that 400-word press release. Furthermore, they have researched the site they are pitching and understand the audience that reads that site.

Public Relations Resource 8-33: PR Experts to Follow on Quora

http://www.prdaily.com/Main/Articles/7443.aspx

Post author Mickie Kennedy, founder of eReleases, should be on this list. So should Mark Ragan, CEO Ragan's *PR Daily.* Maybe neither has signed on to Quora, which would explain this otherwise obvious oversight? Or perhaps it's modesty in Kennedy's case?

By the way, Quora defines itself as a "continually improving collection of questions and answers created, edited and organized by everyone who uses it."

So who, in Kennedy's opinion, are the 20 top PR experts that one should "follow" on Quora. It's an interesting list that not only names the names, but also offers brief biographies that, in total, looks like a "Who's Who" of modern PR.

Public Relations Resource 8-34: PR Advice—
What Are the Best Tips You've Ever Received?

http://www.arikhanson.com/2010/10/06/whats-the-best-pr-advice-you-ever-received/

What better way to end this section that with some generic advice that will help any public relations practitioner—no, it will help anyone—who is interested in using social or any other media to build relationships.

Arik Hanson has a wonderful blog—you'll find his name elsewhere in this book. The blog is entitled "Communications Conversations," and it's a blog you might consider making part of your regular social media fare. He said a friend of his stopped him dead in his tracks with this question, so he thought about it and put down a few tips of his own.

Never burn a bridge is Hanson's tip number one.

Work smarter not harder is his second one. We always liked the story of the guy who submitted a bill to a client for some advice he'd given. The bill seemed a bit higher than the client anticipated. "How much time could it have taken you to come up with the solution?" the client asked. The PR guy responded by saying that he doesn't get paid for pushing buttons, he gets paid for knowing which buttons to push.

Hanson went to several of his friends, at least a couple of which ought to be familiar names to our readers.

Deirdre Breakenridge told Hanson her best advice involved *becoming a better listener*. Many of the female PR executives echoed this kind of line—a particularly important thing for men in the PR business to hear, if you ask us.

Mark Ragan's advice was a bit more basic. "Learn how to write better than anyone else in your organization or market," advice that echoes the results of the study we had talked about earlier. PR supervisors are very unhappy about the writing skills of entry-level professionals.

As Shandwick PR social media expert Jud Branam told one of our classes: If you can write, you can work.

Extra Point: Keeping up to Speed

Public Relations Resource 8-35: David Meerman Scott's lecture feature "You broke my guitar"

http://www.amazon.com/gp/mpd/permalink/m34J78KOWTDWHD/ref=ent_fb_link

This resource speaks for itself. Need we say more?

Public Relations Resource 8-36: Derek Mehraban's Digital PR Advice

http://newmediadl.com/blog

Derek has posted some of his best digital PR advice on the New Media Driver's License® website for several semesters. Here's a sampler.

Monitoring, Digital PR and Blogger Outreach

The great thing about new media is it allows you to tap into a massive resource of unsolicited comments and market intelligence. If you are a savvy marketer, you are constantly monitoring these sites to listen to the buzz going on about and around your product/company/brand.

Media Monitoring

There are many sites the offer a one-stop solution for monitoring:

http://trackur.com
http://twendz.waggeneredstrom.com/
http://www.monitter.com/
http://technorati.com/
http://www.google.com/alerts
http://search.twitter.com

I also suggest opening an account using either www.hootsuite.com or www.cotweet.com and setting up some monitoring on those sites. You simply create some columns and you can track key terms, and #hash tags or @usernames.

Blogger Outreach

Bloggers are always looking for new topics to write about, one PR tactic is to pitch them your stuff! If you can get another blog to write about you, that is very valuable for both SEO links—and because of that bloggers readers can learn about your product from an objective outside source. Much more powerful that if you were writing about your own product or service.

Before you can pitch a blogger, you need to get to know them. Visit their blog, comment on their blog, and build a relationship, take an active interest in the topics that blogger writes about. Bloggers appreciate an interest in their work, so start an online relationship. After you've done the legwork, you can solicit your own material for publication on his/her blog. NOTE: Blogger outreach is not easy, it takes time and effort. I suggest reading more on the topic, and starting off slow. If you are good at this, then you may have a future at a digital PR agency.

Check out the resource below for a good article on how to pitch to bloggers.

News Releases

Press releases are no longer strictly for the press. Online news has opened up PR to the public, so you want to be in front of users. Digital PR pulls together social media monitoring and blogger outreach. These days you don't have to beg for press from the media—you can simply publish it yourself.

Some favorite places to submit your digital PR - www.prlog.com (free), www.pr.com, www.prleap.com, www.prweb.com You can also often submit your digital PR to news outlets and they will publish it for you, or you can publish it yourself on their page. Poke around on their site to see if they have a "Submit your PR" link.

Five Things You Need to Know about Digital PR

Don't be shy. If your company did it, write a press release.

Monitor and engage with your peers online—it could pay big dividends. Great places to engage or forums or groups (LinkedIn and Facebook.)

If someone else says it about your business—the value goes up!

Be interesting and bloggers (after you've done your blogger outreach) may pick up your story.

Digital PR is an SEO Booster—so write optimized content.

Public Relations Resource 8- 37:
Future Leaders Need More than Digital PR

http://www.prconversations.com/index.php/2011/04/future-leaders-need-more-than-digital-pr/

Heather Yaxley posted in PRConversations.com on one of the most important subjects for young PR practitioners—even for college students who think they may have a chance to make it in PR:

> Everywhere you look, those starting out on a career in public relations are urged to focus on developing skills in Digital PR.
>
> But as such competencies shortly will be little more than a commodity possessed by most young graduates and practitioners in the field (as well as many with years of experience), future leaders will need much more than an ability to craft a Tweet or build a network of Facebook friends.

Among the tips Yaxley provides those who don't want to get sucked into what Nick Lucido described as the "black hole of social media":

"Look to gain a wider experience than simply communications."

For an individual to have a hope of rising into a high-level job in PR—in other words to get a seat at the table with the dominant coalition that runs the operation—you simply have to understand the business. You have to be able to speak the language of the industry in order to be able to do the essential translation job of PR.

"If an ability to write—or use social media—is the primary skill we can offer to organizations, PR will never be respected as a strategic function," Yaxley says.

We agree.

Perfect Practice Makes Perfect

Five tasks that will help you understand the concepts and ideas talked about in Part V.

Concept: *PR practitioners use PR for offensive and defensive purposes. Go to a major on-line news site (or otherwise search out) and identify three stories about organizations or individuals (celebrities) in crisis that are currently generating major interest by news organizations.*

Exercise 1. Relying on the framework provided in the "concept paragraph" above, identify three ways that social media either were or could have been used, prior to the crisis, to have advanced the interests of the organization in the news. Give examples of how social media were used and/or examples of how other organizations facing similar situations have used social media.

Exercise 2. Relying on the framework provided in the "concept paragraph" above, identify three ways PR practitioners were or could have been monitoring social media to recognize a potential crisis and how that might have defended the organizational reputation against the impact of the crisis. Provide examples of "listening post" applications or technology describing how it works to monitor and track key issues.

Exercise 3. Relying on the framework provided in the "concept paragraph" above, identify three ways social media could be employed once the crisis has subsided to restore the organization's reputation. Image restoration involves a complicated set of strategies. Use your search skills to identify articles and posts describing how companies have employed image restoration strategies to regain public confidence after a crisis.

Exercise 4: Go to the Edelman Trust Barometer (2011) http://www.edelman. com/trust/2011/ and download and review the results of Edelman's study. The data presented are showing a disappointing and declining trust in US business institutions. Provide three examples of how social media may be contributing to a decline in trust in US businesses. Also provide three examples of how US companies may be standing out as trustworthy as a result, to some degree, of corporate behavior that is being validated through social media policies and accounts.

Exercise 5: Social marketing is often described as the application of tested commercial marketing tactics and techniques to behavior-change objectives that are in the public interest. Examine the wide variety of social marketing campaigns and activities that are being directed at reducing childhood obesity. Turn the tables. Highlight three unique ways that social media have supported any of these social marketing campaigns, and speculate on how these kinds of social media tactics might be applicable to a commercial marketing campaign.

Part VI

INTERNET
MARKETING

CHAPTER 9

Internet Marketing through Customer Conversations

> When it comes to online marketing (and information in general), we just need the truth about what works and what doesn't. And the truth is there is no miracle product for our business, meaning that while there are great things on the market, nothing eliminates the strategy work that the small business owner is responsible for.

Unfortunately there aren't any miracle solutions or tactics when it comes to online marketing. In this quote Jamillah Warner describes how, instead we have an overwhelming and confusing mix of Internet marketing strategies, tips and tactics clouding our vision of what is really important in the business in his Small Business Trends post "Teach Me How to Think about Internet Marketing" http://smallbiztrends.com/2011/05/how-to-think-about-internet-marketing.html

Warner's post examines the theory on web presence posed by Mike Blumenthal (aka *Professor Maps*—the man behind understanding Google Maps—http://blumenthals.com/blog/: "Mike believes in building your core marketing first. He teaches small business owners, via GetListed Local University, to focus first on the marketing elements that you can control and then build from there."

Google executive Michal Lorenc reminded us to let our readers know that one of his colleagues at Google has written an e-book on Internet marketing. Jim Lecinski titled his book *Zero Moment of Truth*—ZMOT. The book walks the reader through what Google calls a "fundamental shift" in the nature of marketing.

You can preview the book here. http://google-zmot.appspot.com/

A major theme of the preview (and of the book, which can be downloaded at no charge) is that a major change occurred in marketing, and if you don't get it, you will pay (and your customers won't).

Dialog is rapidly replacing persuasion as the central modality of marketers. Google calls this change the "Zero Moment of Truth":

To ease your exploration of the resources identified in this book, please go to the Link Listing—www.NewMediaDriversLicenseResources.com

> The way we shop is changing and marketing strategies are simply not keep-
> ing pace . . . the Internet has changed how we decide what to buy.
>   Today we're all digital explorers, seeking out online ratings, social
> media-based peer reviews, videos, and in-depth product details as we move
> down the path to purchase.

As Rishad Tobaccowala, chief strategist at VivaKi says: "When consumers hear about a product today, their first reaction is 'Let me search online
for it.'"

The change is occurring in the way we select the products and services we
want to buy. And it's occurring in the vehicles we use to buy them. Ethan
Block wrote about this aspect of marketing through social media in a Flow-
town.com post he titled "Social Media Demographics: Who's Using Which
Sites?" http://www.flowtown.com/blog/social-media-demographics-whos-
using-which-sites?display=wide

You'll have to spend a few minutes with this post. It has an 'eye chart'
effect in the beginning that's a bit tough to wrap your head around. But you
ought to get the point as you look at social media sites like Digg, Stumbleupon (personalized recommendations), Reddit (what's new online), Facebook,
LinkedIn, Twitter, MySpace, and Ning.

You can get top-line views of which "demos" are populating the sites by
age, income, gender, and educational levels.

Surprisingly many businesses and entrepreneurs are under the impression
that using social media is an easy and relatively inexpensive way to reach customers to generate brand awareness and increase profits. 'Tain't exactly so.

Clement Yeung's post in SocialMediaExaminer.com injects a dose of reality. http://www.socialmediaexaminer.com/how-to-get-the-m-o-s-t-from-social-
media-marketing/?doing_wp_cron: "Many small businesses and solo
entrepreneurs dive into social media marketing strategies without visualizing
a bigger plan." Approaching social media marketing in this fashion is lethal.
Social media marketing is serious business and deserves serious attention.

Yeung stresses the "importance of developing a Marketing plan and identifying detailed Objectives, Strategies and Tactics."

Social media platforms, the importance of blogging for business, and tips
for developing a successful sales funnel round off the insightful social media
marketing guide.

This part of the book attempts to provide a deep dive into what we consider major aspects of understanding and using Internet marketing to its
fullest advantage. Thus, the resources we present reflect a bias for information
that is both understandable and (almost immediately) usable.

But before we start, there's the question about how exactly we decided to
classify what is Internet marketing (as distinct from the stuff we talked about
in the social media, Google, blogging, and other sections). As a couple of the
resources we have included in the book make clear, the lines between many of

the subject areas within this book are blurry, at best, and blurring more and more every day. We decided to have a broad chapter on Internet marketing that begins with trends, tips, techniques, tactics and tricks of the trade, and ends with other broad categories of Internet marketing.

And so as not to discriminate between the world of commercial marketing through social media and the use of social media to aid social marketing (behavior-change related pro-social), we're carrying Search Engine Marketing (Section I), Search Engine Optimization (Section II), Pay-Per-Click (Section III) and Social Bookmarking (Section IV) as sections within this chapter.

Trends and Concepts in Internet Marketing

Internet Marketing Resource 9-1: 4 Current Trends That Will Change Marketing Forever

http://www.twistimage.com/blog/archives/four-current-trends-that-will-change-marketing-forever/

To all of the people who thought Twitter, Facebook, and YouTube were fads, Cheers! Social media is here to stay, and so is Internet marketing. In fact, there's mounting evidence that new Internet marketing is rapidly replacing stuffy old business models.

Despite this mounting evidence to the contrary, some business owners are acting as if they still believe that the Internet isn't important. President of TwistImage.com Mitch Joel explains why, in his opinion, they are dead wrong.

Emphasizing the impact of the Web on individuals and businesses Joel says, "The Internet and social media have changed everything. They are not fads. They are a new way for people to connect, gather information, share, collaborate and build their business."

Revealing the very trends that have evolved and continue to shape the market place the post describes how touch screen technology—one of Joel's four key trends changing marketing—is shaping the way children learn.

"Some are saying that kids today will learn to type on glass, others (my hand is raised) think that kids will soon be learning to type on air. . . ."

Internet Marketing Resource 9-2: Why Real-Time Marketing Matters Now

http://adage.com/mediaworks/article?article_id=146436

This interesting conversation in AdAge.com between Simon Dumenco and social pioneer Wiredset CEO Mark Ghuneim is chock full of interesting background on stuff digital.

Of special interest to Dumenco was the announcement of the launch of

Trendrr v3. Dumenco describes Trendrr "as both a research tool and an excuse to explore how culture and conversation is manufactured these days."

He calls Trendrr v3 a major event that will "vastly expand its strategic value and utility to marketers and media people who need to track campaign/brand performance in the social-media space and beyond."

Internet Marketing Resource 9-3: Online Ads and Search Results Leave Lasting Impressions, Even If Consumers Don't Click

http://www.internetretailer.com/2010/11/02/online-ads-and-search-results-leave-lasting-impressions

Here's more good news for online advertisers. Online ads and search results work. Katie Deatsch, Associate Editor of InternetRetailer.com, describes how effective online advertising is in this post.

"A new study released today finds online ads and search results can stick—even if the consumer doesn't click," according to Deatsch.

Deatsch's post reports on a comScore Inc. poll that examined how consumers react to content after performing an organic search and viewing paid search results and online display advertising.

"When it comes to brand favorability, paid search listings have the most impact. . . ."

Robert Murray, CEO of iProspect told Deatsch: "This study demonstrates that there is a lot more value to digital media than just direct conversions."

Internet Marketing Resource 9-4: What Facebook Mail Will Mean for Marketing

http://www.utalkmarketing.com/pages/Article.aspx?ArticleID=19642&Title=What_Facebook_Mail_will_mean_for_marketing

Facebook continuously changes. New features, privacy settings, and display options regularly evolve.

An UTalkMarketing.com article by ecommerce product manager and SEO specialist at Actinic, Bruce Townsend, provides an interesting perspective on Facebook's email feature:

> Facebook email will obey the same privacy settings as the current Messages. This means that users can choose to share their message stream with their friends—potentially drawing messages to the attention of many more people.

Fairly new advancements permit open settings and less privacy restrictions leaving an opening for marketers to creep in early and begin emailing, messaging, and texting information to Facebook users. The article warns marketers to be cautious when using Facebook messaging due to the threat of spammers, who will ultimately determine the fate of the new messaging innovations.

Internet Marketing Resource 9-5: Announcing the "Validation Era"

http://adage.com/article/guest-columnists/marketers-ready-validation-era/226892/

As far as social media is concerned, is it possible that we have had too much of a good thing? Steve Rubel (see also the end of this chapter for a list of Rubel's favorite resources), in this AdAge.com post, says there are "early signs that the social-media boom is fraying at the edges and that we are entering a new age of intimacy."

Including Internet Marketing in a Business Strategy

Internet Marketing Resource 9-6: How to Use Internet Marketing within Your Marketing Strategy

http://www.howtodothings.com/business/how-to-use-internet-marketing-within-your-marketing-strategy

Stephen C. Campbell gives some great general tips in HowToDoThings.com on adding Internet marketing to give new zip to your overall marketing strategy. Be prepared to say "I knew that" after you read his tightly written four-step model for building your Internet strategy.

One piece of advice drawn right from Campbell's playbook almost seems, on its face, unnecessary at this point in the history of American industrialization, but it too often turns out to be a very important part of the conversation about business and marketing:

> Think of yourself as living in a global marketplace. Consider your customers to be people on the other side of the world as well as individuals in your neighborhood.

So do we.

Internet Marketing Resource 9-7:
5 Stages of Integrated Digital Marketing Life Cycle

http://socialmediatoday.com/irakaufman1/150079/5-stages-integrated-digital-marketing-life-cycle

The digital marketing life cycle begins with set up and ends with viral growth. The article, "5 Stages of Integrated Digital Marketing Life Cycle," by Ira

Kaufman on SocialMediaToday.com explains the role each step plays in the process of integrated digital marketing:

> During an Integrated Digital Marketing campaign, the campaign will experience five stages in the life cycle. During each time period the number of touch points, client marketing efforts that touch the customer, are expanded.

The insightful article provides a detailed time line analysis of "touch points" for every stage of a digital marketing campaign.

And if you are interested in knowing if, let alone how, your digital campaign worked, consider consulting Kaufman, and writing partner Bob Bengen's compelling post, and accompanying chatter, on their Beyond Social Media Marketing Blog http://www.beyondsocialmediamarketing.com/2010/03/5-steps-to-evaluating-social-media-roi/

Internet Marketing Resource 9-8:
Top 10 Internet Marketing Tips for Builders
http://rinf.com/alt-news/web-development-news/top-10-marketing-tips-for-builders/9234/

Think you're website is special? Chances are it's not. Countless business websites crowd the web and it can be impossible to make it stand out over every other business. But almost all can get better.

You'll enjoy the advice on-line marketing expert Jamie Fairbairn offers in this post.

Promoting a business online, Fairbairn says, requires creativity and ingenuity. Creating a website and using a professional email address are only the beginning steps to reach success.

In the Rinf.com article, Fairbairn suggests that you should find "what sets you apart. In marketing speak this is known as your USP or unique selling proposition. If there are other builders in your area doing the same as you, have a think about how you could make your business stand out."

Read his piece, but as a clue to what you'll find, Fairbairn's other tactics include; creating a video, offering something free and tactics to get a business's name out to promote your business to the top.

Internet Marketing Resource 9-9:
5 Tips for Marketing Online to an International Audience
http://mashable.com/2010/11/01/international-marketing-online/

Going Global? Mashable.com can help your brand's Internet marketing campaign be a success across borders with some interesting advice from Erica Swallow:

> Expanding your marketing efforts to an international audience can be a great opportunity to grow your company and reach potential customers that may not otherwise discover your brand, products or service.

That may be so, but the key question is:

> How do you even prepare and strategize the implementation of a business's marketing campaign on the Internet global marketing landscape?
> Start with cross-cultural competency.
> Having your site translated into other languages is a huge advantage to marketing to an international audience, but having a deep understanding of your own and others' cultures is also important.

We might say "All so important."

Beyond some basic no brainers, Swallow's post provides tips on how to personalize the marketing campaign for a brand according to a specific country's preferences:" Learning about and respecting other cultures will help you localize your brand's message," says Swallow.

Internet Marketing Resource 9-10:
A 3-Month Plan for Adding Social Media to Your Marketing Mix
http://www.imediaconnection.com/content/27277.asp

Search, display and email marketing are considered traditional forms of online marketing. Can traditional online marketing and social media marketing work together? Bill Flitter thinks it can and he says so in his article posted in imediaconnection.com.

Beyond his opinion, Flitter provides an outline for integrating traditional and online marketing in the form of a three-month action plan.

Learning this month-by-month plan can help you properly segment an audience and craft targeted unique campaigns and advertisements.

Tips, Tactics, Tools and Tricks of the Trade

Internet Marketing Resource 9-11: Target Your Market with Appropriate Ad Copy
http://www.entrepreneur.com/advertising/adcolumnistroyhwilliams/
article76978.html

Here's a 10-second upload that's worth the wait. Roy H. Williams, posting in Entrepreneur.com, advocates doing an advertising experiment. "In your next advertising experiment, why not try targeting through the content of your message rather than through demographic profiles."

Williams slips in a really cool example of what he means. Click on the word *message*, and you'll see this is a guy who practices what he preaches. He uses a "sharply targeted message" he designed for the Canon PowerShot S500 camera as to make his point.

And it should not be surprising in the genre of the social-media post: Williams has a "four-step" plan for deciding who you can attract into your advertisement, and who you should lose. And his copy is among the best we've seen:

> That's why no one ever replaces his or her PowerShot S500. Go to your local pawnshop and see if you can find one. We're betting you can't. But you will see several of those "prettier" cameras available cheaper than dirt. So if you're looking for a great price on a sleek-looking camera, that's probably where you should go.

Internet Marketing Resource: Steve Rubel's Favorite Resources

Steve Rubel is SVP, Director of Insights for Edelman Digital, a division of Edelman, one of the world's largest public relations firms.

In his role, Rubel maintains a focus on the long view. He studies trends and innovations in media, technology and digital culture and fuses these into actionable insights that help Edelman and its clients remain at the forefront. We asked him to give us some insights into some resources he just couldn't live without. Here's his list:

Techmeme
http://www.techmeme.com
"Techmeme tracks the zeitgeist of the technology news media, including traditional sources and upstarts. It's my first visit to catch up on the world of technology."

Mediagazer
http://www.mediagazer.com
"Mediagazer is Techmeme's sister site. It's the best resource for all the twists and turns from the media world."

Google Reader
http://reader.google.com
"I subscribe to more than 1,000 news feeds that are automatically delivered to all my devices, allowing me to peruse content in-depth at my leisure."

Term.ly
http://www.term.ly
"Term.ly is a simple dictionary and thesaurus that's ad free and just works."

Instapaper
http://www.instapaper.com
"This site helps me capture all the articles I want to read later, but for which I don't have time to do now."

Rubel identifies a host of new social media networks that are emerging that will make it harder for strangers to enter our circle of trust. He identifies a number of new software products—Path, Beluga, InstaGram, GroupMe and others—that individuals and companies can use to validate relationships.

He describes three viable implications of this validation trend.

Extra Point—New Four P's of Marketing

Internet Marketing Resource 9-12: New "4P" Rules Needed

http://www.bangkokpost.com/business/economics/198521/new-4p-rules-needed

The four P's of Internet marketing are permission, participation, profile, and personalization.

Sound different? That's because it is, at least according to Prapasri Vasuhirun, writing in the Bangkok (Thailand) Post. The traditional four P's of marketing—product, price, promotion, and place (location)—don't apply in a digital market.

"A social network is like a party. Marketers have to fit in it with the right mood. Brands must place themselves as a guest, rather than a host of a conversation, as they have done in traditional media," said Dr. Ian Fenwick, who also writes for the Bangkok Post.

Vashuirun says, "Digital marketing can influence consumers to become aware of brands and products with less spending than traditional media. Many brands have realized the importance of social networks but they still do not know where to start."

CHAPTER 10

Buying Your Position with Search Engine Marketing (SEM)— and Pay-Per-Click (PPC)

Search Engine Marketing (SEM) is one of the most important things you can learn to become a valuable, marketable resource.

SEM is using the Internet and search engines to drive traffic to your website through paid search advertising. This may mean using banner ads on websites, or it could mean the text ads you see on the side of a Google search result. Companies are spending on SEM because it works. But figuring out how to make it work best for you will take some time, effort, and practice. Let's get started.

There are a lot of different ways of differentiating between Search Engine Marketing, Search Engine Optimization, and Pay-Per-Click, but we are choosing to follow the description of Elmer Cagape, posting in his blog, SEO Hong Kong. http://www.seo-hongkong.com/blog/seo-vs-sem-vs-ppc-understanding-search-marketing-terms-2949.html:

> When someone says 'we do both SEO and SEM,' he actually means 'we do (organic search marketing) and (organic + pay per click search marketing)' . . . this sounds all right, except that when you mention SEM, it's enough to cover both organic and pay per click search marketing.
>
> Search Engine Marketing should be the parent category whose subsets include both SEO and Pay Per Click and should not refer only to the latter.

Here's a brief overview of how this works.

When people want to buy a product, schedule a vacation, or find a new service they use *Google*, *Bing*, or *Yahoo* to search for what they want. A Google search generally returns 10 results per page. So millions of results from a search would result in hundreds of thousands of pages to review. And there are only ten spots on page one of a Google search.

Has it occurred to you that you and your company are competing with millions of other websites that want to be on Page One? The function of Search Engine Marketing is to move you to Page One and keep you there. There are ways to accomplish that.

As a company or brand you can purchase keywords that will give you placement on the top of the *Paid Search* area of search results. That's SEM. And even though your intuition might lead you to believe that most prospects would prefer natural search results over paid "advertisements," that's not necessarily true.

Paid results often produce more relevant and accurate information. And they should. After all, someone is paying the search engine—Google or Yahoo, for example—so they'll show up for that *search phrase*. And the companies that are producing the ad campaigns for paid results are making sure that paid results deliver.

While there are companies that will do almost all the heavy lifting of SEM for you, you can learn to do some of it on your own, and you can become very good at it. In fact, at some point you may become *Google Certified.* http://www.google.com/adwords/professionals/ This badge states that you are *Google AdWords* proficient, and it can be displayed on your website to advertise your expertise and help you win new customers.

Here are some important elements Derek proposes that you consider:

1. Your landing page should be simple and have a clearly defined goal and action. Do you want someone to purchase a product, join your email list, or to download your white paper or any number of things? Your landing page should be written clearly. It should be obvious what you want the visitor to do. And the page should be very specific to the ad that drove the traffic.

2. You need to *think value*. What is a new customer worth to you? How much does the average existing customer purchase in a year? What is the cost to get that customer? Think value in your transactions. The reason is because SEM costs money, but you can quantify the costs to win a new customer, and to show the value of that customer over time. If they match up, then SEM could be a good investment for you. Essentially, the key question is did the customer deliver more in profits to your company than the cost you spent to get that customer?

3. Relevance and targeting is important. SEM allows you to segment your audience and reach them where they are on search engines attempting to find products and services to buy. You can write an ad for each search term, and each audience member. You can have a landing page for each search term too. You want to be very specific and clear in your ads, and on the corresponding landing page. Then you can drive qualified traffic, and get them to take the desired action on your site.

4. With SEM, you can track and test every concept, ad, and landing page. Split testing works. Take your two ads and figure out which one performs better. Then drop the one that didn't work and write a new ad. Track and test and you can improve results over time. It's much easier to test Google ads than testing magazine or TV ads. So businesses are wise to conduct their research in the hand-to-hand combat that is SEM.

The SEM resources listed below will give you a great start in becoming an experienced search-marketing practitioner. And even though SEM favors those who are good with numbers, it can be done by anyone. It just takes a little time, effort, and tenacity.

So, let's start with a basic refresher on how some people differentiate SEO and SEM. Not everyone agrees, but we like to think of it as a bit like some people characterize the difference between the publicity functions of PR with advertising—as "earned" versus "paid" media.

Understanding the Basics

SEM/PPC Resource 10-1:
What's the Difference between SEO and SEM?
http://adage.com/digital/article?article_id=125716

SEO, SEM, PPC . . . confused? It's okay. Many online marketers like the umbrella concept of SEM. Abby Klaassen provides a somewhat different take on the subject. Search engine optimization and search engine marketing are as similar as they are different. If you don't understand the difference between the two, don't worry about it. You'll *get it* soon. Klaassen, an editor at Adage.com, posted this article for AdAgeDigital.com that will help you clarify the difference between SEO and SEM.

Klaassen asks that you think of SEM as "paid search" and SEO as natural or "organic search," think "free listings."

Regardless of whatever definition makes you most comfortable, you'll be interested to see how different search engines compare to each other.

"Google leads the (search engine) category in the U.S.—but what's surprising is the giant continues to gain or maintain share, even off such a high base," Klaassen states.

The AdAge.com post will help you grasp basic search concepts and learn about the benefits of paid search and how it is done, and see the impact it can have on a real business.

SEM/PPC Resource 10-2: Online Marketing:
The New Word of Mouth

http://www.clickz.com/clickz/column/2032780/online-marketing-word-mouth-

Here's another great ClickZ.com post to match an earlier one about Face-book.

In this one, Jonathan Shapiro uses an impending April 15 "Tax Day" to remind us that online marketing has really become the new word of mouth. Industries or professionals who have traditionally relied on word of mouth for prospects or new clients need to modernize their online strategies.

Using tax preparation services as the example of a professional segment that could benefit from a little new thinking, Shapiro says this:

> With consumers turning to the Internet to find such solutions, it is as cer-tain as death and taxes that successful service providers, like the tax prep crowd, will need to leverage online marketing tools to be sure they get the word out.
>
> There are a number of tools service providers can deploy to be part of the conversation when the client is ready to buy.

And, you guessed it, Shapiro uses his post to provide some insights into how the service professions can be more findable.

SEM/PPC Resource 10-3: Search Engine Marketing Glossary

http://www.seobook.com/glossary/

It's okay if you aren't a SEO super nerd versed in techy search marketing jar-gon. This resource can help you BS your way through almost any meeting with a client—or a search consultant, for that matter.

Here's the argument. With the Search Engine Marketing Glossary you can quickly reference search-marketing terms from A-Z and stop wasting time shuffling through Google's search results—results that could be clouded with information you don't want.

SEM/PPC Resource 10-4: Search Engine Marketing Resources Library
"Wiki"

http://www.searchenginewiki.com/HomePage

The Search Engine Marketing Resources Library is a quick way to reference a variety of marketing resources.

More than 10 years worth of resources have been contributed from across the web universe and compiled in this SEM database. Users can look up search engine optimization (SEO) links to search engine marketing articles, popular blogs, SEM tools, and more, and it's all in one central location.

The SEM Resources Library eliminates searching through pages and pages of highly optimized search engine resources and compiles relevant and useful information into one place. This is a great resource for beginners as well as for industry practitioners.

Of special note is our ongoing attempt to articulate the subtle distinctions some people see between Search Engine Marketing (SEM) and Pay-Per-Click Advertising (PPC).

> *Search Engine Marketing* (SEM): Marketing and advertising via search engines that can include Search Engine (SEO), Pay-Per-Click (PPC) Advertising and Return on Investment (ROI) analysis. Activities can include Keyword Research , Link-Building Campaigns, Web Site (both for readability leading to conversions and for optimizing content for search engine results) and Web Site Usability studies (to aid in assuring that site traffic is able to achieve the desired outcome, be it sales, newsletter signups, etc) and Log File Analysis of results of SEM campaigns (also known as Web Site Metrics or Web Site Analytics). Ideally these SEM efforts will be cyclical and the results of initial efforts will be analyzed and insights used to further improve SEM campaigns.
>
> Here's Search Engine Wiki's definition of *Pay-Per-Click*: Also known as PayPerClickAdvertising or PPC, PayPerClick is an advertising model utilized in online marketing campaigns, in which advertisers pay for ads based on the number of times the ad is "clicked," after which action the person clicking is taken to the web page of the advertiser's choice. There are a number of search engines offering PPC advertising, with the largest including Google Adwords, Yahoo Search Marketing and Microsoft Ad Center.

The Search Engine Wiki people choose to characterize the phrase *Search Engine Marketing* as the umbrella term that covers both Search Engine Optimization and Pay-Per-Click Advertising. We like to use the phrase Internet Marketing as the umbrella phrase to cover paid and earned find-ability. So we lump Search Engine Marketing in with Pay-Per-Click Advertising and keep earned Search Engine Optimization as a separate category.

SEM/PPC Resource 10-5: Pay Per Click Advertising— PPC Using Google Adwords

http://homebusiness.about.com/od/internetmarketing/a/pay_per_click.htm

In contrast to the hard work and creativity that accompanies building your position through organic searches, all advertising takes is money. And the money you pay is directly tied to clicks.

"Pay per click (PPC) advertising may be one of the easiest ways to generate traffic to your website and score some decent profits from your search engine marketing campaign," says Randy Duermyer in this posting in the home business section of About.com.

Duermyer's article is a great resource and starting point to learn about PPC advertising.

SEM/PPC Resource 10-6: PPC—Learn Effective Pay Per Click Optimization

http://www.wordstream.com/ppc

WordStream.com is straight to the point. This is a great reference for PPC-related terms and definitions. The article also discusses different tools that can help you track and perfect PPC advertisements.

But caveat emptor (buyer beware): this site is set up—and very openly so—to sell you PPC software that accomplishes a couple of functions according to this article—automation and PPC management.

We're not endorsing the product, nor suggesting that there are not other products out there that you could use, but we think reading the WordStream copy is a pretty effective way to understand some of the ins and outs, and complexities and idiosyncrasies, of the PPC world.

One of the things we like about this WordStream Internet Marketing Software site is that each pertinent phrase from pay-per-click to PPC search engine is linked to a relevant definition within the WordStream domain.

SEM/PPC Resource 10-7: All about Pay Per Click Advertising

http://www.payperclickabout.com/why_use_pay_per_click_advertising.php

Here's another promotion about a proprietary service designed to enhance your PPC advertising campaign. This resource will take you to a sophisticated and copyrighted newsletter. There's a wealth of free information on their site—great articles on various PPC issues.

You might want to check it out.

SEM/PPC Resource 10-8: Pay Per Click 101

http://www.youtube.com/watch?v=Zyj5r_RcSJY&feature=related

Google isn't the only search engine option to consider when advertising. Paying attention to PPC advertising on other search engines will help expand a business.

Take a break from your reading, turn the volume down on your computer, sit back and listen to this YouTube video, Pay Per Click 101. The visuals won't knock you out, but the tutorial will get your PPC campaign started in the right direction.

The video shows viewers how to use different tools for finding keywords and what to do once you have the keyword information.

SEM/PPC Resource 10-9: Pay Per Click Geeks— How to Keep Up-to-Date

http://www.ppcgeeks.com/

If you're serious about PPC and new media, then you will feel right at home on PPCGeeks.com. This is a great resource for all things digital. Registering and creating a website gives you an all-access pass to every resource on the website.

Information about Smartphones, applications, web browsers, search engines and PPC, in general, are only a few of the subjects covered on the website.

SEM/PPC Resource 10-10: The 3 Laws of PPC Success

http://www.sbwire.com/press-releases/sbwire-60612.htm

From British Columbia, Canada, comes this SBWire.com post from Rohit Kumar of Pitstop Media who shares three tips on how to run a successful PPC ad campaign. His advice is simple and concise, and may be seen by some as simply common sense. Common sense is OK.

"Get intimate with MS Excel," Kumar says. "This is a must. Once you add more keywords to the account, you will need to analyze . . . thousands of rows of data and columns."

SEM/PPC Resource 10-11: SEO vs PPC: The Pros and Cons

http://www.mikesquarter.com/seo-vs-ppc-the-pros-and-cons-378/

We found this posting from Internet Marketing Online by "Mike" published in Mike's blog www.mikesquarter.com.

This resource is quite instructive in that it lists both the positive and negative aspects of using PPC and SEO techniques. You might not agree with every one of Mike's opinions on the subject.

SEM/PPC Resource 10-12: PPC HERO

http://www.ppchero.com/

This resource intrigued us from the minute we found it. Never fear the PPC Hero is here. This blog is an excellent resource for all things PPC.

PPCHero.com was established in 2007 to "educate the world on the finer skills and basic techniques of successful pay per click management," the *About* section of the website says. You'll find PPC case studies and review strategies developed from the PPC Hero team that will help advance your PPC efforts.

PPC Hero may not be faster than a speeding bullet and more powerful than a locomotive, but at least it would seem to give a business's Internet advertising campaign quite a boost.

SEM/PPC Resource 10-13:
When Is PPC Better than SEO for Public Relations

http://www.toprankblog.com/2009/05/ppc-seo-public-relations/

One of the things that people often forget is a great deal of public relations work involves developing and directing paid advertising, as it should. Advertising, it turns out, can be a great way to get a relationship-supporting message to key constituents quickly and in a way that guarantees it will go out in the language you write.

Here's a parallel situation—a case for using search engine marketing, specifically pay-per-click tactics, as a way "to attract visitors to news related content."

Lee Odden, posting for TopRankBlog.com, makes a great case for this technique and uses examples of *The New York Times* "using Adwords to promote a story about Twitter":

> PR professionals can do the same with brand names, company names or executive names that often get searched on. PPC can be used to attract attention to specific news items, stories and content that is likely to be passed along once people get a chance to see it.

This is another one of the posts than need to be explored in further detail. Odden is a straight shooter and his graphics are very helpful.

Creating Your "Find-ability" Strategy

SEM/PPC Resource 10-14: Developing a Pay-Per-Click Strategy

http://www.ppchero.com/developing-a-pay-per-click-strategy/

The PPC Heroes are working overtime to help advertisers and marketers get the best PPC results. Amy Hoffman seems to be one of those heroes.

What's in it for PPC Hero to give away all this free information, like Hoffman's recent post? Well, they have advertisers too. So they sort of practice what they preach.

Developing a great PPC strategy can make or break your Internet marketing campaign. In fact, everyone from SunTzu to Kid Rock will tell you that without a good strategy, you are . . . well, without a good strategy you don't have much of a chance. You see, strategy is a word that was taken from the Greeks. The word *strategos* means general, as in the guy in charge of the battle plan. Where would any army be without a general?

This wonderful little post by Amy Hoffman not only talks about how to develop a good PPC strategy, but, more than that, it helps give you an understanding of what a strategy is and how to differentiate it from a goal or from the tactics that are used to put the strategy into play.

"This article is aimed at helping you to understand and devise a strategy for your pay per click accounts," Hoffman says. And then she goes on to instruct readers in how to create measurable goals, strategies and tactics for a PPC campaign.

"The best strategy development practices are clearly and concisely outlined, making PPC development easier," says Hoffman.

People who call themselves "the creative employees" in the advertising business often bristle at the thought of seeing their precious creative talents harnessed by a clear strategy. Sometimes we call these people former advertising employees.

The real creative wizards in advertising—whether they are the wordsmiths, the commercial artists, or the planners, traffickers, account executives, or media buyers—understand what Norman Berry, a former creative director at Olgivy Advertising, once said: "Give me the freedom of tightly defined strategy."

SEM/PPC Resource 10-15: Effective Search Marketing Strategy Determines Fate of Organization
http://searchenginewatch.com/3641478

Here's a case study about a strong retail brand that died. Since David Dalka, a specialist in SEM strategies, wrote it, you might think he'll try to sell the position that you're either into Internet marketing all the way or your dead. Quite the contrary, Dalka is an advocate for integrated marketing and promotes SEM as part of a strong, "balanced, multi-channel marketing strategy."

In this SearchEngineWatch.com post, Dalka stresses that most everyone knows "that executing an effective search marketing strategy is important to a business. However, have you ever stopped to wonder how businesses that aren't adapting to a search marketing centered business world are faring?"

Posing this question, Dalka's article describes how a 150-year-old, high-prestige Wisconsin furniture store was wiped out, in part, due to a relative upstart's multichannel campaign that included a strong dose of SEM:

> Search marketing is rapidly becoming the lead strategic marketing process as brand creative diminishes in importance in a content-driven world. We must demonstrate to business leaders across the globe that is the current reality.

SEM/PPC Resource 10-16:
Optimizing Your Site for Search Engine Marketing
http://www.openforum.com/idea-hub/topics/marketing/article/optimizing-your-site-for-search-engine-marketing-ben-parr

Buckle up and get ready for an SEM crash course. An OpenForum.com post by Ben Parr will quickly inform you about what SEM is and how to use it.

Parr, a respected tech writer and editor at Mashable.com said, "I'm going to focus on some of the key issues and best practices for optimizing your site for search." And he did just that.

Parr's OpenForum.com post is it short and sweet, providing a definition of SEM, helping you quickly learn the tools to maximize the impact of your

Web pages. Learn what keyword research is, how to do link building and some pay-per-click techniques to increase the rank of a Web site.

As an aside, Parr helps explain some of the confusion or ambiguity involving the very phrase SEM in this newly developing discipline.

"Essentially, there are two ways of defining SEM: either it's an umbrella term that encompasses SEO, paid search, contextualized advertisements, and paid inclusions, or it only covers paid advertising, inclusions, and search and is separate from SEO."

As we have pointed out before, the second form is the preference we have expressed in this book.

SEM/PPC Resource 10-17: Five Ways Social Media Can Build on Search Engine Marketing

http://smartblogs.com/socialmedia/2010/08/05/5-ways-social-media-can-build-on-search-engine-marketing/

Some people see social media (and free search engine optimization) and search engine marketing (and pay-per-click advertising) as being somehow pitted against one another in a struggle for marketing dominance. Some of us never saw SEM and SEO as anything other than somewhat separate components of the rapidly evolving world of Internet marketing.

In this post, Smartbogs.com social media blogger Rob Birgfeld responds to an earlier *New York Times* article by Ariana Gardella. http://boss.blogs.nytimes.com/2010/07/28/trial-and-error-with-adwords-and-s-e-o/

Gardella describes a series of expensive and frustrating Google Adwords (read: SEM) efforts of online retailer La Grande Dame. No Adwords campaign seemed to work for them, so the owner fell back on SEO.

> Finally, she gave the company a social media presence.
> La Grande Dame recently had 2,200 Facebook fans, and more than 1,500 Twitter followers. They read tidbits on things like La Grande Dame sales and the best hairstyles for large women and updates on Ms. Hill's pregnancy. . . .
> [The Grand Dame owner told the *Times*:] These tactics are more personal, bring in more qualified customers, and cost significantly less. Better yet, they're effective.

"The battle between (paid) search and social (free) isn't really a battle at all," Birgfeld says. Rather, he designed his post to help readers learn how "social media (SEO) and SEM can work together to increase the search results of a business."

Easier said than done, perhaps, but by demonstrating "how SEM provides data about the right keywords, locations, costs and conversation," Birgfeld's tips may help increase search result rankings while also expanding social media presence.

SEM/PPC Resource 10-18: Pay Per Click Advertising and How It Fits into Your Internet Marketing Strategy.

http://www.portentinteractive.com/pay-per-click-1.htm

Here is another site we are crazy about.

One of the reasons we like this resource so much is that it shows you the good, the bad and the not so ugly side of PPC advertising. Many facets of PPC are explained on the Portent Interactive site, for sure, though we can't vouch for the site's objectivity. Another reason we like it is that the post has been updated twice since its original publication nearly eight years ago.

Looking for a deeper understanding of PPC?

"This article will provide you with a high-level view of pay per click advertising, provide some general strategies and provide an example of what to do, and what not to do," says Seattle's Ian Lurie of Protent Interactive.

As so many others, this article provides a general definition of what PPC is and how it is used, but then it goes way beyond that. You can learn how PPC can be costly, but also learn how to use PPC efficiently to avoid cost.

The article discusses the role PPC plays in an advertising campaign and how you can use it at its best.

SEM/PPC Resource 10-19: 3 Ways to Market Your Retail Business to Millennials

http://www.allbusiness.com/marketing-advertising/marketing-advertising-overview/15630673-1.html

"Millennials (18-30 year olds) eschew produced, trite, dumbed-down marketing in favor of efforts that are creative, true to their brands, able to connect in a way that feels authentic," something Mike Kraus says he has been talking about for years.

Now we know more about Millennials than we may have before thanks to a McCann Worldgroup survey. McCann called the survey "The Truth about Youth global survey." You can read more about the study on Adweek.com. http://www.adweek.com/news/advertising-branding/mccann-millennials-social-media-and-brands-132289

Kraus, whose career spans general management, marketing, internet/e-commerce and operations explains the "three important elements of a marketing campaign (needed) to connect with Millennials."

"Inform, inspire and educate your audience," Kraus advises, to help you connect with Millennials and attract them as customers in the new social media world.

SEM/PPC Resource 10-20: A PR Pro's Guide to Choosing Keywords for Your Web Content
http://www.prdaily.com/Main/Articles/8552.aspx

What keywords are you using? Have you done your keyword research?

Pete Codella, who conducts a popular *PR Daily* webinar series on social media tools for PR professionals, has these questions and more.

"Sure, some of you may have a set of keywords you use in news release titles and blog headlines, but do you have a strategically crafted keyword list that's vetted against actual online searches?" Codella asks.

Take Codella's advice and you may be surprised at how easy it is to formulate your own list of keywords. But his post doesn't stop there. If you'll focus on this post you'll see that he'll tell you when, where, how, and how often to use these keyword search terms.

Starting and Running a Google Ad Campaign

SEM/PPC Resource 10-21: An Introduction to Google Adwords
http://www.youtube.com/watch?v=uFzoM59bIQ8

British accents (in our Midwest-biased opinion) make almost everything seem more serious.

This quick video provides an overview of how Google search results work and what influences them. You can't be an expert by watching a three minute video, but it's amazing how easy it is to understand how to designate target audiences and when and where Adwords ad will show up.

SEM/PPC Resource 10-22: Google AdWords Marketing Tutorial: For Beginners
http://www.youtube.com/watch?v=ZmXsOJtv1UE

In this YouTube tutorial, Ben Heart describes Google Adwords quite simply as an important search engine-marketing component that "allows you to target precisely and exactly your most likely buyers."

Heart wants to help you make money, not waste it. His stated goal is to help you cheaply achieve top paid search results.

SEM/PPC Resource 10-23: Create Google and SEO Friendly Page Titles
http://www.youtube.com/watch?v=MjIEPT3tEtk&feature=channel

This Free SEObook.com video is a cool summary of titles that will enhance website traffic and search engine optimization.

SEM/PPC Resource 10-24: Google Display Network

http://www.google.com/adwords/displaynetwork/#utm_source=gdn&utm_medium=r
edirect&utm_campaign=gdn_redirect

This should probably be your first stop in your search for how to create your own Google ad campaigns—and this is straight from the horse's mouth.

Google Display Network's step-by-step guide walks you through the process of creating a new campaign, creating ad groups, the targeting and bidding process, creating display ads, and measuring your performance.

> Under the **Networks** tab, you can easily see a performance report for all of the Display Network sites on which your ads have appeared. Coupled with Conversion Tracking, you can quickly understand which sites are resulting in sales, leads or registrations and which aren't, and make decisions based on this information.
> For example, you can use this information to:
> Monitor site-level performance for each of your ad groups, seeing which sites are meeting your performance goals. You can even view page-level performance within specific sites, and, as this resource point out, you can take several other important steps toward running a successful campaign.

SEM/PPC Resource 10-25: Free Adwords Help

http://www.freeadwordshelp.com/

Here's another website we like that is dedicated to helping you set up a successful Google Adwords endeavor. Go to the first minute of the video, for example, and you'll get a nice overview of Adwords Insights for Search. (More about Adwords Insights later.)

This link also whets your appetite for a variety of other useful tutorials.

SEM/PPC Resource 10-26: Google Adwords Tips

http://www.webmasterworld.com/forum81/2839.htm-

Check out this WebmasterWorld.com post to get 15 high-quality tips for using Google Adwords most effectively. This modestly written, but very useful, anonymous post offers suggestions and detail like "Don't use broad matching."

The comments on this are nearly as interesting and useful as the post itself—often true in *blogosphere*. Here comment #1 from Bufferzone:

"What took you so long? I have been looking for this for ages, not wanting to go into Adwords before I was pretty sure about getting it right the first time. . . ."

SEM and PPC Mistakes and Miscalculations

SEM/PPC Resource 10-27: The Top 10 SEO Mistakes #1: Keyword Research

http://www.youtube.com/watch?v=H2M1tXtAc18

This YouTube video stresses the importance of keyword research and how to do it. It also shows how to use Wordtracker to optimize keyword search.

SEM/PPC Resource 10-28: Top 14 Search Engine Marketing Mistakes "Etailers" Should Avoid

http://www.businessknowhow.com/internet/topmistakes.htm

Put yourself in timeout or slap yourself on the wrist if your search engine marketing campaign is guilty of committing one of the SEM crimes described in the BusinessKnowHow.com article.

The guide is a great resource for forming and executing an SEM strategy, and it has been for seven or eight years.

In this post, Hollis Thomases states that "search engine marketing has proven to be an extremely successful and effective means of achieving online sales growth, but not all etailers know how to properly execute their search engine marketing campaigns."

There is a lot of information on the Web that can get misconstrued and important facts and guidelines are often lost in translation. It's important to avoid these industry no-nos. Reading this article should help you identify current mistakes and avoid others. Thomases post can help you eliminate the risk of wasted money, time, and, worst of all, your reputation.

Extra Point—Staying Ahead of the Game

SEM/PPC Resource 10-29: Google Releases Best SEO Tips Ever

http://www.iblogzone.com/2010/04/google-releases-best-seo-tips-ever.html

Here's a pretty self-explanatory resource from IBlogZone.com, posted by Ditesco. For example, the post turned us on to this Google "+1" tip:

> Sometimes it's easier to find exactly what you're looking for when someone you know already found it. Get recommendations for the things that interest you, right when you want them, in your search results.
>
> The next time you're trying to remember that bed and breakfast your buddy was raving about, or find a great charity to support, a +1 could help you out. Just make sure you're signed in to your Google Account.

SEM/PPC Resource 10-30: Search Engine Watch

http://searchenginewatch.com/

Everything from search engine industry news to analytics and new technology information can be found on SearchEngineWatch.com. It's the "Mashable" for search engine enthusiasts and Internet marketers.

"Search Engine Watch provides tips and information about searching the web, analysis of the search engine industry and help to site owners trying to improve their ability to be found in search engines," the website states.

This post should help you learn how to combine SEO with social media and take advantage of analytical advice to make your company stand out on the web.

Search Engine Watch promises to keep you updated on the latest trends and advice for the best SEO practices.

SEM/PPC Resource 10-31: Search Engine Guide

http://www.searchengineguide.com/marketing.html

Typical SEM information doesn't directly address online reputation management, vertical search and copywriting, but the Search Engine Guide provides this kind of information detail for search engine marketers.

Topics are supported with regularly updated blogs from industry professionals, constantly keeping you in the know in a rapidly changing industry.

SEM/PPC Resource 10-32: How to Stay a Step Ahead of Your Hungriest PPC Competitors

http://searchengineland.com/how-to-stay-a-step-ahead-of-your-hungriest-ppc-competitors-71025

Staying ahead of the hungry bear is a familiar, but useful, metaphor Matt Van Wagner uses to open this post in searchengineland.com. When the bear comes into the village, you don't have to run faster than the bear to get away. You just have to run faster than the competition.

His point in this post is that both the bear and your competition are getting faster, and it isn't getting any easier to keep ahead in the PPC. It's the slower runner that gets eaten by the bear, or so goes the metaphor.

In the post you may learn how to create a better process for PPC advertising, including what might just be the most important point of all—setting aside time for learning and discovering new PPC tactics and tools.

SEM/PPC Resource 10-33: How to Use Google Insights for Search to Improve Your PPC Management

http://www.ppchero.com/how-to-use-google%E2%80%99s-insights-for-search-to-improve-your-ppc-management/

In this PPCHero.com post, John lays out an effective and efficient, step-by-step way to use Google Insights for Search tool to promote digital marketing and PPC marketing.

John likes the SearchEngineLand.com description of the tool: "The tool offers a comprehensive set of statistics based on search volume and patterns. You can compare seasonal trends, geographic distributions, and category-specific searches, and you can group all these variables together to get extremely specific."

We're not alone in liking John's PPCHero.com description. Commentator Sim Garner told John that "the information you are sharing on the use of Google trends and PPC keyword research can be the catalyst to help a sharp-minded person increase their profits and expand their resources."

SEM/PPC Resource 10-34: PPC Advertising Enhanced by Google Instant Effect

http://thebrilliantstories.com/ppc-advertising-enhanced-by-google-instant-effect/452036/

Grace Taylor assesses the effects Google's new instant search will have on PPC advertising in this post in TheBrilliantStories.com:

Introduction of Google Instant: Enhancement PPC Advertisement

Google Instant, a system termed as *search before you type* is a novel search enhancement showing results as one types.

Introduction of Google Instant: Enhancement PPC Advertisement

Google has been promising three main benefits to come through Google Instant.

This means that users should be expecting faster searches, instant results and smarter predictions. Nevertheless, it is said that it might be affecting PPC advertising because of the usage of longer tailed phrases as well as campaigns that are locally targeted.

SEM/PPC Resource 10-35: PPC for a Day or for a Lifetime

http://www.searchengineguide.com/mike-fleming/ppc-for-a-day-or-for-a-lifetime.
ph,p

Mike Fleming, posting in SearchEngineGuide.com, walks the reader through a "theoretical progression of how solid PPC search campaigns are started, developed and used to build a foundation for the long-term growth of your brand and website."

Using the Chinese proverb about teaching a man to fish, Fleming cleverly advises on everything from "building the net" to how to "bait, hook and reel." Albeit somewhat of a mixed metaphor (What do you need a hook for if you are net fishing?), Fleming's overall message is right on the money.

He also makes a large number of other resources available to you with a simple click of the *articles* button next to his smiling face. Thanks, Mike.

CHAPTER 11

Earning Your Position with Search Engine Optimization

We've said it before (see the introduction to Chapter 10), and we don't want to belabor the point. But just in case you skipped ahead to this chapter before fully understanding the difference between search engine marketing (and its sibling pay-per-click advertising), we'll say this once more.

Think about this. Marketers pay to improve their client's position in the marketplace by buying space on television, radio, magazines, billboards—the list goes on and includes the Internet. Paying for space increases the likelihood that the message the marketer is sending will appear as planned. And while no assurances can be made, the idea that the message appears as it was designed also increases the likelihood that the consumer will interpret it in the manner the marketer desires. We call this advertising.

When marketers elevate the find-ability of their client's brand, products, services—whatever—by paying for their search position, we call this search engine marketing, and the ads are called pay-per-click advertising.

There are many reasons why individuals and organizations are turning to a more "organic" process to optimize their find-ability in search engines like Google.

Marketers increasingly are turning to the management field of public relations for the model on how their clients can earn, rather than or as well as, buy their position in the minds of their consumers through the process called search engine optimization (SEO).

MarketingTerms.com offers this simple definition of SEO as the "process of choosing targeted keyword phrases related to a site, and ensuring that the site places well when those keyword phrases are part of a Web search."

This description goes on to emphasize the difference between the SEO process and spamming.

"Generally, legitimate search engine optimization adds to the user experience, while search engine spamming takes away from the user experience. . . ."

www.marketingterms.com/dictionary/search_engine_optimization/

There's obviously a good deal more behind fully understanding the role of SEO in a comprehensive campaign—whether it's a pure marketing campaign or one designed to enhance a corporate reputation or build support for a non-profit cause.

Understanding the Basics

SEO Resource 11-1: Search Engine Basics

http://www.youtube.com/watch?v=YhMwwfCtdW0

Learn SEO, clear up some common misconceptions, and do it in less than five minutes. This MarkTheGlobe SEO agency YouTube video will refresh your memory or introduce you to the most basic, but important search engine optimization concepts.

The video covers search engine terms and how relevant and important they are to optimization. You'll quickly learn what search engines look for and what you must include in all of your work in order to rank well.

SEO Resource 11-2: Visual Guide to SEO

http://infographiclabs.com/infographic/complete-seo-guide/

Here's another resource to help you learn about SEO. The Visual Guide to SEO provides a visual conceptualization of what SEO is, how it works, and where it fits in the marketing mix.

The creative souls from InfographicLabs.com collaborated to create their graphic to communicate complicated concepts, and data. The Visual Guide to SEO defines and describes basic SEO terms and procedures including keyword search, page optimization and link building.

SEO Resource 11-3: Google's Starter Guide for SEO!

http://googlewebmastercentral.blogspot.com/2008/11/googles-seo-starter-guide.html

Google won't tell you all of their SEO secrets but this is pretty close—straight from the source.

Google Webmaster Central wanted to help other Webmasters "improve their sites' interaction with both users and search engines," and we think this resource does just that.

The Google.com 2010 SEO Starter Guide attempts to provide tools to "make it easier for search engines to crawl, index and understand your content."

The delightfully colorful document is complete with photos and links and specific examples to help you create SEO websites and documents and rise to the top of search rankings.

SEO Resource 11-4: Singular and Plural Keywords
Are Not Always the Same for SEO

http://www.searchengineguide.com/mike-moran/singular-and-plural-keywords-are-not-alw.php

Here's a simple tip for optimizing your keywords through which Mike Moran demonstrates how singular or plural endings could make a difference in search results.

In this post in SearchEngineGuide.com, Moran advises readers to be cautious when picking a keyword and research to determine whether or not search results are different based on a singular or plural ending.

If you have any interest in mastering SEO, you might want to take a look at "teacher" Moran's many other articles on related subjects. He has a convenient link from this resource to an index of related articles.

SEO Resource 11-5: Search Engine Optimization (SEO):
Webmaster Tools Help

http://www.google.com/support/webmasters/bin/answer.py?hl=en&answer=35291

Here is search engine optimization defined by the people who probably know best—Google. Google Webmasters supplements the definition of SEO with a healthy pool of basic SEO information. Links connect readers to more in-depth SEO knowledge and how to find outside help.

"Before beginning your search for an SEO," Google suggests you, "become an educated consumer and get familiar with how search engines work" and view the resources they have provided to help you understand this.

The SEO guide will help you or a business understand SEO and make the most informed and safe decisions.

Creating Your SEO "Find-ability" Strategy

SEO Resource 11-6: 10 Basic SEO Tips to Get You Started

http://www.businessinsider.com/10-basic-seo-tips-everyone-should-know-2010-1?op=1

Making a website or blog is difficult enough without considering the implementation of SEO tactics. Where do you even begin?

Getting started on a project is often the hardest part. Luckily a BusinessInsider.com article by Bianca Male can help you. Male stresses that, "every business with a Web site should make Search Engine Optimization a part of their growth strategy."

You can jump-start a successful SEO Web page using the10 basic tips outlined in Male's post.

You'll find the SEO guidance easy to understand. She suggests the kind of media content you should avoid when creating content.

"All it requires is a little effort, and some re-thinking of how you approach content on your site," Male says.

Don't stress; pay attention and consider these guidelines and getting started can be a breeze.

SEO Resource 11-7: What's the Value of Content Marketing?
http://www.flowtown.com/blog/whats-the-value-of-content-marketing

SEO how-to guides have beaten the subject of creating content to death. We get it! Creating content will help search ranking. The content is created and search ranking improves. Is that it?

Flowtown.com helps clarify this issue in an article by Ethan Bloch. SEO depends on content and business must realize this:

> A robust content campaign requires a significant investment of time and money, so if you're going to do it, you need to know where the return comes from. Today we reveal several ways that content marketing can be of great value to your business and recommend certain strategies necessary for success.

The value of content for business extends deeper than most believe. Bloch describes the influence content can have on a business, besides increasing search ranking.

SEO Resource 11-8: 5 SEO Tips Every Website Owner Should Know
http://www.sayeducate.com/2010/11/17/5-seo-tips-every-website-owner-should-know/

In the world of SEO nothing beats good content and inbound links. To help, Lior Levin posted an article with five SEO tips to improve your search rankings.

The SayEducate.com post stresses the importance of "making sure that a website's content is as easy to find as possible by the search engines and that the correct keywords are given weight."

Levin's suggestions do not guarantee an automatic increase in page rank but are still a great idea when posting on the Internet. With SEO, every little bit counts and attention to detail becomes even more important for increasing page rank.

Starting and Running a SEO Campaign

SEO Resource 11-9: Why Is SEO Important for Your Business?

http://ezinearticles.com/?Why-is-SEO-Important-For-Your-Business?&id=2860178

Questioning the benefits of SEO? Then you're in luck! EzineArticles.com posted an article by Beverley Le Roux that examines the usefulness of SEO in developing a business promotion strategy.

Le Roux says: "If you wish to run any form of online business, your primary role in life is to get recognized by the major search engines. SEO is really the only way to do that."

She describes why SEO is a big deal and what can happen if a business doesn't implement an SEO strategy. Le Roux also outlines various SEO tactics and tools to make a business infinitely more findable.

SEO Resource 11-10: 25 Tips to Skyrocket Your Search Engine Rankings

http://www.socialmedia.biz/2010/09/15/25-tips-to-skyrocket-your-search-engine-rankings/

The Internet is full of how-to tips and by-the-number experts. Some of these advice columns are definitely better than others. Karan Singhal's SocialMedia.biz post makes it clear he gets it.

Singhal provides "25 tips that, when used effectively, will skyrocket your search engine rankings, often with little effort." He also shows readers how to "avoid shady techniques that could end up costing you a Google penalty."

The article is a great reference for anyone who wants to get straight to the point—points, that is. And there is little doubt that reading and following Singhal's advice can help boost search rankings.

SEO Resource 11-11: The Concise List of Must-Have SEO Plugins for Wordpress

http://lornali.com/social-media/concise-list-seo-plugins-wordpress

WordPress.com is a platform used by many Web designers and bloggers. To improve search engine optimization there are plugins available that can help.

Lorna Li, a search engine marketing and SEO specialist compiled a list of what she calls, "must have SEO plugins for WordPress."

The list on LornaLi.com will help you optimize your WordPress site organically. Li collaborated with noted SEO guru Joost DeValk to create the helpful post.

If you want to boost your search ranking, and you're using WordPress, adopting the plugins suggested on LornaLi.com should help boost your search ranking and improve the website's overall usability and view ability.

Evaluating Your SEO Campaign and Avoiding Mistakes

SEO Resource 11-12: 10 Golden Rules of SEO

http://www.smartdogdigital.com/blog/10-golden-rules-of-search-engine-optimisation

Constructing a perfectly optimized web page is simple, if you follow a few easy rules. This post by Illiya Vjestica in SmartDogDigital.com is designed to help you make a perfectly optimized page.

Vjestica's "Golden Rules of SEO" post is designed to help clean up, adjust and fix content in ways that make search engines happy.

SEO Resource 11-13: 25 Super-Common SEO Mistakes

http://searchengineland.com/25-super-common-seo-mistakes-51888

Stephen Spencer, blogger and author of *The Art of SEO*, has some suggestions to avoid some of the more common SEO faux pas. Everybody makes mistakes. They are unavoidable. "Some of these things catch even the best of us," he says.

In this SearchEngineLand.com post, Spencer identifies "the innocent mistakes that many SEOs make." Most common SEO mistakes, he says, result from a lack of experience and knowledge and can result in lost time and money.

Taking a second look at some of the more common mistakes may help improve your SEO skills.

Extra Point—Staying Ahead of the Game

SEO Resource 11-14: How Social Search Will Transform the SEO Industry

http://mashable.com/2010/10/18/social-search-seo/

Choose your Facebook friends wisely because on some search engines they help determine what results show up. Social media has integrated its way into search and is changing SEO strategies.

Joe Devine, Chief Executive Officer of The Search Engine Guys, used this Mashable.com post to demonstrate the way SEO is changing:

> Yes, there will be changes to the way SEO professionals run their clients' campaigns. Yes, this will affect the industry as a whole. And yes, we believe SEO professionals will have to adapt to meet ever-evolving needs.

To read how, you'll have to check out this post.

SEO Resource 11-15: SEO Blog

http://www.seomoz.org/blog

Although it may seem impossible, you can take a big step in keeping up to date on everything SEO by following some of the people who understand it and love it the most.

SEO consultants and digital marketing pros blog to keep readers updated and engaged. SEOmoz.org/blog is a go-to spot for the latest in SEO news, trends, tips, and tricks: "SEOmoz develops SEO software, provides a robust link intelligence API, and hosts the web's most vibrant SEO community."

This is a great place for SEO beginners to learn the basics with SEOmoz.com's extensive how-to guide for SEO.

SEOmoz.com says they have, "the Internet's most vibrant SEO community with over 250,000 members willing to discuss and share the latest news about what works and what doesn't."

Who are we to doubt them?

SEO/SEM—Andrew Miller, CEO Your Search Advisor

Andrew Miller is a Search Engine Marketing Consultant in Richmond, VA and blogger at CallTrackingBlog.com. In his free time, well, he has a newborn son so there's no such thing anymore.

Search Rankings Don't Matter (and other SEO metrics)
http://www.yoursearchadvisor.com/blog/rankings-dont-matter/

Adding Phone Call Tracking to the Conversion Optimization Mix
http://unbounce.com/conversion-rate-optimization/phone-call-tracking/

You've Optimized Your Site: Now What?
http://www.yoursearchadvisor.com/blog/optimized-site-now-what/

PPC in 5 Years: An Intractable Problem
http://www.yoursearchadvisor.com/blog/ppc-in-5-years/

How Much Traffic Will I Get From SEO?
http://www.yoursearchadvisor.com/blog/seo-traffic-estimates/

CHAPTER 12

Social Bookmarking: What's That? And Who Cares?

There are more than 15 billion web pages, so how do we save the web pages we like? That's the question Seattle Internet wizard Lee LeFever at common-craft.com answers in this tutorial. Shut off your iTunes now, and you'll learn more about social bookmarking in three minutes than we could tell you in an hour.

Lee explains, better than we ever could, what social bookmarking is, why it's social, and how to use the free public tools at Del.icio.us to save your favorite sites, index them according to purpose, or whatever, and classify the indexed sites so you can retrieve them with ease. http://www.commoncraft. com/bookmarking-plain-english

In their own words: "Delicious is a social bookmarking service that allows you to tag, save, manage and share Web pages all in one place. With emphasis on the power of the community, Delicious greatly improves how people discover, remember and share on the Internet." http://www. delicious.com/help/getStarted

Besides being an excellent tutorial, this saves us a great deal of time by showing how a steady stream of interesting and useful websites is available, right now, for your disposal. That's what makes this bookmarking process "social" and a thousand—perhaps a million—times more robust than the bookmarking tool embedded in your computer.

CommonCraft.com's slideshow video production, "Social Bookmarking in Plain English" is available in five languages. So, you can begin right now taking control of your Internet choices and organize your website through one of the free social bookmarking services.

Understanding the Basics

Social Bookmarking Resource 12-1:
Can Social Bookmarking Help Me?

http://www.facebooksniper.com/social-marketing-can-social-bookmarking-help-me.html

Here's another rather simple, but clear, explanation of social bookmarking:

> It's a public list of your favorites [websites, that is]. Not all of your favorites, just the favorites you want to share with others. . . . When you list a site in your bookmark list, anyone looking for that same type information can do a search at the bookmark site and find the sites you have bookmarked. It's like a search engine without all the trash.

Here's another oft-overlooked perhaps, but certainly not to be underestimated, attribute of social bookmarking:

> The more people who mark a site, the more popular it becomes. . . . It's kind of like a voting system. If your site is good enough to bookmark, other people will want to see what all the fuss is about.

Social Bookmarking Resource 12-2: 125 Social Bookmarking Sites: The Importance of User-Generated Tags, Votes, and Links

http://www.searchenginejournal.com/125-social-bookmarking-sites-importance-of-user-generated-tags-votes-and-links/6066/

Social bookmarking is a great tool, and, as Facebooksniper.com (above) points out, it can even help search engine ranking.

Loren Baker is the Editor in Chief of *Search Engine Journal* and has been involved in SEO for more than a decade.

In this post, Baker uses Del.icio.us, StumbleUpon and Ma.gnolia—three social bookmarking services—as examples to show how search engines use bookmarking services to aid them in finding relevant information for you. The list includes faster and deeper indexing of sites, as well as providing an initial measure of quality.

Baker put together a list of 125 popular and, in some cases, unknown social bookmarking sites to "help share the wealth of social bookmarking."

Social Bookmarking Resource 12-3: Learn Search Engine Optimization Tips: How Social Bookmarking Works

http://portaltechnologiespark-learnseo.blogspot.com/2010/01/how-social-bookmarking-works.html

All the bases—who, what, when, where, how, and why of social bookmarking—seem to be covered in this article.

The blog post on PortalTechnologiesPark-LearnSEO.Blogspot.com is designed to help you understand how social bookmarking works. "Not many exactly know what this process is, how it works, or what its intended purpose is. In fact, you may be doing social bookmarking on the Internet without knowing that you are actually using it."

Tools, Tips, Tactics, and Tricks of the Trade

Social Bookmarking Resource 12-4: How to Use Delicious: The King of Social Bookmarking

http://www.socialmediaexaminer.com/how-to-use-delicious-social-bookmarking/3?doing_wp_cron

We're not pushing any particular brand of anything, let alone free social bookmarking services, but if a prestigious outlet like *Social Media Examiner* describes your service as "The King of Social Bookmarking," as it did Delicious in a recent post by Internet marketing specialist Kristi Hines, you simply have to give it a little extra attention.

Hines describes Delicious as giving you the capacity to, kind of, create your own personal Google "push" service.

"It's hard to read every great blog post that's shared with you through other social networks such as Twitter and Facebook. Why not bookmark them for later so whenever you're looking for information on a particular topic, you have a great compilation of favorite articles and pages to choose from?"

Besides organizing your resources, Hines lists creating action plans (with action tags) sharing important links company wide, and backlink recording. "With Delicious, you can simply bookmark a page you requested a link from and tag it by topic, quality or type for future reference. So if you're making a comment on an .edu blog about pets, your tag would be edu pets blogcomment, and the next time you need to look for one of those three elements for another link, they would be right in your Delicious bookmarks," Hines says.

Social Bookmarking Resource 12-5:
How to Use StumbleUpon: Your Comprehensive Guide
http://www.socialmediaexaminer.com/stumbleupon-guide/?doing_wp_cron

Just to prove its objectivity, perhaps, or to feature a service with a slightly different twist, Kristi Hines also wrote about StumbleUpon. Stumble Upon is famous—or notorious if you can't tolerate any more distractions—for keeping Internet users entertained for hours as they randomly browse web pages and share content with friends and comment on what they are viewing.

"StumbleUpon is a social bookmarking and rating site," where people who literally 'stumble upon' cool web pages can "write review and share their discoveries with their followers. The network is like Delicious," Hines says, "but with a more enhanced social platform and sharing system."

Hines created a comprehensive guide to prevent you from having to 'stumble' through StumbleUpon. So why do you care?

"StumbleUpon can be a great site to organize your favorite bookmarks, although it isn't quite as advanced as Delicious in organization." But, Hines says that as a user you "can easily save items by giving them the thumbs-up using the 'I like it' buttons on the StumbleUpon toolbars for Firefox or Chrome."

The SocialMediaExaminer.com StumbleUpon guide directs you through different processes on the social bookmarking website. Hines's post will help you find friends, share items, join groups, set preferences and learn proper sharing etiquette.

Social Bookmarking Resource 12-6:
How to Get Traffic from Social Bookmarking Sites
http://www.webconfs.com/get-traffic-from-social-bookmarking-sites-article-22.php

Want to really make it big on the web? In one way, we wish there was a single definite way to make this happen. But then, if there were one best way, what would you need this book for?

We can tell you this right off. Simply because something is referred to as the result of organic, rather than paid, search marketing, does not mean it just "comes naturally." In fact, the real truth is quite the contrary.

This WebConfs.com post gives you 20 steps you can take to increase the likelihood that you'll generate traffic from the social bookmarking sites, and this ability will make it easier for dig.com, reddit.com or stumbleupon.com to bring traffic to your website.

"How about getting 20,000 or more visitors a day when your listing hits the front page?"

So, what's the catch to increasing traffic to your website by this much?

WebConfs.com explains that, "getting to the front page of these sites is not as difficult as it seems"—once you are committed to the concept, that is.

Social Bookmarking Resource 12-7:
3 Ways to Expand Your Blog through Social Bookmarks

http://bestbloggingtipsonline.com/social-bookmarking-blogs/

"Are you simply using the standard sharing options—Twitter, Facebook, etc.—or are you thinking of ways you can be a little creative when it comes to sharing your blog socially?" asks Danny Brown.

Brown is co-founder and partner at Bonsai Interactive Marketing, advertised as offering integrated marketing, social media, and digital and mobile marketing solutions and applications.

Brown's blogs have been featured on AdAge Power 150 list. But that didn't happen by accident as his post on BestBloggingTipsOnline.com demonstrates with suggestions to create social-sharing groups with online friends and how to promote your own content. Brown says:

> The most oft-used method of sharing a blog post is via social sharing buttons on the post itself.
>
> These are either located at the top and/or bottom of the post, or to the side. I use a mix of both Digg.com to offer the floating share bar to the left of this post, and ShareThis.com at the bottom.
>
> But why not take this a little further, and create a social sharing group?

Social Bookmarking Resource 12-8: Social Bookmarking & Tagging:
About Social Bookmarking

http://blogs.fredericksburg.com/ackermann/2011/06/13/thing-13-social-bookmarking-tagging/

Here's another demonstration of how organizing websites is easier through the process of tagging on a social bookmarking site.

The blog post on Fredericksburg.com from explains that social bookmarking is a great way to collect a set of resources and share them with others. (By the way, they also link to the earlier Common Craft bookmarking tutorial we showed you earlier.)

This post describes how tagging puts articles into categories based on what is called "user generated categorization," and it emphasizes the importance of user-generated categorization to social bookmarking.

This post demonstrates how to properly tag posts, and it will also drive your spellchecker crazy as you email your friends about the power of "spriptlets" and "bookmarklets."

Social Bookmarking Resource 12-9: Top Social Bookmarking Wordpress Plugins

http://www.hongkiat.com/blog/top-social-bookmarking-wordpress-plugins/

Using Wordpress for blogging is relatively inexpensive. But a great many people are blogging, and there is a ton of content. So the competition for "eyes" is getting more intense by the minute.

Siva Kumar, a Web designer and blogger explains this web market fact. "Today, without a good amount of social marketing effort, chances are people will not come across your website because you are basically free from acknowledgment."

In the Hongkiat.com post Kumar says, "Not everyone is a social media genius, but there are definitely tips and tricks to utilize social marketing tool on your website and blog to increase attention for your articles." Kumar suggests using Wordpress Plugins.

The post examines a variety of different Wordpress plugins to help with social bookmarking for your blog.

Social Bookmarking Resource 12-10: Social Bookmarking for Pictures on VisualizeUs

http://vi.sualize.us/

Everyone's invited to this social bookmarking website.

See something you like and easily bookmark it. Super simple design, vi.sualize.us is Firefox's extension tool that makes bookmarking as easy as right clicking or using a browser button. At least, that's how they put it.

We have to disclose right here and right now, however, that most of these "easy tools" take a certain amount of concentrated effort to install and use. Don't think that just because it's not as easy as the promotional material suggests that there's something wrong with you. But having said that, it's clear vi.sualize.us can help give important marketing exposure to an artist or author.

Here's the deal: Vi.sualize.us allows you to view feeds and even embed a badge onto your own website to make bookmarking for others increasingly simple. You can share detailed images with a simple click, increasing potential viewership and traffic, or simply showing off your own talents, inspiring photographers, artists and photographers—and possibly creating some copycats. Forewarned is forearmed.

Extra Points—Social Bookmarking for Business

Social Bookmarking Resource 12-11: Best Social Bookmarking Websites for Businesses

http://www.helium.com/items/1965584-best-social-bookmarking-websites-for-businesses

Says Murray Lunn in Helium.com:

> Social bookmarking is not only a tool to help others find content on the web without having to hunt it down; it can be a powerful way for business owners to build backlinks and traffic to their websites.
>   Using social bookmarking sites not only help you gain backlinks but it can be a powerful way to send waves of traffic if you reach enough influence.

And ultimately, he says, this will help your business to be more successful.

Lunn says social bookmarking sites allow businesses to make a profile, share their own content, share other content, and build friends within the community.

His favorites for business include: Digg.com; Reddit.com; Delicious; Yahoo Buzz; StumbleUpon; Mixx ("Mixx doesn't get a lot of light, but it's still a great site to submit your content, engage the community and send visitors your way); Slashdot and Newsvine.

Perfect Practice Makes Perfect

Six tasks that will help you understand the concepts and ideas talked about in Part VI.

1. Try out the Google AdWords Tool. Load it up with keywords related to your business and see what you can learn. What are the most competitive keywords? What do you have the best chance of ranking for? Test different keyword phrases, short tail vs. long tail and see what you come up with. The AdWords Tool is a free way to determine search traffic and figure out what keywords you should target for your SEO and SEM efforts.

2. Write a search engine optimized paragraph (minimum 75 words). Body content for a web page. You can never get enough practice because each one is different. Choose 2 short-tail phrases (1–3 word) and 3 long-tail phrases (more than 3 words). The most important thing to remember is that you're writing for humans AND search engines. You need to get your

key phrases as close to the front or top of the content as possible, while making the sentences flow well for the people reading it.

3. Write four search engine-optimized H1 Tags or Title Tags (maximum 70 characters). This is the text you see at the top of your browser window, above the URL. Every page of a web site has its own H1 Tag, so try to optimize each one for a different 1 or 2 key phrases. You want to lead with the most important targeted keywords up front; these should not be complete sentences. See: http://www.seomoz.org/learn-seo/title-tag

4. Write two meta descriptions (about 150 to 160 characters). A Meta Description is a short summary of what an individual web page is about. Search engines use these to determine what that page is about, and often display them in search results. While you do want to use key phrases, again, these are more advertising messages to users. You're trying to draw them in and convince them your page has what they want. See: http://www.seomoz.org/learn-seo/meta-description

5. Take your original search engine optimized paragraph from #1 above, and apply internal linking for SEO purposes. Find your five key phrases (the short-tail and long-tail), link each of the key phrases to another page within the same web site. Every page of your web site should use keyword links to point to other pages within your same web site. This is the making of a good internal link structure.

6. Join some social bookmarking sites. Try at least Delicious, DIGG and Stumbleupon. Then try surfing around on them. Save some articles and give others a thumb's up for vote or comment. See how this works. You will be amazed at how sites like Stumbleupon can drive traffic to your websites. In fact we find that Stumble is a main traffic driver to sites after social media sites like Facebook, Linkedin, and Twitter. Make Social Bookmarking part of your SEO and traffic driving efforts and you could reap the rewards.

Part VII

ACCESSORIZING SOCIAL MEDIA: DESIGN AND ACTION

CHAPTER 13

Basics of Good Web Design

Web Design Resource 13-1: Blog Tutorial

http://www.photoshopsupport.com/tutorials/jennifer/blog-templates.html

Generic-looking blogs are boring. This is a great tutorial by Jennifer Apple that can help you become a better blog designer. This blog tutorial from PhotoShopSupport.com has tips and suggestions to personalize your blog.

Jennifer Apple says: "To be noticed your blog needs to make a splash—as there are more than ten million blogs out there. . . . So what we'll concentrate on here is working with some design elements that can help you add more zing to your blog."

Web Design Resource 13-2: 5 Website Designs That Blew Us Away (Mashable Awards)

http://mashable.com/2010/10/31/breakthrough-website-design/

What does great Web design look like? Mashable.com has reviewed many Websites and writer Jolie O'Dell posted an article highlighting what Mashable thought were five of the best Web designs.

"What we're after is a truly elegant and functional design, and those things are just the icing on the cake," says O'Dell.

Viewing other designs can be inspirational. These websites are using the latest and greatest Web technologies and website building tools and creating intelligent and functional designs.

Tips, Techniques, Tactics and Tricks of the Trade

Web Design Resource 13-3: 40+ Web Design and Development Resources for Beginners

http://mashable.com/2010/07/23/web-design-resources-beginners/

Web designers need to know their stuff. And there are so many tools available and unlimited design possibilities, it could make your head spin.

Brian Casel, Web designer and owner of ThemeJam WordPress Themes and CasJam Media, created this list of basic web design resources for beginners and posted it on Mashable.com:

> We aim to give you an overview of a few (design resources) that are essential to a well-rounded knowledge of web design. These are starting-points, if you will. Below each item, we've listed additional resources for you to continue on in your learning process.

An overview of HTML, CSS, Photoshop, Fireworks, content management systems are just a few topics covered. Every topic is supplemented with links to web design tutorials and great resources.

You can, for example, learn the differences between various content management systems like Drupal, Wordpress and Expression Engine.

Web designing takes many years to perfect, but learning these tools early is a great start to understanding what's behind professional work.

Web Design Resource 13-4: Free CSS Templates

http://www.freecsstemplates.org/

This resource provides an assortment of free CSS templates that are available for download from FreeCSSTemplates.org. You can upload these templates onto your blog to create a different look and get you started web designing.

Web Design Resource 13-5: You Work For Them

http://www.youworkforthem.com/

Use this resource to download graphic designs, fonts, and stock art from the same company that supplies U2, BMW, and Apple with their design needs. YouWorkForThem.com sells creative designs to help you build a website like a pro.

Michael Paul Young, creative director and founder of YouWorkForThem.com created his enterprise, in part, to provide affordable and creative designs for Web designers:

> YouWorkForThem understands that a great brand needs investment and care in order to retain its greatness. For us, that means investing and caring about design and designers. We live and love and breathe design, and we will continue to offer only the best resources available anywhere.

Web Design Resource 13-6: Just Creative Design

http://justcreativedesign.com/

You can get creative with graphic designer Jacob Cass. Cass is the founder of JustCreativeDesign.com and his blog is a great resource. Cass discusses different aspects of web design and can help you design a blog.

"The blog focuses on all areas of design and creativity ranging from but not limited to graphic design, logo design, web design, advertising, branding, typography, designers, blogging, resources, my work, photography, color, marketing, social media, user experience and more," says Cass.

Web Design Resource 13-7:
10 Essential Design Tools for Social Media Pros
http://mashable.com/2010/03/23/social-media-design-tools/

This Mashable.com post promises that you can look like a social media pro even if you are not a professional. Associate Features Editor Matt Silverman posted the article that reviews different tools you can use to enhance the look of your web site.

If you aren't a digital artist but still want to perfect your web design skills here are programs with web designs to help you pull your website together. Silverman offers you suggestions from industry professionals.

"We've talked to the experts about what they use for inspiration, collaboration, and getting down to the business of design in a social media world," says Silverman.

Photo editing tools are very expensive, and the article suggests a few alternatives to standard photo editing software to really make your photos pop.

Web Design Resource 13-8: How to Create Custom Backgrounds for Twitter, YouTube, and Myspace
http://mashable.com/2010/01/14/custom-twitter-youtube-myspace-backgrounds/

In yet one more Mashable.com piece, Matt Silverman vows to ban bland and uninteresting predesigned web layouts on social media networks.

Tiresome blue–and–white backgrounds and repeated color schemes make up the majority of web layouts. Silverman's post is designed to show you how to customize and personalize Web space.

"You need a custom design to make your profile stand apart from the rest and convey important information about who you are," says Silverman.

Changing the background for a social media network is a great way to stand out from millions of other profiles while helping to brand yourself or business. Silverman's post provides resources for photo editing and customization for the web.

Web Design Resource 13-9: Web Design Tips & Advice from A to Z
http://justcreativedesign.com/2011/03/01/web-design-tips-advice-from-a-to-z/

We all know our ABCs, but do you know the ABCs of design? Natalie Schnotz posted a great rulebook for Web design practices on JustCreative Design.com.

Web Design Resource 13-10: The Most Powerful Colors in the World

http://www.colourlovers.com/business/blog/2010/09/15/the-most-powerful-colors-in-the-world

Beautiful bright reds and cool blues illuminate the most popular brand names on the web. The article, in the form of a beautiful infographic from ColourLovers.com breaks down the color spectrum of web brands.

"While the initial reasoning for the colors chosen may be trivial, the impact that these dominant players now have in the web world will surely influence the smaller startups that want to share in the positive color associations created by their bigger siblings," says ColourLovers.com

A rainbow of brand icons communicates the colors that dominate the web.

The article also displays the top 100 web brands ranking with the color of each brand to express what colors are ranked higher and show a larger part of the market share. You'll find this resource pleasing to the eye and a great reference when creating the web image of a brand.

Web Design Resource 13-11: Top 10 Web Design Tips to Improve Conversions

http://www.goodbusinessnews.com/2010/10/top-10-web-design-tips-to-improve-conversions/

Some may say that if you're not on the web you're dead, especially in business. Now, having a website for your business isn't always good enough. There are many other factors that play into this.

"The website's design and search engine optimization plays a critical role in shaping its success," according to this GoodBusinessNews.com article.

"Great website design incorporates effective keyword rich content, an

attractive layout that reflects the business image, engaging colors, and straightforward navigability."

The Good Business News post describes how good design will improve your conversions while providing tips to do so.

Resources for Design Professionals

Web Design Resource 13-12: 10 Principles of Effective Web Design
http://www.slideshare.net/sirferds/10-principles-of-effective-web-design-presentation

This Slideshare presentation lays out many of the most important principles for effective web design. What's even more interesting to us is that it is linked to the Lynda.com inventory of web design tutorials.

If you have never before appreciated the skill-level required of an effective designer, just take a look at their "body of knowledge" as represented in these Lynda.com tutorials.

Web Design Resource 13-13: W3Schools Online Web Tutorials
http://www.w3schools.com/

If you need a quick reference for HTML, HTML5, XHTML, CSS, and other codes then you'll find w3schools.com the perfect resource.

If you're looking for a more extensive education on any of these subjects or scripting, web services and web building, then w3Schools.com is also the perfect resource.

This website allows you to view tutorials, take classes or even type your own code and view the result, which you can then copy and paste into your own website.

The home page states, "w3schools.com offer an online certification program, where you can become certified in the most popular web topics."

Web Design Resource 13-14: 50 Useful Tools and Resources for Web Designers
http://www.smashingmagazine.com/2010/07/26/50-useful-tools-and-resources-for-web-designers/

Designing for the web is tedious time-consuming work. Taking a shortcut here and there is an acceptable way to save time that could be used for more creative and specialized areas of web design.

Vitaly Friedman, editor-in-chief of *Smashing* Magazine, an online magazine dedicated to designers and developers posted a list of useful tools and resource to help web designers.

Friedman posts this list of his 50 favorite tools and time-savers for web designers and developers. Friedman's typography design tips and resources are great for creating typography and viewing type in an HTML format. Links to CSS, HTML and JavaScript generators are also timesaving alternatives to typing mundane codes. Application development tools and interesting programs and apps are also included in the article.

Web Design Resource 13-15: 25 Tools to Improve Your Website's Usability
http://www.hongkiat.com/blog/tools-to-improve-your-websites-usability/

What is the most important web design factor? While there may not be one clear-cut answer, usability is definitely one of the most important.

Siva Kumar, a web designer and photographer, posted his favorite on tools improving website usability on Hongkiat.com.

Kumar's tools aren't for everyone but you will definitely find something to suit you:

> Here are some of the best tools (web services) that track user's actions in various methods, and the output (end result) will deliver you the information you'll need to improve your website's usability. Some of them may not be free but there is always a price to pay for a good return. Have fun hunting for the right tool you need!

Web Design Resource 13–16: Building a Coming Soon Site with Builder
http://webdesign.com/building-a-coming-soon-site-with-builder/

This is a webinar narrated by WebDesign.com professor Benjamin Bradley that will guide you through the important process of building a coming soon website.

Bradley teaches you how to write and create different short codes that will provide a pie chart and/or timer to help viewers understand when the website will be ready.

This webinar takes you through an entire example of building a coming soon site for a Wordpress web page. By the end you will understand how to use different short codes to create a "coming soon" design.

Extra Point—Staying Ahead of the Game

Web Design Resource 13-17: Top Web Design News
http://web-design.alltop.com/

Web-Design.AllTop.com is an awesome resource for all things web design.

News feeds and blog posts are organized on the website's homepage to help you find what is new and trending in the world of web design.

Web Design Resource 13-18: Essential Web Design Advice from a Wire-framing Master
http://mashable.com/2010/11/12/travis-isaacs-web-design/

Web is everywhere, from our phones, to tablets, television and the computer. There is no escaping it. So how do you get the maximum effect of great design?

Mashable.com blogger Christina Warren tackles this subject when interviewing Travis Issacs, who is an experienced designer and creator of Keynote Kung-Fu: "I specialize in bridging the gap between visual and interaction design, information architecture and web development."

Issacs is an awesome resource when it comes to web design's integration across platforms. In this interview you'll learn about Issacs's design process and how he uses keynote to design web sites and applications.

Web Design Resource 13-19: Web Design Mistakes
http://www.youtube.com/watch?v=vPO7lDZbcfA

The margin for error in web design is quite precise and the specific guidelines for specific web sites are as different as the businesses for which they are created.

Watch and listen as the author of E-Consultancy's Best Practice Guides, Dr. Dave Chaffey, describes what to do and what not to do in YouTube video.

Dr. Chaffey attempts, in just less than four minutes, to define the basic rules of web designing, such as creating flexible design that can change quickly with fast-paced technology advancements.

Web Design Resource 13-20: When Web Design Goes Too Far
http://designreviver.com/articles/when-web-design-goes-too-far/

Learning from our mistakes is often the only way to understand the difference between the right and wrong way to do things. Why not learn from other people's mistakes and avoid the pitfalls of bad design all together?

Design Reviewer.com asks "What are the parameters for an artist or web design creator on knowing when to step on the brakes with their design?"

This post identifies what to avoid—like how too much imagery and information is a sure way to make viewers hate your website.

Web Design Resource 13-21: The Top 15 Google Products for People Who Build Websites
http://sixrevisions.com/tools/the-top-15-google-products-for-people-who-build-websites/

It shouldn't come as news to anyone that Google is a great place to search for information to meet your Web design needs. But did you know that Google has many products to help you build a website?

Jacob Gube, Founder and Chief Editor of Six Revision, is a web developer/designer who specializes in front-end development (JavaScript, HTML, CSS) and PHP development, and a book author. He posted this article on SixRevisions.com providing an overview of his 15 favorite website-building products from Google:

> Google's strategy of empowering site developers and owners with free and valuable tools has proven to be effective in garnering a fair bit of geek love for the company.
>   They really do make excellent products that can be instrumental in building, maintaining, and improving websites.

Web Design Resource 13-22: 20 Motivating Design Outlets for Graphic Designers

http://www.graphicdesignblog.org/graphic-design-quotes/

It's time to ignite your senses, get inspired and spark your next creative design. Maybe you're in need some motivation? This blog post may just give it to you.

GraphicDesignBlog.com compiled 20 design quotes, depicted in creative ways, to help inspire your next graphic design:

> This is the magnificence of inspirational quotes, providing us stimulation and motivation to achieve what others have accomplished. It supports our reasoning and gives us an encouragement to do what we believe in.

We could not agree more.

Web Design Resources 13-23: Avoid the 7 Deadly Web Design Sins

http://www.businessinsider.com/7-deadly-web-design-sins-2010-11#putting-your-brilliant-design-first-1

Here's a list of things to avoid when creating a website.

The article posted in BusinessInsider.com advocates "putting your brilliant design first." And it practices what it preaches with a brilliantly designed overview that proves, again, the old adage that a picture (in this case seven pictures) is worth a thousand words.

Web Design: Ross Johnson's Favorite Web Design Blog Posts

Ross Johnson, CEO of 3.7 DESIGNS, lives and breaths web design. Beyond running the agency, he is a published author, teacher, blogger and speaker.

Johnson built his first commercial website in 1996, discovering the web blended his lifelong passions: fine arts and technology. Johnson founded 3.7 DESIGNS in 2005, after studying business, sociology and anthropology. While in college Johnson says he discovered that "contrary to popular belief, design was more science than art." This belief is the foundation for his book *The Six Layers* (of design), which explores design as cognitive science.

Johnson tweets @3pointRoss and blogs on both StylizedWeb.com and 3.7Designs.co/blog.

Johnson provides *The New Media Driver's License Resource Guide* with four of his favorite posts:

Designers are Scientists, Not Artists
http://3.7designs.co/blog/2011/08/designers-are-scientists-not-artists/

How to Design Using the Fibonacci Sequence
http://3.7designs.co/blog/2010/10/how-to-design-using-the-fibonacci-sequence/

Ten Laws to Design By
http://3.7designs.co/blog/2010/07/ten-laws-to-design-by/

The Web Design Process is All Wrong
http://3.7designs.co/blog/2011/01/the-web-design-process-is-all-wrong/

A Special Perfect Practice Makes Perfect for Web Design

Five tasks that will help you understand the concepts and ideas talked about in Chapter 13

1. Learn the basics of HTML and how it describes the content on the page:
   http://www.w3schools.com/html/default.asp (all chapters)
   http://www.webdesignfromscratch.com/html-css/semantic-html/

2. Learn the basics of CSS (Cascading Style Sheets) and how they dictate how a website looks.
   http://www.w3schools.com/css/default.asp
   http://www.cssbasics.com/

3. Learn about your user and create personas.
   http://boagworld.com/usability/an-experience-with-site-personas/
   http://doteduguru.com/id6515-creating-effective-user-personas.html

4. Define the site's business objectives and key performance indicators.
   http://www.viget.com/advance/user-centric-design-is-about-users-and-clients/
   http://cojent7.wordpress.com/2010/04/24/how-to-set-business-goals-and-objectives-101-best-practices-for-your-small-business/
   http://24ways.org/2009/what-makes-a-website-successful

5. Create a sitemap and wireframes for your website.
   http://www.viget.com/advance/ux-101-the-site-map/
   http://www.viget.com/advance/ux-101-the-wireframe1/

CHAPTER 14

You-Tubing in the Streams of Consciousness

These days more people are watching YouTube videos than watching TV. Online video has broken into our living rooms with live streaming on TV's. Videos are being archived and shown in the natural search results. And YouTube is the second largest search engine, right behind Google.

So what's the lesson in all this?

You need to understand online video and how to use it to market yourself and your business. YouTube and Vimeo are two of the leading platforms for online video but they aren't the only ones available. Quite the opposite: the competition is considerable and growing. There are many possibilities.

The website TopTenReviews.com compared and contrasted the top ten video sharing websites and listed the advantages and disadvantages of each. This could give you the basis for "comparison shopping."

Understanding the Basics

Online Video Resource 14-1: History of Online Videos: The Last 5 Years . . .

http://visuallounge.techsmith.com/2010/11/online_video_history_-_the_las.html

You'll find this infographic an interesting review of online video history. Betsy Weber, writer for Techsmith.com, posted an article about this interesting visual of web video.

Weber said her team "worked with The Blog Herald to create an infographic showing the history of online video over the last 5 years. It's awesome to see the data the Blog Herald analyzed, shown visually."

The infographic begins around 2005 when we see the first evidence of web video's Internet prominence. View demographic differences, usage percentages and more.

Online Video Resource 14-2: YouTube Handbook

http://www.youtube.com/t/yt_handbook_home

Here's a simple guide to YouTube basics that will help you view, share, and interact with other YouTube users online.

The handbook from YouTube.com instructs users on the best practices for watching videos, finding, sharing and saving YouTube favorites: "This area of the site is all about helping you to use and enjoy all of YouTube's features, no matter what your level of interest is."

YouTube video production tips and techniques are also part of the handbook.

Online Video Resource 14-3: Vimeo Video Sharing: History and Overview

http://www.reelseo.com/vimeo-video-sharing-history-overview/

Vimeo is another great video hosting service similar to YouTube.

Mark Robertson, founder and publisher of ReelSEO.com posted an article on his website laying out the history of Vimeo.

Robertson describes what he sees as the major differences between YouTube and Vimeo. He describes the types of content Vimeo generally hosts and accepts, and he provides an overview of Vimeo registration and user-video privacy controls.

A Vimeo user video describes the types of videos generally uploaded onto the website, and can help you determine what major video hosting site will be the most beneficial for your own goals.

Online Video Resource 14-4: YouTube, Vimeo or Both?

http://www.edsocialmedia.com/2009/02/youtube-vimeo-or-both/

Using video for Internet marketing can be a very smart idea. There's no doubt about it. But, which way do you go: Vimeo or YouTube?

Peter Baron posted in EdSocialMedia.com as a way to "generate conversation about using video in your social media outreach." And he compares YouTube and Vimeo.

Baron's post displays two different videos—one posted on YouTube and the other on Vimeo—to show the difference in quality of the two web hosting sites.

Online Video Resource 14-5: YouTube Partners Meet in New York City (June 15, 2011)

http://www.youtube.com/user/YouTube - p/u/6/do6piTEkcxc

Members of the YouTube Partnership packed up their bags and headed to New York City to discuss business opportunities, how to generate business and suggestions to increase subscription and attract viewers.

This video from YouTube's own channel is a great resource for creative folks who want to use YouTube successfully. It describes how YouTube partners create content.

If you want valuable information about video editing software, collaboration and editing from YouTube professionals, this video can help your content become successful.

Tips, Tools, Tactics and Tricks of the Trade

Online Video Resource 14-6: Help Center/Vimeo Basics
http://vimeo.com/help/basics

Here's another resource to teach you the basics of Vimeo. It's designed to provide a lot of helpful resources to start you off on the right online video foot.

"Simply put, Vimeo is the home for videos you create. We offer the best tools and the highest quality video in the Universe." What would you expect them to say, you say? Well, here's a good way to hear their case.

This comprehensive site will show you how to upload, share and connect with others. It provides links to other helpful tools like Vimeo Video School where you can learn different video production tools to help you produce and edit better videos.

Online Video Resource 14-7: How to Engage the YouTube Community for Audience Growth
http://www.reelseo.com/embrace-youtube-community/

YouTube users expecting an easy path to becoming the next YouTube superstar are in for a big surprise. Going viral on YouTube is possible, but it requires a lot of hard work, and a certain amount of luck.

Founder and publisher of RealSEO.com Mark Robertson said: "Content creators need to get out there and engage the public."

"If you build it they will come is not a valid video marketing strategy." Robertson says.

This Mashable.com article provides wannabe YouTube stars and online marketers important tips to increase YouTube viewership through audience engagement.

Online Video Resource 14-8: All You Need to Know about YouTube's Promoted Videos
http://website101.com/video/youtube-promoted-videos/

Making a popular YouTube video is part inspiration, and mostly perspiration. But as the worst examples of online video prove without a doubt, there's also an element of skill required for good online video production. Some basic business sense is also very important to getting the exposure your video needs.

Website101.com blogger Merle makes the case that there are some tried and true methods to successfully promoting videos using YouTube's site features.

"The purpose of 'Promoted Videos' is to help your videos stand out from the millions of others on the site," says Merle.

Merle shows you how to promote YouTube videos and enhance your online marketing campaign. His article walks you through the entire video promotion process to drive traffic to your video.

YouTube Resource 14-9: Top 10 YouTube Tips for Small Businesses
http://mashable.com/2010/04/23/youtube-small-business/

The little guys can now get in on the big action in business. YouTube is a great way for a small business to get big business.

A Mashable.com staff writer, Amy-Mae Elliott, posted an article to help small businesses use YouTube. This resource will teach you how to leverage a small business to success on the video-sharing platform.

"Rather than video production hints or content tips (there are tons of other resources that can help you on that front) here are the dos and don'ts of using YouTube from a behind-the-scenes perspective," says Elliott.

Everything from creating and customizing your business's YouTube channel to promoting videos is covered in this article. Different video production techniques are examined to help your small business create quality videos.

Learn how to track YouTube analytics to manage content and continue to create web videos that customers are watching and enjoying and will help make your small business, or any business, shine.

Online Video Resource 14-10:
How To Make YouTube Videos Look Great
http://www.squidoo.com/youtuberight

Squiddo.com blogger, Chinetech, wants to help you do a makeover to your YouTube videos:"The key for YouTube to display your video the best possible way is to upload the best possible quality video that meets or exceeds their requirements."

Chinetech offers tips on how to take low-quality videos and turn them into red-carpet-ready Internet videos.

It may be true that it doesn't help to put lipstick on a pig, but ugly YouTube videos are usually uploaded directly without any real preparation. This resource can help you understand how to encode, compress and optimize YouTube videos to produce higher-quality, if not beautiful, videos.

Chinetech describes tools to match nearly any skill level of a YouTube video producer and makeover your video channel.

Online Video Resource 14-11: 5 Tips for Successful and Professional Online Video Projects

http://www.reelseo.com/5-tips-successful-professional-online-video-projects/

Armed with a webcam, wireless connection and a YouTube account, hopeful viral "vloggers" and YouTube stars begin producing content they deem worthy of fame. Unfortunately these hopefuls don't understand that successful YouTube personalities and videos are more often than not, the result of hard work and strategic planning.

If you're interested in another perspective on how to create credible and interesting web videos, Grant Crowell's post on ReelSEO.com can help.

Crowell, a professional consultant and developer in the online-marketing space and regular ReelSEO blogger described five "Sesame Street" style tips to help you.

"If you want an easy way for people to remember a complex subject like online video, do what I call the 'Sesame Street Rule'—include a single number and letter in your presentation," says Crowell.

What he created is called, "The Five P's for successful and professional video." This resource is an easy way to help you remember what to do when creating web videos.

"I came up with these five P's from my own years of professional experience in online video project management for my own business and clients, so I can testify that each one of these P's will be essential for your own professional needs," says Crowell.

Online Video Marketing and Advertising

Online Video Resource 14-12: Guide to Video Marketing on YouTube

http://www.searchenginejournal.com/guide-to-video-marketing-on-youtube/6381/

"Keeping it real" on YouTube is an important marketing issue.

Joe Whyte wrote this post to help marketers use the video hosting website to drive sales.

Effectively marketing your YouTube video means keeping the content fresh and producing viewer engagement. Creating a YouTube channel specific to your brand and submitting videos in the right category are a couple of other pointers for marketing your video. Whyte suggests some tools and techniques to create engaging materials to gain subscribers, share content, and successfully market your video.

YouTube Resource 14-13:
Social Media Marketing with YouTube: Why?

http://www.youtube.com/watch?v=lFTHOkCj0-I

Understanding the value of YouTube may be difficult for some marketers to comprehend, and it can be even more difficult to convince a business to spend the money necessary to create a successful YouTube campaign. This video may help you or others understand why YouTube is important.

On BlastMediaPR's YouTube channel they state, "The social media team at BlastMedia has a wealth of experience creating successful YouTube marketing campaigns for our clients—from major consumer tech companies to small businesses and startups."

Social media is creeping its way into every aspect of our lives and in marketing. This video describes the reach YouTube has. The number of viewers, videos viewed a day, and the amount of content created are examined in this video. Learn the social aspects of YouTube, where content can be viewed, and how marketing on YouTube will help every other aspect of a social marketing campaign and online advertising efforts as well as engaging consumers.

Online Video Resource 14-14: YouTube Answers: Ads & Advertising

http://www.youtube.com/watch?v=jF—uLxtYlo

Hate it or love it, advertising is important for a successful business, and YouTube may be a great place to advertise your business and/or YouTube Videos.

To help users understand the different types of ads and advertising approaches used on YouTube, Rick Silvestrini answers some frequently asked questions. Silvestrini, Product Marketing Manager at YouTube, is featured in the segment YouTube Answers in the video "Ads & Advertising."

He describes what different ads formats are (for example, home page ads, promoted videos, banner ads) where they are placed (such as homepage and pre-role ads).

This video will guide you to other advertising resources for webmasters who wish to use YouTube's many advertising features.

Online Video Resource 14-15:
10 Tips for Advertisers to Go Viral on YouTube

http://www.socialtimes.com/2010/07/advertisers-viral-youtube/

To help advertisers be successful on YouTube, SocialTimes.com blogger Megan O'Neill wrote an article to help advertisers go viral on YouTube.

O'Neill says, "Advertisers need to stop thinking in the commercial mindset and start thinking about producing compelling content. An informative video that explains the benefits of your product and how it works just won't cut it anymore."

This is a great resource if you want to learn how to produce great content. O'Neill examines popular commercials from television and the web; the article explains how web videos can advertise content without making the audience think it is being "advertised to."

The Old Spice campaign, where commercials were popular offline and went viral online, is an example of thinking long-term and combining online and offline advertising efforts.

The post includes other great tips and examples of alternative forms of Internet video advertising to engage consumers help your brand go viral.

YouTube Resource 14-16: The Secrets of YouTube Marketing Revealed

http://www.socialmediaexaminer.com/the-secrets-of-youtube-marketing-revealed/

Your mom isn't just using Facebook; she may be using YouTube also. It is important that marketers recognize that a diverse group of people is using the web and social media.

A SocialMediaExaminer.com article explores how businesses can market on YouTube. "Whether you work for a high-tech company, a hardware store, or a university, you might want to learn more about using YouTube to publicize your operation," says Ruth M. Shipley.

Shipley's post explains exactly what YouTube marketing is and what businesses can do on YouTube.

"YouTube is all about video broadcasting. And videos are perfect for showing technical equipment, demonstrating a procedure or giving parents of prospective students a virtual tour of the campus," says Shipley.

You'll learn the type of reach you can expect and the market share present on YouTube that will boost marketing efforts. Different ways a business can use YouTube are suggested including introducing a new product, demonstrating a product, and publicizing news.

Extra Point—Staying Ahead of the Game

Online Video Resource 14-17: YouTube Brands: 5 Outstanding Leaders in YouTube Marketing

http://mashable.com/2009/06/01/youtube-brands/

Tutorials that help you fix a toilet, connect with education loans, and indulge in your wildest surfing dreams come from just about anywhere. YouTube marketing takes brand image to another level.

Catherine-Gail Reinhard, creative director at Videasa, reviews five companies that lead the way in YouTube marketing in this Mashable.com post.

"YouTube represents a great opportunity for marketers to reach consumers who are searching for information about a brand or related products and services."

Online Video Resource 14-18: How to Become a YouTube Sensation

http://mashable.com/2010/11/09/become-youtube-sensation/

"Chicken Sandwiches and Waffle Fries," "Hiding yo' Kids and yo' Wife," "Choosing the Right Seat on a Friday," "Charlie Biting a Finger"—believe it or not, these statements describe famous YouTube sensations.

An assistant features editor for Mashable.com, Zachary Sniderman, posted an article to help decode the alchemy that produces fame and stardom on YouTube:

> Becoming a hit on YouTube is no easy task. Actually, correction: Becoming a hit on YouTube on purpose is no easy task.
>   The popular video platform is loaded with viral videos of people doing silly or embarrassing things.

Becoming famous, even if it's on YouTube, is time consuming. Viewers are hungry for funny content they can't find on TV.

We're not sure if you can make silk purses out of sows' ears, but Sniderman's post will give you some insights into how current YouTube sensations achieved their success.

Online Video Resource 14-19: YouTube Blog

http://youtube-global.blogspot.com/

This could by your go-to website for all things YouTube.

The YouTube blog keeps you updated on YouTube news, hottest trending topics, user advice, staff video picks and more.

"Each weekday, we at YouTube Trends take a look at the most interesting videos and cultural phenomena on YouTube as they develop," says the "Official YouTube Blog."

Online Video Resource 14-20: Video Share Websites Review 2011

http://video-share-review.toptenreviews.com/

Online video sharing competition is fierce. YouTube is king, but there are many other video-sharing websites you should consider when uploading video.

The website TopTenReviews.com compared and contrasted the top ten video sharing websites.

"We've scoured the web for the very best video share websites. So after reading about the advantages and disadvantages each has, you may want to try a few sites before choosing one."

The differences between the different video sharing website audience and producer features are compared the various upload formats are reviewed and other important web video sharing topics.

If you are trying to figure out what video sharing websites are compatible with your equipment this is an awesome resource.

Post Script

The resources cited in this book can be found on the publicly-accessible websites we have identified. Going directly to these resources will help you get maximum value out of this book. We have attempted to make these resources easier for you to go to by providing our "link listing" at www. NewMediaDriversLicenseResources.com. We owe a great debt of gratitude to the various individuals and companies that have made these resources freely, available.

We also deeply appreciate the work of the Children's Trust Fund of Michigan social media maven Alan Stokes, himself a holder of a New Media Driver's License® certificate, who provided great support as a contributor to and an editor of our work.

As we said earlier, we owe a special debt of gratitude to all the students who have participated in our New Media Driver's License® Courses and Seminars at Michigan State University. Many of the students (listed below) first identified the resources we chose to include in this book.

2009 Aaron, Samantha; Abbott, Amy; Abbott, Megan; Ahern, Nicholas; Allen, Martha Oneill; Anderson, Keith; Anderson, Ryan; Anderson, Stephanie Marie; Auh, Ye Jin; Bader, Angela Dawn; Baker, Amanda; Bang, Si Hyeon; Banks, Andrew; Bator, Philip; Baylerian, Lauren; Becker, Julie Ann; Berry, Elena Janelle; Billings, Ashley Inez; Blackburn, Krystle Margaret; Bossard, Anthony Richard; Bouchard, Kyle; Boyd, Gregory Michael; Brennan, Jillian Levell; Brittain, Scott Francis; Broome, Amy Lynne; Brown, Stephen Thomas; Burke, Alexander Albert; Butler, Kevin Michael; Caban, Daniel; Calleja, Christopher; Campfield, Scott Thomas; Caples, Michael; Chaklos, William; Cheek, Katie Elizabeth; Ciani, Jonathan; Ciolek, Jacqueline Autumn; Cipparone, David; Clausen, Gregory; Coakley, Sarah; Coley, Chelsea Rae; Cottrell, Christopher; Cummings, Alexander Michael; Curran, Courtney Marie; Daniels, Khadijah; Davis, Latrice Levora; Davis, Monica Ann; Deason, Kelly; Dienes, Abbey Jo; Dixon, Lindsay Marie; Dowling, Cyle Gordon; Doyen, Maximilian; Doyle, Matthew David; Dunwoodie, William; Dziklinski, Megan Ashley; Erickson, Nathan Lee; Fabbri, Nicholas Andre; Fabris, Angela; Fadil, Bashar Farok; Fehrle, Jacqueline Grace; Feinberg, Rachel; Fineis, Monica Rae; Gaskin, John; Gatewood, Tiffany; Gerulis, Daniel; Grabowski, Brian Michael; Graham, Daniel Michael; Graham, David William; Grunewald, Bradley Randall; Gunaseelan, Divyamalthi; Hackett, Melissa Ashley; Halverson, Lauren; Hambright, Jeffrey; Han, Ji Young; Harding, Alexander William; Hardy, Brooke Lynn; Harrison, Jennifer; Hart, Monica; Haupt,

Matthew; Hebden, Katie Elizabeth; Henck, Brandon; Hendrick, Kaylee; Hickey, Jessica Lynn; Hicks, Christy Ann; Hillman, Michele Nicole; Hodges, Cassidy Lawrence; Holmes, Valerie May; Homanick, Katy Lynn; Houser Elizabeth Jean; Huston, Ken; Jackson, Seth; Jazayeri-Nejad, Jessica Aliyeh; Jeong, Jaehoon; Jin, Ju Hye; Jo, Minhee; Johnson, Emmanuel Montez-Curtis; Joy, Jacob Michael; Kafantaris, Kellie Marie; Kaidan, Katherine Leigh; Kaminski, Jaclyn; Kelly, Savannah Leigh; Kemp, Shawn Michael; Kent, Erika Lynne; Kim, Brian; Kim, Soo Hong; Kirby, Candice Lynn; Kleist, Andrew; Klosterman, Gretchen; Knazze, Carly; Kowalski, Patricia Arlene; Kraft, Ryan; Krzewinski, Mary; Leaym, Lauren Wynn; Lee, Hyegyu; Lee, Hyun Joo; Lee, Junghoon; Lee, Seoyoung; Lesley, Richard Joseph; Leung, Brian; Major, John Lynn; Makowski, Sara; Matreja, Supriya; Mattack, Bryan Gerald; Mcelroy, Janai Cherisse; Meade, Megan; Meiresonne, Jacquelyn Leigh; Meram, Marie; Michalski, Lindsey; Mills, Amy Elisabeth; Montgomery, Brian Edward; Moore, Nakeia; Murphy, Michael Joseph; Obrien, Jaclyn Lee; Oconnell, Caitlin Elizabeth; Osuji, Rainelle Idinotuchinonso; Paige, Robert Leo; Patrick, Lauren Elizabeth; Patterson, Zaneta Lynn; Peters, Angela Mae; Pinkney, Delena Lasha; Porcari, Sara Elizabeth; Poston, Natalie; Potter, LaShondra; Pranke, Amanda; Radcliffe, Dennis Floyd; Radcliffe, Kaianne Rochelle; Reincke, Nicole Alyssa; Roeder, Alexander Dale; Roth, Alicia Marie; Rutsyamuka, Mark Ronald; Santucci, Lauren E; Savage, Jade; Savage, Shawn Robert; Schiel, Stacy Marie; Schmidt, J. Max; Schneider, Erik Alexander; Scott, Lauryn Ranae; Sharps, Andrew Dustin; Sheldon, Timothy; Sibiski, Audriana Lynn; Smith, Megan Aubrey; Sojourn, Seneca; Sokoly, Alyson; Stebila, Anthony Michael; Stevens, Amber Lynn; Stokes, Alan; Stowell, Todd; Suh, Young Uk; Sumpter, Britney; Talsma, Bethany Lynn; Taylor, Ryan; Telinda, Amy Therese; Thoenes, Henry Douglas; Thomas, Simone Elise; Townsel, Kristen; Traskal, Kimberly; Tremberth, Kyle; Turek, Carly Anne; Vazquez, Jose; Victoria, Samantha Josephine; Walder, Sarah Elizabeth; Warren, Jessica; Weaver, Susan; Weger, Max; Weight, David Eugene; Weingartz, Lauren Elizabeth; White, Domonique; Williams, Chante; Wilson, Kelly; Wimbush, Kyle; Woelfel, Ryan Michael; Wright, Faris; Wysocki, Kristin Ann; York, Ami; Zamora, Natalie; Zeikus, Alexandra Grace

2010 Ahern, Kara Michelle; Aitch, Lauren Kendall; Alleyne, Darnell Tahj; Allison, Christina Lee; Alston, Jasmyne T; An, Jongwoo; Ansel, Tayler Layne; Argersinger, Adam Joseph; Arseneau, Alyssa Kaye; Bacigalupo, Lindsay Breann; Barber, Michelle Rose; Barber, Sarah Jean; Batchelor, Adam Richard; Becker, David John; Becsey, Katherine Mary; Berg, Patrick Michael; Beson, Kara Ann; Bindus, Michael Charles; Blanchard, Kevin Michael; Bodnar, Marie Elizabeth; Bonk, Richelle Renee; Bourgois, Deborah Lynn; Boydell, Erin Marie; Bradley, Caitlin Mary; Bremer, Cole James; Brzezinski, Jerome Francis; Cameron, Adrienne Gail; Campbell, Kyle Scott; Campbell, Lauren Kathryn; Caponi, Gina Marie; Cardin, Caitlin Grace; Cervo, James Anthony; Chang, Donghoon; Chen, Yu-Chen; Cheng, Jack Hsu; Cheon, Hyun Soo;

Chiarini, Dario A; Chmill, Zachary John; Cho, Tae Yuen; Churchill, Jennifer Anne; Clark, Ebony Monique; Clark, Teresa K; Contois, Adam Wayne; Cope, Breanna; Cosme-Petersen, Elaine; Crawford, Cierra Michelle; Creswell, Lindsay Catherine; Daien, Laura Gayle; Dams, Melissa Jo; Danto, Ashley Sue; Dargan, Mollie Martay; Debiasi, Danielle Victoria; Decker, Marci Rose; Diclaudio, Michael Steven; Dingersen, Katherine Rose; Dinkgrave, Ryan Michael; Doback, Caitlin Elise; Dodge, Carly Lauren; Dodson, Katrina Kay; Donerson, Erica Danielle; Doyle, Emily Lauren; Dragisity, Ann Patricia; Dudek, Martin Scott; Dueweke, Stefanie Lynne; Dukes, Courtney Chanel; Edgerly-Costigan, Cathleen Marie; Eisenstein, Emma Marian; Eizis, Alda Katrina; Elias, Nina Marie; Elrod, Katherine Lynn; Emington, Joshua David; Ennis, Ashley Christian; Ensing, Nicole Lynn; Epstein, Samantha Lynn; Esmer, Julie Kay; Eyre, Michelle Lee; Fedrigo, Kayla Kristina; Fifarek, Lauren Noel; Figlan, Lisa Marie; Finegood, Lindsey Helaine; Finkbeiner, Nicole I; Fleming, Megan Nicole; Freer, Kaitlin Marie; French, Ashley Marie; Fuelling, Valerie; Fussman, Alexandra Jean; Galbraith, Alaina Maria; Gardella, Sara Renee; Gatewood, Heather Ann; Gendernalik, Margaret Anne; Gibbons, James Michael; Gillespie, Carl Derrick; Gilliam, Sharde Brechette; Gordon, Carly Helene; Gossman, Meredith Ann; Gougeon, Laura Jin; Grant, Tatiana Desiree; Grove, James Jeffrey; Gurney, Jenna Rose; Hagerman, Lauren Anna; Hale, Katie Lynn; Hale, Lauren Miranda; Haley, Briggs James; Harding, Alexander William; Harris, Sarah Anne; Hayman, Thomas Daniel; Hendershott, Jacqueline Susanne; Hertzberg, Briana Leigh; Hicks, Kelly Nicole; Hill, Ashley Nicole; Hinsberg, Sarah Jean; Hoagland, Claire Ann; Hoang, Dat Trong; Hoffman, Jessica Lynn; Hohendorf, Austen Frahm; Hopkins, Janelle Rose; Howard, Alyssa Lynn; Hsu, Chun-Ting; Huang, Ni; Hughes, Ashley Lyn; Hung, Hsiao-Han; Isaac, Jacob I; Janus, Samantha Lynn; Jaques, Paul R; Jeong, Sun Hee; Karas, Lauren Marie; Katsarelas, Maxwell George; Kaufman, Ashley Jean; Kazanjian, Stephanie Vera; Kelly, Katherine Irene; Kemp, Jason Elias; Kerwin, Lauren Jill; Khire, Kirsten M; Kim, Dong Min; Kim, Dowan; Kim, Gu Youn; Kim, Ji Young; Kim, Ki Jung; Kim, Suhyun; Kindt, Lindsey Honora; Kirchmer, Elizabeth Ann; Kline, Evan Joseph; Kmiec, Erica Rachel; Krausman, Pamela Grace; Kuptz, Ainsley Kristine; Kurian, Jonathan J; Kussmaul, Lindsey Rae; Kustantin, Lina Marie; Kwaselow, Lindsay Michele; Laabs, Ashleigh Victoria; Langen, Chelsea M; Langley, Katherine Elizabeth; Lauhoff, Danielle Dawn; Le, (Sammy) Van-Kieu Thi; Lee, Hsin-En; Lee, Jung Yoon; Lenart, Kelly Marie; Leonard, Emily Kim; Lessens, Eric Timothy; Lester, Scott Aaron; Levison, Carly Grace; Lewis, Matthew Mark; Liang, Zi; Lin, Man; Liu, Siwen; Liu, Yi-Peng Zoe; Liu, Yining; Livesay, Guy Anthony; Lo, Tengyao; Lopatofsky, Emily Ann; Lundmark, Emily Christina; Luxon, Thomas Warren; Mach, William Christopher; Maciarz, Sandra Lynn; Maier, Katherine Marie; Maki, Emily Anne; Mancuso, Andrea Rose; Mangalick, Tina Rani; Mann, Andrew Monroe; Marble, Nicole Renee; Marshall, Brittney Patrice; Mason, Jill Marie; Mateer, Andrew Jay; Mattos, Joao Marcos; Mayfield, Jaimee Latrice; Mcconkie, Kallie Marie; Mcgregor, Morgan

Marcella; Mcnamara, Shara Joan; Meldrum, Megan Ann; Metts, Katie Nicole; Meyer, Alexandra Jean; Miller, Casey Katherine; Miller, Lindsey Corrine; Minock, Melissa Lynn; Moon, Brian Russel; Morgan, William Robert; Morrison, Madeline Coyle; Morrissey, Jeffrey James; Murninghan, Jessie Danaher; Murphy, Mike Joseph; Musial, Gennafer Claire; Nagashima, Rina; Namatevs, Alexander Bryant; Napolitano, Angela Victoria; Natale, Mary Bridget; Newell, Melissa Jane; Nguyen, Trang Ngoc; Nichols, Katelyn Marie; Niffin, Nicole Alana; Novak, Emily Ann; Novato, Adrian; Ortiz, Juliana Kay; Osborn, Andrew Alexander; Overacker, Jill Louise; Paczas, Kenneth William; Parks, Domenique A; Patterson, Ashley Nicole; Peters, Danielle Sue; Peterson, Christopher Andrew; Pitts, Nicolas Lamarr; Pointer, Evelyn Joy; Poort, Kailey Marie; Porter, Amanda Elizabeth; Pulcipher, Morgan Marie; Rademacher, Renee Ann; Recker, Eric James; Revard, Mary Beth Bridget; Rose, Tyler James; Rossi, William Stoll; Roznowski, Taylor Stanley; Rozzisi, Amber Marie; Rullo, Matthew Anthony; Sabo, John Steven; Scheier, Stacy Lynn; Schepel, Zachary James; Schloss, Matthew Barrett; Schmidt, Laura Beth; Schofding, Elizabeth Ann; Schullo, Marissa Marie; Schumann, Erica Marie; Schussman, Aprill Lillian; Schwartz, Sean Arthur; Seal, Seangho; Seidl, Emily Anne; Sendek, Mike; Shaffer, Bonnie Jean; She, Jiang; Shekell, Erica Lynn; Shin, Ah Young; Sibiski, Audrianna Lynn; Siekirk, Courtney Joy; Simms, Ashley Evelyn; Simonetti, Lauren Joy; Skubisz, Ronald James Willett; Slater, Erika Monique; Smith, Megan Aubrey; Smith, Ragina Lynay; Smith, Taylor Brittany; Son, Hyun Woo; Sorge, Jeannine; Spellicy, Kristen Lynn; Staples, Ashley Margaret; Stefanides, Brittni Lee; Stephenson, Carly Ann; Stickler, Amanda Jean; Stofflet, Stephen John; Stuard, Jennifer Leigh; Suarez, Mauricio Andres; Sun, Xiaoqing; Sung, Kee-Chan; Swope, Christy Lee; Targosz, Shawn Anthony; Terwilliger, Nathan L; Thinnes, Jill Marie; Tindall, Kathleen A; Tomburrini, Steven Daniel; Tripp, Rachel Elizabeth; Troutman, Brittney Vivian; Tschirhart, Emily Marie; Veldman, Shelby Lyn; Wang, Miao; Weinstein, Emily; Weiss, Jourdan Taylor; Wernette, Jessica Lynn; Wesson, Elizabeth Eileen; West, Courtney Allison; White, Michael Thomas; Wolff, Jennifer Joann; Woodington, Ashley Marie; Wu, Joan Qiong; Xia, Lingna; Xia, Lingzi; Xu, Qian; Xu, Saisai; Yagley, Andrew Michael; Zalewski, Shelley; Zavala, Elizabeth Lauren; Zhang, Yan; Zylstra, Rachael Lynn

2011 Abbgy, Kelsey Nicole; Abrahim, Venus; Abundis, Adriana; Adams, Kelsey; Aho, Katelind Diane; Alexander, Donjana; Antioho, Kristen Ann; Argue, Sarah; Armstrong, Lauren; Austin, Elisabeth; Avram, Nickolas Brian; Bae, Junhan; Balks, Bethany Marie; Banker, Brigette; Barden, Kiya Adrianna; Barnes, Kyle; Beltowski, Lauren; Berens, Elizabeth; Berger, Chelsea; Berkowitz, Corey; Bertrang, Shaina; Bisson, Craig; Blackman, Danielle; Blackmore, Samantha Robyn; Briolat, Evan Arthur; Brooks, Nicole; Broucek, Samantha; Budaj, Michelle; Budziszewski, Elissa Jolene; Bulgarella, Anthony; Burroughs, Jordan; Burton, Naomi; Buskirk, Lauren; Butkunas, Liana; Butterfield, Nicholas; Carpenter, Tayler; Carr, Katelyn; Carter, Brittni Felicia Lyn;

Carter, Jessica Anne; Chiquito, Priscilla Marie; Chung, Hoyeon; Clevenger, Alexander Todd; Cocke, Kelsey; Coleman, Meghann; Colt, Kelsey; Cooley, Devon Marie; Crisan, Rebecca; Cullen, Erin Jeannine; Damec, Joel; Danford, Kiersten Marie; Darby, Joanna Joy; Davis, Brittany Nicole; Deegan, Kevin Michael; Dellicolli, Brendan; Dion, Rita; Doherty, Lauren; Dugan, Brandon Weldon; Edmondson, Kaitlin Ann; Emerson, Jillian; Eum, Young Seok; Flanagan, Lauren; Forchione, Ashlie Michelle; Foy, Lauren; Frierson, Laporsha Shelia; Fritz, Sara Jean; Fuller, Christian Alyse; Funk, Marilynn; Gambino, Angelia Maria; Gargaro, Joan; Glasper, Shawn; Glover, Holly; Gonzales, Kelsey; Gradwhohl, Louise; Greenspan, Sara; Grobbel, Allison Ann; Guzik, Kate; Halfhill, Nicholas; Hamilton, Davina; Han, Lu; Hawthorne, Megan; Hayden, Cameron; Heck, Katherine; Hermans, Alexs; Herrinton, Kelsey; Hill, Heather Marie; Hill, Steven; Ho, Chia Yuan; Holli, Jessica; Hyun, Myounghae; Iceman, Ami Michelle; Jaber, Nahed; James, David William; Janutol, Jeanne; Jarosz, Melissa Kay; Jeong, Kristin; Jobin, Kristen; Joyce, Carolyn; Jusick, Kylie Victoria; Kastelic, Stephanie; Kelly, Patrick Richard; Kim, Sangwoo; Kim, Se Jun; Knowlton, Katie; Kranz, Elizabeth; Kristl, Sean; Larson, Laura Marie; Lashley, Kaitlyn; Lee, Sang Hoon; Letwin, Daniel Nelson; Lhota, Ashley; Liao, Chen-Hsiu; Lin, Po Chun; Loftus, Kate; Loughrige, Marissa Ann; Lowe, David Charles; Macdonald, Maeve; Machasic, Alexandria; Maher, Alexandra; Mann, Molly; Marsh, Amanda; Marzec, Victoria Elizabeth; Maurici, Tess; McCallum, Melissa; Mcdonald, Jessica; McGuire, Garrett; McInerney, Ryan; Mckeen, Elizabeth; Mercer, Melinda; Michael, Angela; Michaels, Emily; Miller, Jordan; Miller, Michael; Miller, Trent; Moore, Cam Ariel; Moorehead, Justin; Morris, Lauren Nicole; Mulder, Kyle; Muscat, Matthew; Muskovitz, Amy; Nguyen, Lien Thanh; Norris, Jeremy Edwin; Oginsky, Joseph Alexander; Oleszkowicz, Ashley Marie; Ortega, David Anthony; Otting, Jenna Lynn; Pansoian, Darcy; Park, Heesang; Park, Ji Hae; Pascaretta, Natalie; Pellegrino, Brittany; Phiungkeo, Nisa Ratana; Pine, Melanie; Ramson, Ashley; Ransdell, Kelsey; Renwick, Bridget; Rigan, Samantha; Roberts, Dirk; Robson, Julie; Roman, Kimberly; Rottman, Andrea; Runions, Kerri; Sasinowski, Maria Teresa; Satkowiak, Chelsea; Schofding, Scott; Silver, Ashley Marie; Simmons, Megan; Soave, Andrew; Sosnowski, David; Stalker, Neal; Stevens, Mark Douglas; Stewart, Jamie Leigh; Stewart, Lisa; Stewart, Tara; Strank, Jody C; Stuart, Amy Nicole; Sulier, Jessica; Sullens, Courtney; Swade, Samantha; Thayer, Jillian Lynne; Thomas, Scott; Thompson, Lisa; Tibbs, Erin Kristin; Trelenberg, Kristen Rose; Tsai, Hui-Ju; Vanderschaaf, Thomas James; Victory, Lauren; Vlietstra, Charles Ross; Vuong, Julie Ngoc; Walker, Leo; Wallach, Shelby; Walsh, Bailey Kathreen; Walter, Elyse Jean; Wang, Pei-Lin; Wayne, Melanie; Wendzinski, Julia; Wickham, Cody Edward; Wieber, Stefanie Marie; Williams, Shirla; Winn, Jessica Rita; Winton, Jasmine; Wu, Julie; Wu, Yue; Yang, Yi; Ybarra, Roque; Yeh, Yi Feng; Youtsey, Olivia.

About the Authors

Dr. Richard T. Cole (http://en.wikipedia.org/wiki/Richard_T._Cole) is a recognized expert in PR, which he calls "public relationships." He has owned a PR company and served as the Press Secretary and Chief of Staff to a Michigan governor. He also headed up communications and other functions for America's largest nonprofit health plan and was chief administrative officer of a nine-hospital system. His is currently a full professor of public relations at Michigan State University, East Lansing, where he lives with his wife Deborah.

One constant in Cole's career is that he has always encouraged people—his bosses and employees, his clients, his colleagues and his students—to understand that PR and marketing are two separate and distinct disciplines—a theme that he repeated often in this book.

While serving as chairperson of MSU's Department of Advertising, Public Relations and Retailing, Cole brought Derek Mehraban to MSU to help him develop and teach the New Media Driver's License® Course that provided the inspiration, and much of the material, for this book.

Cole sees the power of social media for the great capacity it has to create open dialog between the management of any organization and its constituents. And in that sense, he sees social media as helping PR reach its true meaning as a way to help PR practitioners to adjust organizational behavior to better conform to the values and aspirations of the public upon which the organization depends for survival and to stimulate dialog.

You can stay in touch with Rick at:
http://www.facebook.com/DrRichardCole
http://www.linkedin.com/pub/richard-t-cole/5/30b/a28
Email: DrRichardCole@gmail.com

Derek Mehraban is a graduate of Michigan State University and owner of Ingenex Digital Marketing, a full-service digital agency located in Ann Arbor, Michigan. Mehraban is co-creator of the New Media Driver's License Course and teacher of the course since its inception at MSU in January 2009.

A Crain's (Detroit Business) "40 under 40" award winner, Mehraban is passionate about marketing education. He founded 501c3 non-profit Lunch Ann Arbor Marketing (LA2M) in 2008, and has organized hundreds of programs on a variety of digital marketing topics. Archived presentations are available at http://la2m.org/live.

Mehraban is married to University of Michigan professor Amy Pienta Mehraban and has "two amazing daughters, Abigail (age 9) and Lucy (age 7), who are both great kids and fabulous swimmers." As those who know him would say, Mehraban is a father first and a businessman and educator second.

Mehraban owes a big debt of thanks to social media for making it easier than ever to stay connected and help others through new media. "And to Dr. Richard Cole, who asked me to help him start the New Media Driver's License Course and co-author this book you are reading, thanks Rick."

You can stay in touch with Derek on Facebook, LinkedIn, and Twitter, or by reading his blog http://thedigitalbus.com

http://facebook.com/derek.mehraban

http://linkedin.com/in/mehraban

http://twitter.com/mehraban

Index